The Secret Doctrine of the Gaon of Vilna

Mashiach ben Yoseph and the Messianic Role of Torah, Kabbalah and Science

Joel David Bakst

City of Luz Publications
www.cityofluz.com
Manitou Springs, CO

Cover Design by J.D. Bakst

Cover Graphics by Margalit

Editing and electronic layout by Miriam Leah Ben-Yaacov

Cover Fractal Art by Ken Keller http://fractalartgallery.com

Published by City of Luz Publications, www.cityofluz.com

City of Luz Publications
www.cityofluz.com

Printed in the United States of America

*"Accept upon yourself a master teacher
and acquire for yourself a learning partner."*
(Mishnah Avot)

~ ~ ~ ~ ~

Dedicated to
my Rebbe in *pshat* who
taught me the terrestrial secrets of Talmudic
methodology and the living dynamics of rabbinical
thinking; and to my *chavrusa* in *sod* who showed me
the celestial pathways of the language
of the Kabbalah and the four
rivers that flow from
the *Eitz Hayim*.

Without either one this
work would not be possible.

S hallow ideas can be assimilated; ideas that require people to reorganize their picture of the world provoke hostility.

James Gleick, *Chaos – Making a New Science*

I n the 600th year of the 6th millennium (1840), the gates of wisdom [Kabbalah] above together with the wellsprings of wisdom [science] below will be opened up and the world will prepare to usher in the seventh millennium.

Zohar

T hrough his divine inspiration, our master the Gaon established the necessity of learning the Seven Sciences from below. It is known that they are like the patterns and models on the "bottom side of Mt. Sinai" that can be used to explain the secret wisdom of the Torah and accelerate the redemption.

Rabbi Hillel of Shklov

O ur exodus from the exile is therefore dependent upon the study of the Kabbalah.

Gaon of Vilna

N ot every mind can handle this.

Zohar

Table of Contents
(Volume One)

The Secret Doctrine of the Gaon of Vilna

The following three chapters appear in
Volume II of *The Secret Doctrine of the Gaon of Vilna*
(Available at cityofluz.com)

Preface

The Lost Gifts   "The Holy One bestowed three gifts (*hashpa'ot*) to the world and the Torah community of Israel. By not grabbing each of these gifts at the time they were given, the Torah community lost all three to the External Forces (the "Other Side"). *Chochmah* — wisdom — was lost and fell into the hands of the scientists. *Eretz Yisrael* — the Land of Israel — was lost and fell into the hands of the secular Zionists. *Teshuva* was lost and fell into the hands of assimilated Jews — the *Ba'al Teshuva* Movement."

The Gerer Rebbe[1]

Kol HaTor (Call of the Turtledove) is possibly the most extraordinary and revolutionary book in modern Jewish history. It is certainly Judaism's best-kept secret. *Kol HaTor* defies standard classification and is an esoteric work in all senses of the word: mystical, abstruse, and requiring in-depth initiation. Although on one hand *Kol HaTor* is a profound intellectual challenge, necessitating years of prerequisite study of Talmud and Kabbalah, on the other hand it is a simple, no-nonsense, step-by-step manual for grass roots, communal, and national activism that virtually everyone — men and women, adults and teenagers, Torah scholars and laypeople, Jews and even non-Jews — can utilize and apply on a daily basis. (By non-Jews I am referring here to *Torah oriented non-Jews,* which includes the rapidly evolving groups of righteous gentiles, Noahides (*B'nai Noach*), "Ephramites," and any spiritual truth-seeker who is beginning to look, in fulfillment of the ancient biblical prophesies, to the Torah and her sages for direction.)

Kol HaTor is also a metaphysical tool kit to understand, integrate, and apply the ever emerging new paradigms of science and technological breakthroughs from an unexpected messianic perspective. Additionally, *Kol HaTor* contains the keys to unlock transcendent states of consciousness and divine transmission (*ruach hakodesh*), in order to effect one's personal spiritual growth, as well as to directly stimulate cosmic rectification in the messianic process.

Entering the universe of the Gaon of Vilna's *Kol HaTor* necessitates a complete paradigm shift in one's world view and in one's relationship to God, Torah, and *mitzvot* (Torah directed acts and deeds). At this unique period in human history, this mandate applies to both Jew and Torah oriented non-Jews. The explicit purpose of the *Secret Doctrine of the Gaon of Vilna*, in fact, calls for a covert, messianic master plan, centered in the ancient, eternal city of Jerusalem. This is in order to stimulate a series of cosmic triggers that will literally "quantum jump" humanity and all reality into a higher dimension of existence — back to our true Adamic home in Gan Eden (the Garden of Eden) and beyond.

Kol HaTor challenges us with its numerous enigmas – its history, its authorship, and its contents. *Kol HaTor* has only recently become available in print, after being closely guarded by family members and disciples of the Gaon of Vilna for two hundred years. Originally composed as a secret journal (*"megilat setarim"*) intended for an elite group of initiates, it remained virtually hidden from the public for two centuries, only to resurface in 1968 when two separate parties (unbeknownst to each other) published it simultaneously from the last two remaining manuscripts. Even following a number of Hebrew reprints since the two 1968 editions, with the last (and most complete) edition in 1994, as well as an (incomplete) English edition, *Kol HaTor* remains unknown to the vast majority of academic and religious scholars – not to mention the public at large. Indeed, it appears that *Kol HaTor* has a supernatural ability to remain concealed from the world even when it is revealed!

At the heart of the mystery surrounding this work is the astounding and ostensibly unbelievable claim that *Kol HaTor* asserts. The author, Rabbi Hillel Rivlin of Shklov, maintains that the entire source for this secret doctrine is his own master, teacher and relative, the illustrious 18th-century sage-mystic, Rabbi Eliyahu ben Shlomo Zalman, the Gaon of Vilna, who arguably was the most revered rabbinic and kabbalistic authority in the last two hundred-fifty years, if not more. Moreover, challenging the traditional notions surrounding his teacher, R. Hillel makes the incredible, but documented claim that the soul of the Gaon of Vilna was sent from above to the world below with the actual keys to hasten the messianic process, to return the Jewish people to the Land of Israel, to overturn the current order of society, and to usher all humanity into a new world order.

Kol HaTor is a systematic presentation of the Gaon's secret messianic mission and teachings about the End of Days, including direct quotes and events attributed to him. According to *Kol HaTor,* the Gaon of Vilna (popularly, but inconclusively known as the religious arch conservative *par excellence*, as well as the inexplicable historical nemesis to the emergence of the Hasidic movement) was none other than a Messiah himself! *Kol HaTor*, composed over two hundred years ago, states that not only was he the Messiah, but also that the Gaon of Vilna continues to fulfill the role and function of the Messiah to this day even two hundred years after his death! However, as we will see, this "messiah" is not the oversimplified and primitive, Occidental "Judeo-Christian" view of a messiah, rather that the Gaon of Vilna is the mysterious and paradoxical "First Messiah", the Messiah from the House of Joseph. And *Kol HaTor* is the guide book and instruction manual that he has given to us — we who are the long prophesied "Final Generation".

I have several personal connections to the legacy of *Kol HaTor*. Raised in a liberal Conservative Jewish home (until I entered yeshiva at the age of 20), I grew up knowing very little about Torah and my Jewish tradition. The one thing I did know, however, was that I was related to a famous rabbi by the name of the *"Vilna Gaon"*. I had no idea who he was, and at the time it had no relevance to me. Yet, many years later, the Gaon of Vilna, his teachings, and his disciples would have an immeasurable impact upon my life.

According to public genealogical records, I am, on my mother's side, an eighth generation descendant of the Gaon's younger brother, R. Avraham Ragoler (1742-1807), a renowned Torah giant in his own right and the author of a book that is studied in yeshivot to this day. His work, *Ma'alot HaTorah* (*Virtues of the Torah*), develops the ascendancy of in-depth Torah learning as the most direct, as well as obligatory path to serving and knowing God. He served as the communal *maggid* (preacher) of the town of Shklov, Lithuania, where the Rivlin family is originally from, and where the actual legacy of *Kol HaTor* began.

Once, long before I began studying the works of my ancestral uncle, the Gaon of Vilna appeared to me in a dream. Whatever may be the source of that appearance, it certainly deepened my connection to the Gaon and the legacy of *Kol HaTor.* (Following in the footsteps of the disciples of the Gaon, my great-grand parents, R. Yoseph Nissan Rosenblum and Ita Pesha (nee Kroskal) made *aliya* from Chicago, Illinois to *Eretz Yisrael* in their old age in the year 1930. They are buried on the Mt. of Olives. Additionally, my grandfather, Rabbi Elihu Rosenblum, was named after Rabbi Eliyahu, the Gaon of Vilna.)

I first encountered *Kol HaTor* over twenty-five years ago, while a yeshiva student studying Talmud in Jerusalem. An elder colleague of mine (a Torah bibliophile, as well as a true scholar) knew of this obscure document, and he thought I would be interested in it. For years it remained just another interesting, but obtuse and inaccessible book sitting on my shelf. Only after many years of additional in-depth study of the writings of the Ari (Lurianic Kabbalah), and specifically of the Kabbalah school of the Gaon of Vilna, was I able to begin to decipher this highly coded digest.

As I struggled to understand the language and concepts of *Kol HaTor,* what I saw unfolding before my eyes was like nothing I had seen throughout the entirety of all the kabbalistic and Hasidic writings I was studying. This book was a virtual manual for personal and collective cosmic redemption! Every time I picked it up to decipher and study the work (and this continues to this very day), I felt like a spiritual archaeologist uncovering long hidden secrets — not only of the past — but also of the messianic future. In order to more fully comprehend the arcane cosmology of *Kol HaTor,* I have continued to be engrossed in, and transformed by, the study of the most important and influential expositor of the Kabbalah school of the Gaon of Vilna, the famed Lithuanian kabbalistic Rabbi Shlomo Eliyashiv (known as the "*Leshem*").

I also have another personal connection to *Kol HaTor*. In the early 1970's I had the honor to be acquainted with the Torah sage, Rabbi Chaim Shraga Feivel Frank, rabbinic judge and rabbi of the Jerusalem neighborhood of Yemin Moshe. He was the nephew of R. Tzvi Pesach Frank (1873–1960), who himself was the chief rabbi of Jerusalem, a *halakhic* authority, and a direct descendant of Rabbi Hillel of Skhlov, the author of *Kol HaTor*. Rabbi Frank wrote (in his Approbation I have included below) that he received a tradition, from generation to generation, that his "grandfather, the sage and kabbalist, Rabbi Hillel, merited to stand before his master, the Gaon of Vilna, many years and received from him hidden secrets concerning the process of the final Redemption." In the formative years of the yeshiva where I studied, Rabbi Frank was a spiritual mentor. During that period while I was living at the yeshiva, on Shabbat, the students would walk over to Rabbi Frank's *shul* in Yemin Moshe and *daven*/pray together with him. Shortly thereafter, I again had the honor to be present at his burial, while his only three daughters recited the *kaddish* prayer for him, as he left this world for the next world.

As the reader begins to hearken to *Kol HaTor's* strange, yet familiar, "voice of the turtledove," several things should be kept in mind. The challenge of deciphering and rendering a coherent and understandable translation of the text of *Kol HaTor* has been, and continues to be, a work in progress. Even after studying and contemplating this most unusual book, with the grace of the Almighty, now for well over two decades, I have only touched upon its surface.

This sacred book, with its corollary studies of Talmud, Kabbalah, and science, welcomes, and even requires, a group effort. And so should it be. Just as Mashiach ben Yoseph is a living *gestalt* – many discreet parts coming together to complete an integrated whole – so should be the human effort that encounters the Light of the Gaon of Vilna and his disciples within the soul of *Kol HaTor*. Indeed, this is one of the necessary *Seven Characteristics of Redemption* explicitly stated in *Kol HaTor*.

One of the central factors in the success of our

work is the establishment of Inner Circles (lit. "Men of Truth", i.e., spiritual fraternities) for the purpose of implementing the Agenda for Redemption, as expressed by the sages: "Jerusalem was only destroyed because the Inner Circles ceased to exist."

Over the past decades, a number of colleagues and scholars have directly and indirectly contributed to *The Secret Doctrine of the Gaon of Vilna*. I am indebted to their contributions and suggestions as well as for the assistance I have received from family members. Additionally, if you are one who hears the "call of the turtledove" and has a contribution to make to the living legacy and mission of *Kol HaTor* — questions, corrections, critiques, or additional Torah sources — please contact me through my web site: www.cityofluz.com. Newer versions of this work will include those changes or notes.

J.D.B.

---

[1] Rabbi Simcha Bunim Alter (1898-1992), the fifth Rebbe in the Gerer Hasidic dynasty and brother of the previous Gerer Rebbe, the *Beis Yisrael*, was well known in Gerer circles for the statement that he made concerning the Three Gifts, (commenting upon the Kotzker Rebbe's commentary to the Zohar 1:117a). In view of *Kol HaTor's* doctrine, as presented throughout this work, of the messianic illumination of Mashiach ben Yoseph at key moments in history being forced into exile and going undercover, the following would be an explanation of his statement.

After almost 2,000 years of foreign rule, the Land of Israel, instead of falling back into the hands of the Torah leaders, fell into the hands of secular Zionism and became the secular State of Israel, (i.e., the "backside" of the Holy Land). Secondly, as will be explained at length below, the prophesied accelerated modern discoveries of the Seven Sciences, which should have been spearheaded by the Torah and Kabbalah elite, became instead the domain of the secular and atheists. Thirdly, the fact that the grass-roots *Teshuvah* movement fell into the world of predominantly secular and assimilated Jews should not be taken for granted. *Teshuvah* — in the form of an intense spiritual revival, returning to the inner teachings of the Kabbalah unified with the Talmud together with an outpouring of brotherly love — could have taken place among the different Orthodox camps themselves. Instead, something that was logically impossible to foresee occurred. Tens of thousands of highly assimilated Anglo Jews have since proclaimed, "Moses is truth and Torah is truth." Since the 1960's, and seemingly out of nowhere, masses of these Jews have had their collective spirit transformed, have returned to Torah, and have become a powerful force ever affecting the face and direction of contemporary Judaism.

(In addition, we could add that a similar phenomenon may now be occurring with the Kabbalah teachings of the Gaon of Vilna and the doctrine of *Kol HaTor* that has had virtually no visible impact upon the Torah community. Will the ever-accelerating, global grass-roots Noahide movement, in its desire and commitment to embrace the Torah authority and messianic direction of the Gaon of Vilna, reveal yet another unexpected "backside," orchestrated by the Holy One in the enigmatic unfolding of the covert mission of Mashiach ben Yoseph?)

Introduction

"The blossoms have appeared in the land; the time of singing has arrived and the call of the turtledove is heard in our land."
(Song of Songs 2:12)

Rabbi Eliyahu ben Shlomo Zalman — the Gaon of Vilna (Genius of Vilna, Lithuania, 1720-1797) — is universally recognized as one of the greatest Torah authorities of the last several centuries. Known for his extensive commentaries covering the full range of Jewish exoteric teachings, the Gaon (also known as the Gra, an acronym for Gaon Rabbeinu Eliyahu — the Genius our Master Elijah) personifies the epitome of talmudic scholarship. His penetrating clarity into the complexities of Jewish law, and his absolute commitment to its divine nature, has determined the character of much of Orthodox Torah study and observance to this day.

What is not widely known is that the Gaon was also a mystic and a scientist of the first order, whose vision of the ultimate unity of all knowledge was the subject of the vast body of his esoteric writings. It was in these writings, and in the oral teachings transmitted to his closest disciples, that the Gaon revealed a comprehensive mystical doctrine. This doctrine reveals that the discoveries of modern science will interface with, and directly affect our ability to understand, the ancient esoteric teachings of Judaism — the Kabbalah. He thus exhorted his followers to sanctify the Name of God by applying the secrets of the Kabbalah to all branches of secular knowledge. Only thus could they perceive the Divine wisdom that is embedded in the laws of the physical universe and grasp the underlying unity of all knowledge, both earthly and Divine. The goal was nothing less than a plan — a virtual spiritual conspiracy — to hasten the Redemption: a quantum leap in consciousness that would inaugurate a new era of human history and encompass the entire cosmos.

The most explicit source for the Gaon's mystical approach to science is found in the book *Kol HaTor* — Call of the Turtledove.[1]

This unusual work was written by a relative and intimate disciple of the Gaon, R. Hillel Rivlin of Shklov (1758-1838). The text of *Kol HaTor* began to take form during the period when R. Hillel was still serving and studying under the Gaon. It only became available to a limited public in 1968, after being closely guarded by family members and disciples of the Gaon for nearly two hundred years. Indeed, as a result of its mysterious history and unexpected content, attributing the text's complete authenticity to the Gaon of Vilna has been challenged. Even among those who do know of its existence, it is either not seriously studied or, if it is, remains a "closed book" to most people, due to its unfamiliar kabbalistic terminology and initially, many strange concepts. None the least of these bizarre concepts — embarrassing to some, blasphemous to others — is that *Kol HaTor* reveals that Rabbi Eliyahu, the illustrious unparalleled Genius of Vilna, was none other than a Messiah himself — Mashiach ben Yoseph.[2]

Kol HaTor is a detailed account of the Gaon's prophetic vision of the future, in which the secret wisdom of the Torah — the Kabbalah — is the key to the long awaited final evolution of global consciousness. It is a highly sophisticated instruction manual, comparable to virtually nothing in its genre. It was originally intended only for an elite circle of Torah scholars initiated into the Gaon's esoteric cosmology, and it assumes a familiarity with the *Zohar* and Lurianic Kabbalah (not to mention Talmud, Jewish law, and rabbinic methodology). Thus, either because of its terse Kabbalistic terminology, its often-cryptic style, and/or its revolutionary approach toward secular knowledge, the text has remained largely inaccessible to all but a small circle of scholars.

The Gaon's forceful position on the messianic confluence between Torah and science is only one facet of his complete master program of redemption. *Kol HaTor* also deals with the vital concepts of the cosmo-historical role of the Jewish nation, the role and the progressive revelation of its secret wisdom as the "End Times" approach, the centrality of the Land of Israel, and the nature, influence, and different aspects of the Messiahship. Because of these crucial elements that are the warp and woof of *Kol HaTor*, some have considered it only as a manual for religious Zionism. *Kol HaTor*, in fact, has been known and studied since its publication in 1968 in religious Zionist circles in the Land of Israel. But as will be shown below, the Gaon's absolute imperative for all Jews to return to Israel, to reclaim its biblical borders and rebuild the land with Jerusalem as a global spiritual and scientific metropolis, is only a part of the entire thrust of his secret doctrine.

The book is composed of seven chapters. Initially, only the first five chapters were discovered and printed in 1968, followed by the discovery and printing of a missing last page of Chapter 5, Part I in 1990, and the complete sixth chapter in 1994. The seventh chapter, aside from a short description of its contents, has yet to appear.

•**Chapter One** discusses the role of human effort in the steps toward global evolution, together with the gradual interpenetration of higher dimensional realities. The key to this concept is the "First Messiah," Mashiach ben Yoseph (the Messiah from the House of Joseph or the "Josephic Messiah").

•**Chapter Two, Part I** examines 156 different aspects of this process, each based on a biblical verse. Together, these 156 Aspects – which is the numerical value *(gematria)* of each of the Hebrew words "Yoseph" and "Zion" — reveal the complete form, texture, and contour of the enigmatic phenomenon of the "Hidden Messiah," Mashiach ben Yoseph.

•**Chapter Two, Part II** develops the concept of the *Trein M'shechin*, the Two or "Twin" Messiahs: Mashiach ben Yoseph as the immanent force expressed through human actions "from below" and Mashiach ben David as the transcendental force, divinely revealed "from above."

•**Chapter Three** reveals the Gaon's methodology of how to utilize scriptural formulas and encrypted Torah codes. This is a prerequisite so that each one of us can know his soul root and earthly mission in order to help stimulate the messianic process. Even though we no longer have leaders, priests or prophets to guide us in the Last Generation, the Gaon in his mission as Mashiach ben Yoseph and his vision of *Kol HaTor* has been vouchsafed from Above to instruct and direct us. The Gaon emphasizes that it is the study of the Kabbalah that specifically arouses this Redemption process.

•**Chapter Four** describes a three-fold framework through which the final redemption process operates and how we can recognize and stimulate these key juncture points. These are the messianic Signs, Times, and Agents — interdependent with each other. The human agents are alerted by specific signs or events, which in turn can stimulate specific time periods.

•**Chapter Five, Part I** outlines the Gaon's doctrine to accelerate the Redemption through the power of "Formula 999". Through specific mental and physical acts, whose spiritual reverberations generate spontaneous, "quantum-like" evolutionary leaps, we can consciously stimulate our own global redemption.

•**Chapter Five, Part II** *(Sha'ar Be'er Sheva)* explains the underlying *raison d'etre* of rapid technological development, specifically since 1840. This chapter is a systematic presentation of an unparalleled vision of the synthesis between traditional Jewish mysticism and modern scientific development. Here the Gaon reveals the concept of the messianic role of accelerated secular wisdom, which demands a radical paradigm shift in the relationship between religion and science. This includes the responsibility of Torah scholars to reveal the principles of Kabbalah within scientific discoveries and to use the emerging maps, models, and metaphors from science and technology to understand the depths of the Kabbalah, now also being revealed at an unprecedented rate.

•**Chapter Six** outlines the seven essential practical acts to be implemented in the beginning of the redemption process. Overall, the process of the return of the Jewish people to the Land of Israel, and its reconstruction, will manifest in a "natural" manner, as was the case during the initial period of the rebuilding of the Second Temple. One of these acts is the establishment of "Inner Circles", i.e., a network of spiritual fraternities to redeem the truth and sanctify the Name of God.

•**Chapter Seven** mandates that everyone living outside of Israel must participate in the building and expansion of the Land of Israel, and especially in the rebuilding of Jerusalem, through acts of righteous *tzedaka* ("charity"), i.e., contributing to the financial and material needs of their brethren living in Israel. Contributing financially to the rebuilding of Jerusalem is as much a spiritual act as it is a material one.

The centrality of the present work, *The Secret Doctrine of the Gaon of Vilna*, is Chapter Five, Part II of *Kol HaTor* entitled in the original manuscript as *Sha'ar Be'er Sheva*. In the Orthodox Jewish circles where *Kol HaTor* was first published, the nature of this chapter was so controversial that it was censored from one of the two 1968 published editions of *Kol HaTor*. (This chapter is providentially, again, also missing from the more recent 1994 English translation of *Kol HaTor*.)[3]

This chapter, titled in the original as *Sha'ar Be'er Sheva* (Gate of the Well of Seven [Sciences])[4] details the Gaon's unprecedented and futuristic integration between science and Torah. Part I, Chapter 4 of *The Secret Doctrine of the Gaon of Vilna* contains the complete translation of this astounding and truly messianic document. In addition, I have supplied the reader with extensive notes, enabling laypeople, as well as scholars, to clearly grasp the revelatory message of the Gaon and its implications. Aside from scores of passages from the other chapters of *Kol HaTor* that are necessary to understand the dynamics of Mashiach ben Yoseph and its cosmic role in the phenomenon of modern technology, I have also translated and annotated a more recently discovered fragment of *Sha'ar Be'er Sheva* (the last page of Chapter 5, Section I) that was not included in the two 1968 editions.

Preceding the text of *Sha'ar Be'er Sheva,* I have collected a short history of the Gaon of Vilna. This is followed by the legacy of the family of R. Hillel Rivlin of Shklov, in order to familiarize the reader with the historicity of *Kol HaTor* and the Gaon of Vilna's virtually unknown messianic movement, *Chazon Tziyon* — "Vision of Zion". This movement, spearheaded by R. Hillel, his father, R. Benyamin

Rivlin, and others, preempted the term "Zionism" by more than a century. Included are the genealogy and events of two hundred years of *Kol HaTor* that led up to its providentially dual publication in 1968, following Israel's Six Day War.

I have also included the original Approbation, by a leading Jerusalem sage, to one of the 1968 editions of *Kol HaTor*. Along with other primary source material, much of the historical information provided here has been drawn from the introductions to these two editions, as well as from feedback from colleagues and interviews with a number of scholars, whose assistance was invaluable.

Kol HaTor, due to both its content and style, is a very unwieldy book, and it is challenging even to trained scholars. The present work, *The Secret Doctrine of the Gaon of Vilna*, only translates in full Section II of Chapter 5. However, in order to enable the reader to glimpse the larger picture of *Kol HaTor*, I have included four sets of summaries ("Overviews") of many of the essential tenets of *Kol HaTor*. These four summaries, each containing seven aspects, are enumerated within *Kol HaTor*. Additionally, I have included the original content headings of each chapter prepared by R. Shlomo Zalman Rivlin for the 1947 edition. (The Overviews and Content headings are found below in Chapter 3.)

In addition to the material presented in Part I, I have composed Volume II, entitled The Josephic Messiah, Leviathan, Metatron and the Sacred Serpent – The Secret Doctrine of the Gaon of Vilna. This second volume contains four chapters that seek to explain the extensive and profound kabbalistic underpinnings of the Gaon's Kabbalah doctrine, as applied throughout *Kol HaTor* in general and in *Sha'ar Be'er Sheva* in particular.

These additional four chapters are the first ever – in English or in Hebrew — to introduce the reader to a coherent, thematic overview of the arcane theosophy of the virtually unknown Kabbalah School of the Gaon of Vilna. Specifically, these four chapters lay the prerequisite foundations for understanding the Gaon's utterly unique synergistic interface of Torah and science. Here the reader is introduced to an exploration of the most awe-inspiring "secrets of secrets" *(razay derazin)* to be found from among the entire corpus of the kabbalistic teachings of the Jewish sages: Mashiach ben Yoseph and the Twin Messiahs, the Sacred Serpent and its role in technology, the futuristic "skin" of Leviathan, and Metatron — Prince of the Presence — the ultimate key to unlocking the Gaon's Kabbalah system, specifically the doctrine of *Kol HaTor*, and, for that matter, the entire Torah.

These specific, highly esoteric matters, although seldom elaborated upon in detail throughout the entire scope of kabbalistic and Hasidic literature, are "the matters that stand in the height of the Heavens."[5] The secret of the Twin Messiahs, the Sacred Serpent, Leviathan, and Metatron are literally the backbone of the Gaon's cosmology of creation and his understanding of the purpose and mission of the Jewish Nation. The Gaon's school of Kabbalah virtually stands alone in the in-depth exploration of these challenging, intimidating, and even fearsome, fundamentals of existence in his necessary plan for Redemption.

According to the Gaon, these four phenomena are but one trunk of the same tree, the actual higher dimensional Tree of Dualistic Knowledge, and its infinite branches and twigs all woven together. All are fractals ("fractured fractions") of one singular underlying cosmic structure. The new science of fractal geometry, and its corollary of modern chaos theory, is, as mandated in *Sha'ar Beer Sheva*, one of the most important messianic tools to understanding the newly revealed teaching of the ancient Kabbalah. It is for this reason that I have titled the chapter subheadings of Part II as "Fractal 1", "Fractal 2", "Fractal 3", etc.... Each one of these fractal sections stands on its own, but can, and must, be integrated into all the others. In this sense they are also modular — they can be taken apart and plugged into one another. It is then up to the reader to "understand one thing from another." (For an initial explanation of fractal geometry and chaos theory see *Tachtit HaHar* in the Appendix.)

A few other applications from *Sha'ar Beer Sheva* will also be explained. These are the geometrical model of

"Flatland", enabling us for the first time to actually get a glimpse of the higher dimensional Garden of Eden and the forgotten sacred serpent, and the topological model of the Möbius strip, which will allow us to understand the Gaon's secret of *Tachtit HaHar* — the "under" or "backside" of Mt. Sinai. Also, the "coherent superposition" – a revolutionary tool to understanding the secret of rabbinic and kabbalistic thinking - will be introduced.

Within the four chapters of Volume II we will encounter other teachings germane to the Gaon and his school of Kabbalah that are virtually unknown outside of a relative handful of devotees. They include the secret messianic Formula 999 that stimulates personal and collective evolution, the secret of the primordial split in *yesod* whose revelation was so forbidden that it is not even explicitly mentioned by the Ari (Lurianic Kabbalah), the soon to be revealed "New Torah" that is ancient beyond time, and the Gaon's self-proclaimed greatest revelation of his life — the secret of the two Jewish "heretics" Sasson and Simcha. And then there is the mysterious symbol of the Uroboros - the universal archetype of a snake with its tail in its mouth. The Gaon, however, reveals that the Jewish Uroboros has *two* tails that curve around and reunite back into its mouth! This is the secret of the Zohar's "Two-Tailed Leviathan" that frolics in a messianic ocean of universal knowledge encompassing all humanity and existence.

For the Gaon, these ostensibly dissimilar esoteric traditions of Judaism are but different bands in a single spectrum of evolving Divine Consciousness. Each one cannot be wholly understood unless it is interfaced and integrated with each of the others. These kabbalistic secrets lie at the root of the Gaon's Torah cosmology, and thus place his personality, biography, teachings, and mission into an unexpected, yet coherent and awe-inspiring, perspective. It is my opinion and studied observation that without these keys, the Kabbalah teachings of the Gaon, and certainly the secrets of *Kol HaTor*, will remain a closed book.

---

[1] Based on the verse, "The blossoms have appeared in the land; the time of singing has arrived, and the call (i.e., voice or cooing) of the turtledove is heard in the land" (Song of Songs 2:12). The *Tor* (in Hebrew, from which the word *tur*ledove is likely derived) is a beautiful bird with colorful feathers that is noted for its plaintive cooing and affectionate disposition. It is recognizable by the bright stripes at the side of its neck, which become an iridescent red when the bird matures (Rashi, Talmud Chullin 22b). Large flights arrive in Israel in spring, and the cooing, which fills the woods, heralds the advent of spring. The turtledove was used, like the dove (*yonah*), for sacrificial offerings in the Temple. It was also one of the animals used by Abraham in the Covenant Between the Pieces (Genesis 15:9-10) in which it represented the Nation of Israel (Rashi, ad. Loc.).

[2] It is evident throughout this work, however, that the Gaon's concept of the Messiah has little to do with the Christian, or even a "Judeo-Christian", concept of the Messiah.

[3] *Voice of the Turtledove*, Rabbi Yechiel Bar Lev, Israel, 1994. The book is subtitled (translated from the original Hebrew), "In The Footsteps of the Mashiach, A digest of 7 chapters on the Redemption, by the Great Kabbalist, Rabbi Hillel Shaklover, relative and student of, Rabbi Eliyahu, the Gaon of Vilna z''l". His translated text (minus many of the key words and phrases in the original Hebrew that are included in the hard-bound printed edition) is also currently available, on his website: www.yedidnefesh.com. However, the entire *Sha'ar Be'er Sheva* is not included, nor is the last page of Chapter 5, Part I. An additional section, comprising some six pages and found at the end of Chapter 5, Part II, following *Sha'ar Be'er Sheva*, entitled *The Rectification for the Sin of the Spies*, is also not included in the Bar Lev translation.

[4] This is the only chapter, or section of a chapter, that was given a title that is more than simply a description of the contents. The term *"Be'er Sheva"* can also refer to the ancient biblical city of Beersheba, with all of its kabbalistic allusions, to "Well of Oaths," as well as to "Well of Seven."

[5] This is a kabbalistic expression found in Talmud, *Berachot* 6b: "These are the matters which stand in the height of the Heavens and yet people treat them lightly."

Part I

The Lost Doctrine

Chapter 1

The Living Legacy of *Kol HaTor*

- The Gaon of Vilna
- The History of *Kol HaTor* and the Rivlin Family
- "The Call of the Turtledove is Heard in Our Land"
- "Zion has no one to preach for her"
- The Kabbalah Teachings of the Gaon of Vilna
- Messianic Synthesis

Chapter 1

The Living Legacy of *Kol HaTor*

The Gaon of Vilna
The Gaon of Vilna, Rabbi Eliyahu ben Shlomo Zalman (1720-1797), was a legendary figure in his own lifetime. Born into a distinguished rabbinic family, he was a descendant of the great Lithuanian Talmudist, R. Moshe Rivkes (died in 1671), who authored *Be'er HaGolah* (Fountain of the Exile), a classic commentary on the *Shulchan Aruch* (Jewish Code of Law) that is included in all editions.

For the Gaon, the study of Torah included all knowledge, from the most recondite secrets of heaven to the most mundane concerns of earth. Indeed, he saw the study of the natural sciences as necessary for understanding the Torah in its entirety. In the introduction to his translation of Euclid (from Latin into Hebrew), which was done at the Gaon's behest, R. Dr. Baruch Schick of Shklov records a now well known dictum of his master: "To the extent that one lacks knowledge of the properties of the natural forces, he will lack one hundred-fold in the wisdom of the Torah."[1]

It is only in Chapter 5, *Sha'ar Be'er Sheva,* of *Kol HaTor,* however, that the esoteric meaning of this statement is revealed, along with many far-reaching implications that recast even the image of the Gaon as the Kabbalist par excellence in a totally new light.

As R. Hillel states in *Sha'ar Be'er Sheva*, the Gaon mastered all the "Seven Wisdoms" of science that included mathematics, astronomy, physics, chemistry, engineering, pharmacology and medicine, musicology, parapsychology, and the brain sciences. Non-Jewish scholars and scientists seeking answers to perplexing questions also frequented his home in Vilna. Although his original solutions to their problems won him the title of the Gaon of Vilna ("Genius of Vilna"), even among the non-Jewish population, his main intention was to sanctify the Name of God in the eyes of the nations and to hasten the final redemption.[2] To this effect he encouraged his students to master the Seven Sciences as well, so that they too could apply them wherever and whenever possible, to sanctify the Name of Heaven and to accelerate the redemption process.

Beyond the mastery of any single branch of knowledge, be it religious or secular, was the Gaon's vision of their unique confluence as integral to the process of the final redemption of the Jewish people and the advent of the Messianic Era. Only with the return to the Land of Israel, and the reestablishment of the physical and spiritual center of the Jewish people, could the vision of total unification come to fruition. The Gaon transmitted this vision to his disciples, especially as it is contained in the body of R. Hillel Rivlin's *Kol HaTor* that has come down to us today.

This vision began to take shape through the Gaon's relationship with his cousin and close disciple, R. Hillel Rivlin's father, R. Benyamin Rivlin of Shklov (1728-1812).

The History of *Kol HaTor* and the Rivlin Family

Among the Gaon's disciples and followers from throughout Lithuania and Byelorussia, the Torah scholars from the city of Shklov were a unique class, set apart onto themselves. From a worldly perspective they appeared to be integrating components of gentile culture and science into traditional Torah, and they have been referred to as "Russia's First Modern Jews".[3] Yet, many of those same "modern Jews" were also deeply rooted in the Kabbalah and in the Secret Doctrine and messianic mission of their master the Gaon. At the head of this covert mission was R. Benyamin Rivlin of Shklov.

The distinguished Rivlin family also claims descent from R. Moshe Rivkes, the author of *Be'er HaGolah* and grandfather of the Gaon. R. Benyamin Rivlin of Shklov was the Gaon's second cousin. He was one of the Gaon's most outstanding disciples and colleagues (*talmid-chaver*), as well as a doctor who was conversant in a number of languages.[4]

A history of the Rivlin family, first published in 1915,

provides us with a vivid image of R. Benyamin foraging in the fields a few hours every day during the summer months: "He would collect herbs, roots and flowers from which he would manufacture medicines according to the rules of pharmacology. He knew this science well from the books of the wise gentiles, written in their own languages. In order to practice medicine he also familiarized himself with other branches of the natural sciences, mineralogy, botany, and zoology. He would administer the herbs and the cures, which he had prepared to aid any ailing person who sought his services."[5]

Under the Gaon's direction, R. Benyamin and his business partner, R. Yehoshua Zietlin,[6] established a large, well-financed yeshivah in Shklov. Due to R. Benyamin's efforts, the unique study method of the Gaon was introduced for the first time on a large scale. Aside from Talmud and the legal codes, there was a special department for the study of Kabbalah, and the students were required to learn and attain complete fluency in *Tanach* (Torah, Prophets and Writings), all according to the system of the Gaon. Another innovation was that classes were given on the Hebrew language and its grammar. A small group of students also studied the science of healing with R. Benyamin himself.[7]

As a result of its high level of scholarship, the yeshivah gained tremendous prestige and became known as the "Yavneh of Raisen" (Belo-Russia, Byelorussia), after the 1st-century center of talmudic learning. R. Benyamin was called the "Builder of Shklov and its scholars." At the age of fifty-two, R. Benyamin suddenly amassed a fortune, when his company sold a large tract of forest area, rich in medicinal herbs, to the Russian government. A short time afterward, he experienced a vivid dream in which he beheld an awesome vision of Jerusalem. Sensing that the extraordinary sum of money had been sent to him for the purpose of fulfilling a great mission, he traveled to Vilna to seek counsel from the Gaon. The Gaon immediately perceived a profound connection in these events. The dream, he explained, was a sign from Heaven. R. Benyamin and his son Hillel were being commissioned to initiate the first steps in the Messianic process: the ingathering of the exiles and the resettlement of the Land of Israel.

The long awaited time had arrived; *Chazon Tziyon* ("Vision of Zion"), as the Gaon named it, was to become a movement that would arouse the hearts of the Jewish people to begin the prophetic return to Zion. (It should be kept in mind that this "Zionist" activity was taking place at the end of the 18th-century, long before the acknowledged beginning of the Zionist movement that would take root in the 1840's and 1850's, with its real objectives only being realized in the 1880's. The term "Zionism" was not coined until 1890.)

One of R. Benyamin's sermons, passed down in the Rivlin family from that period, speaks in fiery language about the return of the Jews to Israel. Commenting on the verse, "Behold, I will bring them from the northern land" (Jeremiah 31:7), he explained that the "northern land" refers to Russia, and particularly the city of Shklov, which is to the extreme north of Jerusalem. The initial arousal for the return to Zion and the rebuilding of Jerusalem would begin in Shklov. (The great and last wave of Russian emigration to Israel in 1990 is, in many regards, the culmination of the initial arousal that began in the "northern land" in the 18th-century with the Gaon's Vision of Zion.)

The eyes of Diaspora Jewry turned toward Shklov when, in 1808, the first group of *olim chadashim* (new immigrants) departed for the Land of Israel. Thirteen years later, in 1822, R. Benyamin himself left to join the new settlement, but died in route before reaching the Holy Land. However, the Vision of Zion that had been his dream was already well established and had been passed on to his son, Hillel Rivlin (1758-1838), who had been initiated into the secret process of redemption by the Gaon himself.

"The Call of the Turtledove is Heard in Our Land" Just as the call of the turtledove each year fills the woods of Israel, heralding the advent of spring, so the Vision of Zion proclaimed the immanent beginning of the redemption process. In 1778 the Gaon had unsuccessfully attempted to immigrate to the Holy Land.[8] In 1783, when he realized that Providence would not permit him to "dwell in Zion," he handed over the mantle of leadership of gathering the exiles and resettling the land to his disciples. Together with R. Benyamin, who was alive at the time, the Gaon chose R. Hillel to lead this mighty campaign, the Vision of Zion.

Although only twenty-five years old at the time, R. Hillel was an outstanding prodigy in Torah. In addition, he had learned languages and medicine from his father, and was gifted with a superlative singing voice. On occasion, the Gaon would request that R. Hillel chant the prayer liturgy before him, in order to elevate his soul even higher while contemplating the esoteric wisdom. All together, he was a close attendant of the Gaon for seventeen years, during which time he assisted his mentor in transcribing his commentaries on the Kabbalah.[9]

Now, as leader of the new movement, the Gaon transmitted to him its mystical foundations, which included the particular actions the returning nation would need to perform in order to accelerate the complete redemption. As R. Shraga Fivel Frank writes in his Approbation to the B'nei B'rak edition of *Kol HaTor* (quoted in full below), "We, the descendants and the grandchildren of the [Rivlin] family, have received the tradition in solid succession that our grandfather, the sage and mystic, R. Hillel, may his merit protect us, merited to stand before his master the Gaon z"l for many years. He received hidden secrets from him concerning the resettlement of the Land of Israel..." The doctrinal teaching that R. Hillel received from the Gaon was a vast and complex system that he arranged in a large and detailed book. The abridged form of that book is what has come down to us today. It is *Kol HaTor*, "The Call of the Turtledove."

Although the Gaon passed away in 1797, never having reached the Land of Israel, his esoteric Doctrine of Redemption remained alive and active among his many followers. It was this doctrine that gave these men and their families the courage to endanger their lives on the long and perilous journey and in the trials of resettling and rebuilding a desolate and poverty stricken land.

The first caravan left Russia for Israel in the fall of 1808. R. Hillel headed the seventy-member group that included fourteen of the Gaon's personal disciples. After ten months of difficult travel, the first convoy arrived in Tzfat on the 5th of Elul, 5509 (September, 1809). Tzfat was already an established Jewish community. Sensing the immanence of the redemption, a previous wave of immigration had been initiated in the latter half of the 18th-century by the disciples of R. Israel Baal Shem Tov (who was also unsuccessful in his attempt to enter the Promised Land). These disciples had settled in Tzfat, Tiberius and Hebron. Nonetheless, the living conditions were terrible, and the new immigrants experienced untold hardship in their struggle to survive.

In 1812, seven of the Gaon's disciples, led by R. Hillel, departed for Jerusalem to begin the resettlement of the ancient Jewish capital. They left Tzfat in the hands of another one of the Gaon's disciples, R. Israel of Shklov, a brilliant scholar and leader. He authored the classic work *Pe'at HaShulchan*, a compendium of the many agricultural laws unique to the Land of Israel.

On their arrival in Jerusalem they found only twenty Sephardic and nine Ashkenazic Jews living among the non-Jewish population. R. Hillel and his comrades immediately set about establishing the necessary institutions vital to Jewish communal life — charity funds, a hospital, a yeshiva and a civil guard unit. The tests that awaited them were enormous. They suffered from severe food shortages, roving bands of marauders, diseases and plagues, and libelous defamations from their non-Jewish neighbors. In addition, communication with the Diaspora was extremely difficult. This meant that they were almost totally isolated from the rest of world Jewry, which was their one source of financial support. It was only the Gaon's powerful vision of the messianic destiny of their mission that gave this first group of pioneers the strength to persist and overcome, against all odds. Finally, when word reached home that R. Hillel and a handful of men had succeeded in resettling Jerusalem, a great fervor was generated that led many Russian Jews to attempt further immigration to the Holy Land. R. Hillel passed away in 1838, at the age of eighty. To world Jewry, he left a well established Jerusalem community. To his family, he entrusted the collection of writings that constitute the doctrine of *Kol HaTor*.

"Zion has no one to preach for her" Moshe Rivlin (1781-1846), R. Hillel's oldest son, was fifteen years old when the Gaon told him that he had been blessed by Heaven with the gift of oratory. In accord with the Talmud's homily on the verse, "Zion has no one to preach (*doresh*) for her" (Jeremiah 30:7), the Gaon intimated that it was his mission to become *Doresh Tziyon*, a "Preacher for Zion."

For thirty years, first in Russia and then in the Land of Israel, R. Moshe delivered powerful sermons expounding the Gaon's vision of redemption, based on his father's and the Gaon's own writings. As the Gaon had predicted, he became known as "Rebbe Moshe, the Preacher of Zion." When he died in 1846, he handed this mission over to his son, R. Avraham Benyamin Rivlin (d. 1871), who was an outstanding scholar and the director of the famous Etz Chaim Yeshivah in Jerusalem.

R. Avraham's son, Yoseph (Yosha) Rivlin (1837-1896), became the head of the Ashkenazi community in Jerusalem. In his hands, the movement to rebuild Jerusalem took another historic step. Until his time, the entire Jewish settlement of Jerusalem was located behind the fortified walls of what is now the Old City. Each night the gates would shut tightly to protect the inhabitants from the dangers lurking outside. In the summer of 1869, R. Yoseph Rivlin built one of the first Jewish homes beyond the Old City walls. For one and a half years, he dwelt there alone until, in 1872, fifty families followed his lead and built their homes around his. This was the historic neighborhood of Nachalat Sheva.[10] Barely two years later, in 1874, after his wife died of heart failure, after valiantly defending herself against an Arab horseman, R. Yoseph once again uprooted his family in order to build another neighborhood, the now historic Meah Sh'arim. This was his way throughout his life, to move and build, move and build. Thirteen new neighborhoods, including the town of Petach Tikvah, were the direct results of his efforts.

R. Yoseph Rivlin also composed a number of poems and articles based on the Gaon's teachings, as he received them from his father and grandfather. In essence, the entire doctrine of *Kol HaTor* is contained in these writings, many of which were published in journals and periodicals of the period. His "mystical-Zionist" poetry was collected in the book, *Brit Avot B'Se'arat Eliyahu*, "(Covenant of the Forefathers in the Storm Wind of Elijah)," written when he was eighteen to twenty years old.[11]

R. Yoseph Rivlin's son, R. Shlomo Zalman Rivlin (1886-1962), was a scholar, composer and *chazzan* (cantor). As director of a school of music in Jerusalem, he created a unified musical style based equally on the European and Oriental traditions. His reputation as an outstanding teacher was spread by his students, many of whom became notable chazanim. He also trained many of his students in homiletics and published his own sermons in *Midrash Shlomo* (1953) and *HaMagid Doresh Tziyon* (1960).[12] In 1946 he wrote and published *Chazon Tziyon - Shklov and Yerushalaim* with Alter Dov Vishnitsky and Yeshayahu Luria. This work is a detailed history of the original immigration to Israel of the Gaon's disciples and their descendants, and of their struggle to lay the foundations for the renewed settlement. It tells of an era that has been forgotten by most of contemporary Orthodoxy, while intentionally overlooked by secular scholars. In *Chazon Tziyon*, R. Shlomo Zalman discusses the ideology of *Kol HaTor* extensively and clarifies many of R. Hillel's statements in light of the Gaon's other writings. A note at the end of the preface states, "[P]roceeds from the revenue of this book are pledged towards the printing of the book *Kol HaTor* — an *Outline of Redemption*, by R. Hillel of Shklov, disciple of the Gaon z"l, founder of the Ashkenazi settlement in Jerusalem."

Five generations after R. Hillel of Shklov, in a rebuilt Jerusalem, the vision of the Gaon was about to shine forth. Until this time, the original manuscript of *Kol HaTor* had remained solely in the hands of an elite circle of Jerusalem scholars and kabbalists. In the years 1946-1947, fulfilling the pledge that he had made in *Chazon Tziyon*, R. Shlomo Zalman prepared a version of *Kol HaTor* to be printed for public use. "In past generations," he wrote in his introduction, "the great Jerusalem kabbalists would speak with great fervor about the exalted principles and wondrous secrets that were to be found in R. Hillel's manuscript of *Kol HaTor*. This text served the leaders of the Jerusalem community as a veritable *Shulchan Aruch* (Code of Jewish Law) and *Urim V'Tumim* (Divine Oracle) in every aspect of their work of founding the Jewish settlement in the Holy Land. In all circumstances, and especially during times of trouble, they turned to the masters of *Kol HaTor* to solve every problem related to the development and administration of the settlement."

R. Shlomo Zalman had inherited the original manuscript from his cousin, R. Yitzchak Tzvi Rivlin. R. Yitzchak Tzvi was known as the "Living Talmud," as well as the "Master of the Settlement" and "Master of the Holy Tongue" (for his emphasis on reviving the Hebrew language). Together with a number of other scholars, it was R. Yitzchak Tzvi who helped prepare and authorize *Kol HaTor* for publication. R. Shlomo Zalman thus writes in his introduction, "With the help of heaven, I have invested much travail and toil over a period of many years. I was aided in this holy endeavor by the great kabbalists of Jerusalem, especially my teacher and master, the Gaon and Saint R. Yitzchak Tzvi Rivlin, R. Tzvi Hirsch Kahana Shapira, R. Shimon Horowitz (Leider), R. Shlomo Luria, R. Yaacov Charlap, R. Yitzchak Auerbach and others." With the help of these men, R. Shlomo Zalman took a text that was filled with abstruse terminology and kabbalistic allusions and produced an abridged version for the layman. To this he added a complete commentary and cross-index to other writings of the Gaon and his students. "In this way," he writes, "it will be possible for every learned individual, and certainly those initiated into the esoteric truths, to understand this book."

Originally intended to be seven chapters, he succeeded in typesetting only as far as the second section of the fifth chapter, apparently due to insufficient funds.[13]

Furthermore, the book was never actually published as planned and, instead, approximately one hundred copies, without his introduction or commentary, were circulated among relatives and followers of the Gaon living in the Land of Israel in 1947. In the post World War II upheaval, with the flood of immigrants and the Israeli War of Independence, the original manuscript of *Kol HaTor*, and nearly all of the abridged editions, subsequently disappeared, with the apparent exception of two remaining copies in the hands of R. Shlomo Zalman Rivlin's two sons, Asher Rivlin and Shmuel Rivlin.

It was in 1968, following the 1967 Six Day War and the reunification of Jerusalem, that these two copies were simultaneously published by two independent parties, unbeknownst to each other. The Asher Rivlin copy was appended to the book *HaTekufah HaGedolah* (The Great Era), by R. Menachem Mendel Kasher of the *Torah Shleimah* Institute, just as it was going to press. The Shmuel Rivlin copy was printed separately by the Organization for the Dissemination of *Kol HaTor* in B'nei B'rak.[14] The *Torah Shleimah* edition included a lengthy introduction by R. Kasher, as well as, the important commentary by R. Shlomo Zalman himself on the first chapter, missing from the original one hundred copies.

In the Kasher edition, however, an entire eight page section of the fifth chapter, describing the Gaon's formula for the confluence of Torah, Kabbalah and science, *Sha'ar Be'er Sheva*, was deleted. The B'nei B'rak edition did include this section, together with R. Shlomo Zalman's original 1946 introduction, but without his commentary on the first or any other chapter. The additional two chapters, to which R. Hillel himself refers, and which were part of R. Shlomo Zalman's original work, were missing from both editions and, as of that time, had yet to be discovered.[15] Although the *Torah Shleimah* edition has since been republished numerous times (without *Sha'ar Be'er Sheva*) and is currently available, the B'nei B'rak edition with the chapter on the sciences is no longer obtainable. A new and more complete 1994 Jerusalem edition, however, does contain *Sha'ar Be'er Sheva* (and the missing sixth chapter and the missing last page of Chapter 5,

Part I).

The section in question is the second part of the fifth chapter, entitled *Sha'ar Be'er Sheva* (Gate of the Well of the Seven [Sciences]). In a clear and concise manner, R. Hillel outlines, according to the oral doctrine that he received from the Gaon, the prophetic role of secular wisdom and the obligation of Torah scholars to help direct that wisdom. R. Kasher mentions (p. 532) that he deleted these eight pages, because he did not consider them directly related to the rest of the text. It is evident, however, that he did so because the Gaon's powerful doctrine of "mystical Zionism" was already too radical for some segments of the Orthodox community, without including the ostensibly heretical concept of the messianic role of secular wisdom.[16] In truth, *Sha'ar Be'er Sheva* should not be studied by either the observant or the non-observant without the necessary explanations. Great effort and time has been invested in the present work to supply the extensive commentary that this profound treatise requires.

The difficulties in making *Kol HaTor* accessible to the public, and the controversies surrounding its contents, are not new and have, in fact, followed its two hundred year history from the beginning. R. Shlomo Zalman Rivlin, in his introduction, offers the following six possible reasons that he believes accounted for this:

1. In addition to the profound kabbalistic secrets that it presents, *Kol HaTor* alludes to various climactic "End Times" in the process of redemption. These were not to be revealed except to select individuals. [One such passage, the last page of the first section of the fifth chapter, was not published in either of the two 1968 editions. It was only discovered afterwards and included in the 1994 edition.][17]

2. There was concern about political repercussions. *Kol HaTor* deals with the fall of "*Seir* and his father-in-law," the biblical Esau and Yishmael, understood to be the archetypes of the ruling Christian and Moslem governments. [Russia was then under the Russian Orthodox Church and the

Land of Israel was under Turkish Moslem rule.]

3. There was fear of triggering a messianic fervor that would result in a premature rush of immigration to the Holy Land. Such a rush of immigration did occur. In 1877, an article by Dr. Tzvi Lipshitz appeared in the journal *HaLevanon*, entitled "Concerning the Report on the Matter of the Messiah and the Triumphant Return of the Ten Tribes in the Year 1815." The author describes how a panic swept Russian Jewry when a letter arrived from the new settlement in Jerusalem. Hundreds abandoned their property and businesses to travel to Israel, sustaining serious losses.

4. *Kol HaTor* strongly advocates a system of social equality in the establishment of the new settlement. During the 19th-century, when both the Russian and Turkish governments were monarchical, such a form of socialism was bound to arouse animosity. [Paradoxical as it might seem, it appears that the Gaon was advocating a form of socialism and a kibbutz-like system, at least during the initial and most difficult stages of the ingathering.]

5. The author, R. Hillel, speaks of the obligation [of Torah scholars] to master the seven branches of science, according to the system of the Gaon. He emphasizes that the Gaon had actually commanded a number of his disciples to do so, among them his father, R. Benyamin Rivlin of Shklov. This idea met with great opposition from a number of religious factions in Jerusalem and Russia. Before R. Hillel immigrated to Israel he, along with his colleagues, suffered from this opposition. These included R. Dr. Baruch Schick of Shklov, R. Menashe of Ilya, R. Dr. Zalman Luria of Mohilov and others.

6. In addition to the above reasons, there was simply a lack of funds for the production and necessary explanations. In the last fifty years [this was written in 1947] many attempts were made by the

elders of our family to arrange to have this important document published. It has been twenty years since, with the advice of the great Kabbalists of Jerusalem, we decided to publish a condensed version of this lengthy and difficult treatise, keeping the terminology as simple as possible.

After studying and contemplating *Kol HaTor* for well over twenty years now along with the Kabbalah writings of the Gaon (together with the other schools of the Kabbalah) I believe there is an additional reason that must be added to R. Shlomo Zalman Rivlin's six reasons listed above. A seventh reason, as to why this work has been a secret for two centuries and continues to remain a virtually sealed book, is also the key to unlock the hidden door to *Kol HaTor* as well as to the enigmatic personality of the Gaon. This is the specter of the strange yet ubiquitous entity known as Metatron, which quite literally is the backbone running through the entire body of *Kol HaTor*.

Metatron is by far the most controversial and challenging phenomenon in the whole of biblical and rabbinical literature. Yet, it is *Kol HaTor* that reveals that the fundamental force behind the Gaon and his messianic mission is the "meta-archangel" Metatron, the root of Mashiach ben Yoseph as well as the collective Oversoul and celestial guardian of the Nation of Israel. Because of the extreme mystical and potentially dangerous nature of misunderstanding the phenomenon of Metatron, and the role it plays in the implementation of *Kol HaTor*, this book has been hidden. The identity and role of Metatron is discussed in Volume II.

Over all I believe there are at least six additional esoteric reasons, each one radical enough on its own to be rejected by mainstream Judaism, as to why *Kol HaTor* continues to remain virtually unknown, and studied and practiced by only limited individuals and select groups.[18]

1. *Kol HaTor* explicitly reveals the Gaon of Vilna as a Messiah from the House of Joseph and that his role in this function continues till this day through his unique

teachings especially through the direction of *Kol HaTor*. Moreover, the Gaon was consciously incarnating the Oversoul of Metatron which is also the soul root of Moses.

2. *Kol HaTor* demands in-depth study of the Kabbalah (together with Talmud, *halacha* and ethics) and the secrets and formulas of the sages encrypted into the talmudic aggada. This is in order to stimulate the incoming stages of global evolution and *Kol HaTor* is the key to understanding the system of the Gaon's Kabbalah.

3. *Kol HaTor* alludes to the hidden keys to the Gaon's otherwise unknown methodology of prayer, which is predicated upon an intimate and direct experience of Metatron, Leviathan, and the Sacred Serpent as well as the polarity of *hasadim* and *gevurot* (the "yin-yang" of the Kabbalah, see the Appendix).

4. *Kol HaTor* is the only source that covertly reveals the answer to the otherwise unsolved mystery as to why the Gaon was inexplicably and almost superhumanly opposed to the Hasidic movement.

5. *Kol HaTor* is the only source that develops, *for practical application,* the details of the paradoxical rules that govern the First Messiah, Mashiach ben Yoseph.

6. *Kol HaTor* is explicit and adamant about the absolutely necessary messianic role of science and technology. This requires everyone, especially rabbis and Torah scholars to familiarize themselves with the new sciences in order to understand the Kabbalah and the secrets of talmudic aggada, which they are also required to learn.

The Gaon and his branch of unique disciples from the sages of Shklov methodically planted seeds of the messianic light for world redemption, both in the holy ground of the Land of Israel and in the secret text of *Kol HaTor* itself, which would bear its fruit at different stages in the future. The difference of opinion regarding the often paradoxical nature of this fruit, and how it will continue to evolve, is another reason why there is such a wide range of opinions concerning *Kol HaTor* among the leaders of the different non-Zionist, anti-Zionist, secular Zionist, religious Zionist, and kabbalistic based Zionist groups. But then again, this is exactly what should be expected in the mystery of Mashiach ben Yoseph — "And Yoseph recognized his brothers, but they did not recognize him." Zion (and thus "Zionism"), as rabbinical sources reveal and *Kol HaTor* emphasizes, is another name for Mashiach ben Yoseph.

It is not the purpose of the work being presented here to debate the contested authenticity of *Kol HaTor* as a whole, or of the controversial fifth chapter, *Sha'ar Be'er Sheva*. Today there are numerous Torah scholars, religious groups and kabbalists, for whom *Kol HaTor* is a guidebook and instruction manual, who have no question as to its authenticity. The letter of approbation to the 1968 edition of *Kol HaTor* speaks for itself.

There are, however, some scholars and Jewish leaders who do know of *Kol HaTor*, yet reject it (most Jewish leaders and scholars still do not even know of its existence or have only the vaguest notion of what it contains). They make the accusation that the work is a forgery, claiming that R. Hillel Shklover's original *Kol HaTor* has been tampered with by "modern Zionists." Yet, whoever "tampered with" *Kol HaTor* was clearly a God-fearing, master Torah scholar, visionary genius and modern prophet steeped in the Kabbalah of the Gaon, the Ari and the *Zohar*! It is implausible that such a Torah master and kabbalist would put heretical words in the mouth of the revered and saintly Gaon of Vilna. Four points, however, should be mentioned:

1. There is virtually no idea propounded in *Kol HaTor* that is not developed elsewhere in the writings of the Gaon and/or in those of his disciples.[19] Many of these corresponding sources have been supplied, discussed, or indicated in the notes.

2. *Kol HaTor* has been mentioned by name in books, newspaper articles, and periodicals, as well as, by leading rabbinic authorities, from R. Hillel Rivlin's time until its partial publication in 1947. The introduction to the *Torah Shleimah* edition gives numerous such examples. In R. Shlomo Zalman Rivlin's *Chazon Tziyon - Shklov and Jerusalem*, the historical and ideological development of the Gaon's system of "mystical Zionism", as implemented

by the Rivlin family over a 150 year period, is well documented.[20]

3. The Gaon's Doctrine of Redemption, as outlined in *Kol HaTor*, is a historical fact attested to by many of his disciples who immigrated to Israel and helped found the new settlement.

4. R. Yoseph (Yosha) Rivlin's collection of poems, entitled *Brit Avot B'Se'arat Eliyahu*, expounds the history and ideology of the Gaon's Doctrine of Redemption and contains virtually the same material found in *Kol HaTor*. It essentially comprises the seven chapters of *Kol HaTor* in verse form and makes extensive use of word plays, having identical numerical values (*gematria* — to which the third chapter of *Kol HaTor* is devoted). These poems were written in 1857, almost one hundred years before the establishment of the State of Israel, thus making the accusation that *Kol HaTor* has been "tampered" with by modern Zionists unfounded.

The Kabbalah Teachings of the Gaon of Vilna

The Gaon of Vilna's esoteric teachings form one of the most sophisticated and all-encompassing systems of Kabbalah to be revealed since the time of the Holy Ari, Rabbi Yitzchak Luria (1534-1572, the acronym for his name, the Godly Rabbi Isaac, also spells the word "*ari*", meaning "lion"). In truth, the Gaon's system of Kabbalah, and his secret Doctrine of Redemption that grows out of it, builds upon, and ultimately incorporates, the entire system of Lurianic Kabbalah. Without the foundations of the "Tree of Life" — *Etz Chaim* - the *magnum opus* of Lurianic Kabbalah which is, aside from the *Zohar*, the most authoritative and influential text of Jewish mysticism, the Gaon's extensive esoteric teachings remain sealed. It is therefore a mistake to think that we can understand the Gaon's messianic doctrine solely on the basis of a few sections of *Kol HaTor*. What is required is an intimate familiarity with the larger context of the Gaon's system of Kabbalah.

The four chapters of Volume II of The Secret Doctrine

are an introduction to some of the fundamental aspects of the Kabbalah system of the Gaon and his chief expositors. For now, without even entering into the details of the Gaon's system of Kabbalah, we can gain a general appreciation of its uniqueness by comparing it with the parallel systems of his contemporaries. Four schools of Kabbalah branch out from the Ari's *Etz Chaim*. These four schools were revealed and developed independently by four supreme Torah masters who, although living at the same time, had no contact with each other. They are:

R. Yisrael Ba'al Shem Tov - the Besht (1698-1760)
R. Shalom Sharabi - the Rashash (1720-1777)
R. Eliyahu ben Shlomo Zalman – the Gra (1720-1797)
R. Moshe Chaim Luzzatto – the Ramchal (1707-1747)

The fourth school, of R. Moshe Chaim Luzzatto, is a vital systemization and magnification of the Ari's Kabbalah. The Ramchal's system, however, is easily incorporated into that of the Gaon's system, and the two can be considered essentially as one system and both are often studied together (which is virtually never the case between the other three).[21]

Although these three schools are all based on the same identical principles found in the *Zohar* and in Lurianic Kabbalah, and can be found to interface in countless instances, each one's mode of application and emphasis of personal mission, clearly differs from the other. These three modes can be viewed as analogous to the three aspects of reality mentioned in *Sefer Yetzirah* (Book of Formation): *Olam* (space), *Shanah* (time) and *Nefesh* (soul).

The system of the Rashash, which is the Sephardic "purest" school of the Ari, is the most abstract and mathematical-like of the three. It is also known as the Kabbalistic school of Beit El, but is little known outside of Israel, where it continues to be studied and practiced, both privately and in a growing number of Sephardic yeshivot. It deals with the Ari's meditative *kavanot* (mystical intentions) that must accompany the performance of *mitzvot* and especially the daily prayer sessions. In this approach all the Hebrew words of the prayer book are viewed as discrete spatial "quanta" of divine energy. The Rashash literally maps out every *kavanah* onto a 3-dimensional grid system so that the practitioner can move through and unify each spatial coordinate with the other, and thereby fulfill the Divine Will to make a *tikkun* (mending) in the fabric of creation. The Rashash's Kabbalah calculates and elevates the "space" of the world.

The teachings of Hasidut, fathered by the Ba'al Shem Tov, are primarily involved with the *Nefesh* (soul) aspect of one's relationship to God and creation. In this sense, Hasidut is a spiritually therapeutic application of the Ari's system, bringing his teachings, and those of the *Zohar*, "down to earth." The Hasidic schools of Lurianic Kabbalah are by far the most well known, as it was also directed to the masses from its inception. The system of the Ba'al Shem Tov liberates and elevates the personal "soul" of the world.

The Gaon, however, is primarily concerned with the mystery of time. His cosmology, more than any other, is involved with the historical process of redemption and it's programmed "end times." The Gaon's concept of time, however, differs substantially from the old version of "Newtonian time." In an Einsteinian fashion, the Gaon unites time into one continuum with space. Time becomes a structure that actually follows an underlying divine form. This structure has specific spatial coordinates that we presently experience as "time". For the Gaon, the redemption process, which culminates in the Messianic eras, involves mapping out and rectifying the fallen structure of space-time and history itself. The Gaon's Kabbalah aims to redeem and elevate the "time" of the world.

The Gaon revealed the Torah's blueprint for the redemption process, because his soul and mission were rooted in the mystery of cosmic time. It is for this reason that *Kol HaTor* is a guidebook for analyzing and mapping out the inner dimension of time, as it is currently unfolding. Moreover, it is a manual for "stimulating" the chronological unfolding of time itself and, along with it, all of reality in preparation for a quantum "jump" into a higher state of existence. Here the Gaon, together with the Ramchal, stand alone in identifying and decoding the complex archetypes known in Kabbalistic texts as the *Trein M'shechin* — the Two or "Twin" Messiahs.[22] It is within the context of the Two Messiahs that *Kol HaTor* outlines different plans of action to be applied in different fields of operation, in order to accelerate the cosmic redemption of reality.

According to the Gaon, the unique relationship that is destined to exist between Torah and science revolves around a statement in the *Zohar* (*VaYeira* 117a):

> In the six hundredth year of the sixth millennium (5600 = 1840 C.E.) the gates of wisdom above [Kabbalah] together with the wellsprings of wisdom below [science] will be opened up, and the world will prepare to usher in the seventh millennium. This is symbolized by a man who begins preparations for ushering in the Sabbath on the afternoon of the sixth day.[23]

The Gaon explained that the opening of the "gates of wisdom above" refers to new and profound revelations that would render the Jewish esoteric tradition, the Kabbalah, more accessible from the mid-19th-century onwards. The Gaon was far from being alone in this assertion. The same tradition has been handed down by another unexpected, yet highly authoritative source, R. Yisrael Salanter (1810-1883), the Torah master who spearheaded the Mussar Movement (emphasizing character and ethical development). In confirmation of the statement of the *Zohar*, he is said to have commented: "Prior to 1840 the study of Kabbalah was a closed book to all but the initiated." The master kabbalist of the Gaon's school of Kabbalah, R. Shlomo Eliyashiv, quotes this tradition and continues, "Thus, from 1840 onwards, permission has been granted for those who truly desire to enter within. The Kabbalah is no longer the private domain of the initiated masters."[24]

The "gates of wisdom above" parallel the opening of the "wellsprings of wisdom below." This refers to revolutionary discoveries in the sciences that would completely change our view of the world.[25] We are all only too aware of the fulfillment of this part of the *Zohar*'s prophesy. In retrospect, we have also seen continuing examples of the revelations of "wisdom from above." Although a number of the works of the Ari were circulated after he died in 1572, the most authoritative texts of Lurianic Kabbalah, the *Shemoneh Sh'arim* (Eight Gates) by R. Chaim Vital, remained in closely guarded manuscript until the beginning of the 20th-century. The availability of previously unpublished esoteric manuscripts of the early kabbalists, the teachings of the Ramchal and the Hasidic masters,[26] and finally the esoteric writings of the Gaon and his disciples (including *Kol HaTor*) have given our generation further access to crucial teachings of the Kabbalah.

While it is true that the principle of *hitkatnut hadorot*, the gradual diminishment of each successive generation in its ability to understand the Torah, holds true with respect to its exoteric teachings, the school of the Gaon of Vilna emphasizes that the inverse of this principle holds true with respect to its esoteric truths. Simply stated, this means that as the world travels farther away from the revelation of the Torah at Sinai, at the same time we are approaching ever closer to the Messianic Era, when the inner secrets of ancient kabbalistic revelations become more manifest and available.[27]

This does not mean that our generation is more advanced than our predecessors. To the contrary, our grasp of the "inner" wisdom is decidedly more "external." It does mean, however, that this wisdom is no longer restricted to a select few. In order to hasten the redemption, the inner wisdom has come down into the public domain, with all the inherent dangers that this "descent" suggests. This is born out, on the one hand, by the emergence of the Kabbalah as an accepted field of academic research in universities in Israel and in the world at large. This is in sharp contrast to the Kabbalah's previous "secular" status of belonging to the realm of superstition. On the other hand, this prophecy is reflected in the appearance of Orthodox yeshivot (mainly Sephardic), which openly teach Kabbalah side by side with Talmud and *halachah* (Jewish Law). Further, any longtime student of the Kabbalah cannot but be staggered by the recent proliferation of classical Kabbalah literature, in Hebrew, English, and other languages, which continues to increase in momentum.

The revelations of the "wellsprings of wisdom below" during the past two centuries are better known, but nonetheless astonishing. Stimulated by the Industrial Revolution in the 18th-century, a plethora of theoretical models and new technologies has burst forth with such intensity that a wholly new paradigm of scientific thought, and consciousness, is emerging. Electromagnetic theory emerged midway through the 19th-century. This, in turn, paved the way for the invention of radio, telecommunications, television, and computers. New psychological and neurological descriptions of the brain, black hole phenomena, genetic engineering, and the holographic model, are a few more examples of scientific discoveries that have taken place in our generation alone, which have given us completely new ways to perceive the world in which we live. Perhaps of even greater significance has been the effect of breakthroughs in the field of geometry during the first part of the 19th-century. These new non-Euclidian geometries set the stage for the emergence of Einsteinian relativity, quantum mechanics, and the search for the Unified Field Theory in the 20th-century and beyond. Currently, under the name of "Super Strings," this theory is being proclaimed by leading physicists as an unmistakable genesis of a new physics. Pre-deterministic chaos theory and fractal geometry, beginning in the 1970s, has also now been proclaimed, along with Relativity and Quantum physics, as the third most profound discovery of the 20th-century changing our view of how we see and understand virtually *everything*.

The Gaon was a master kabbalist and a master scientist. As is apparent from *Kol HaTor* itself, his doctrine of "Kabbalah and science" securely grabs hold of both extremities of the separate, and often opposing, disciplines of ancient religious truth and evolving scientific knowledge. According to the Gaon, the true confluence and interpenetration of these systems will only emerge when, paradoxically, the newly discovered models and metaphors provided by the "external wisdom" of science will help illuminate the deepest secrets of the ancient mysteries of the "internal wisdom" of the Kabbalah. Reciprocally, those same ancient mysteries of the Kabbalah's "internal wisdom" will define, explain, and help reshape our perception of the entire phenomenon of the external physical world. Yet there is even more to the Gaon's unique vision of the role that secular wisdom must play in the messianic unfolding.

Messianic Synthesis From a traditional perspective, the necessity of an exchange between Torah and science is certainly not unique to *Kol HaTor*. There are numerous explicit, and even more implicit, references to this idea throughout talmudic and rabbinic literature up to, and including, *halachic responsa* of the last and present generation.[28]

Regarding the need to master the sciences in order simply to understand and solve the technicalities of talmudic law, for example, R. Yehudah Loew, the famed Maharal of Prague (1513-1606) wrote, "The other wisdoms are like a ladder upon which we may ascend to the wisdom of the Torah."[29] The Gaon himself is known for the oft-quoted statement, "To the extent that one lacks knowledge of the properties of the natural forces, he will lack one hundred-fold (literally, 'one hundred gates') in the wisdom of the Torah."

However, although this statement of the Gaon appears to express the same idea as the Maharal and others, it has a missing second half. Transmitted to R. Hillel Rivlin, it is found in paragraph #12 of *Sha'ar Be'er Sheva*. The statement concludes, "And to the extent that the Torah sages attain knowledge of the depths of the properties of nature, they will increase their understanding of the wisdom of the Torah one hundred-fold ('one hundred gates')." The intention of the full statement becomes clear when we remember that throughout *Kol HaTor* the "wisdom of the Torah" refers primarily to its esoteric teachings, the Kabbalah. It is thus significant that the Gaon speaks here of "one hundred gates of wisdom" per the *Zohar's* statement that the "gates of wisdom above" will open together with the "gates of wisdom below." The apparent repetition can now be understood as a reference to a mutual interdependence between science and Kabbalah. These two bodies of knowledge are really two sides of the same coin, two aspects of something greater than their individual parts. When we will no longer view them as opposing disciplines, our understanding of *both* will change radically. But how will this come about?

This statement of the Gaon, regarding the role of secular knowledge in helping uncover the secrets of esoteric Judaism, is almost unheard of throughout the millennia of rabbinic literature. One of the few exceptions is a text that appears in the writings of R. Moshe Chaim Luzzatto. Commenting on the *Zohar's* requirement "to know the [structure] of the human body and to look into the world in order to attain knowledge of the Divine,"[30] he explains that the human body (the microcosm) and the universe (the macrocosm) are physical counterparts of spiritual processes. It is therefore necessary to study their structure and dynamics on the material plane in order to gain a deeper understanding of the divine process itself.[31] Yet even here, the Ramchal does not depict this approach playing a necessary role in stimulating a process of messianic redemption. The fact is that there is no other source as explicit and forceful in redefining the messianic relationship between Torah and science as *Kol HaTor*.[32]

R. Shlomo Zalman Rivlin provided each chapter of *Kol HaTor* with a brief summary of its contents. At the beginning of *Sha'ar Be'er Sheva* he writes:

> Subject contents: The obligation to study the Seven Wisdoms of science according to the Gaon in order to grasp the wisdom of the Torah, sanctify God's Name and accelerate the redemption.

We have seen that the Gaon defines the "wisdom of the Torah" as the Kabbalah. It is the obligation of Torah scholars to master modern scientific thought in order to understand the deep secrets of this Jewish esoteric tradition, and vice versa. This, in turn, will lead to a sanctification of God's Name (*Kiddush HaShem*) in the eyes of the nations. To some extent, this role of the Torah sages is also known from previous sources. R. Moshe Chaim Luzzatto also writes, "One for whom it is necessary to mingle among the learned Gentiles should be knowledgeable in those subjects which will evoke their admiration and respect. God's Name will thus be honored through him."[33] What is novel about the Gaon's system is that here the true sanctification of God's Name is only possible through an intimate knowledge of the Kabbalah.

For the Gaon, science is not only to be regarded as an aid in revealing the teachings of the Kabbalah and vice versa. Neither is its role exhausted in the great sanctification of God's Name that emerges out of this synthesis. There is a third revolutionary aspect to the interrelationship between Kabbalah and science. Kabbalah together with scientific discovery and its technology is essential in ushering in, and even accelerating, the incoming and final stage of global evolution, traditionally referred to as the Messianic Era. Thus, modern science and technology are one of the very manifestations of the messianic process itself.

The doctrine that science and technology play a prophetic and mystical role, alongside the ancient mystical teachings of Judaism, and that this synthesis depends upon the Jewish nation being re-centered in a rebuilt Jerusalem, is unparalleled in Torah literature. This is certainly the case here in *Kol HaTor,* where these factors are woven together and developed within a systematic and comprehensive framework — a virtual *Shulchan Aruch* (Code of Jewish Law).[34] This is not because these principles were unknown to the elite Torah masters throughout the generations. Rather, as R. Hillel Rivlin states:

> "Our master, the Gaon, was sent from heaven
> to reveal the formulas of the Torah on a level
> for which permission had never been granted to
> his predecessors. Even our master, the holy
> Ari, was not granted such permission as he
> lived hundreds of years before the beginning of
> the 'time to favor her' and the 'time for
> singing'." [Psalms 102:14 and Song of Songs

2:12. These are both code terms used throughout *Kol HaTor,* which refer to the period of Mashiach ben Yoseph].

The first two functions of science — to grasp the wisdom of the Torah and to sanctify God's Name — must now be viewed against an even larger backdrop. This is the universal purpose of fulfilling a messianic destiny and serving to guide and prepare all humanity for a major paradigm shift in consciousness. According to the Gaon, the Torah sages' mastery of scientific models and maps is an intrinsic and necessary component of the ancient, prophetic mission of the Jewish nation to be a global and evolutionary "light to the nations" (Isaiah 42:6).

---

[1] R. Menachem Mendle of Shklov, Introduction to *Pe'at HaShulchan,* and in R. Shlomo Zalman Rivlin's introduction to the 1947 edition of *Kol HaTor* (printed in the 1968 B'nei B'rak edition). See Vol II, Chapter 3, Leviathan for more on R. Schick and his statement.

[2] This point is illustrated in an episode concerning the Gaon (*Aliot Eliyahu,* p. 77, note 31).

> It is related that once, upon passing through Berlin [the center of academic enlightenment], the Gaon was a Shabbat guest at the home of the Jewish community's wealthiest and most respected communal leader, R. Yaacov Tzvi of Berlin. A gentile neighbor, who was a leading professor and head of Berlin's three universities, inquired about all the commotion that the Jews were making in their preparations to welcome the Gaon. R. Yaacov Tzvi replied that a great genius was to be hosted in his house, who was a master of all the sciences as well as being a holy man and great Torah sage.

> The Gaon arrived on Friday afternoon to a palatial estate that was teeming with all the Torah scholars of Berlin. All of these men had been invited to the Shabbat meal so that they could hear the Gaon's Torah novella and exchange dialogue with him. Upon witnessing the jubilation of the crowd and great honor that they were awarding this Jew, the professor approached R. Yaacov Tzvi and expressed his desire to converse with the Gaon about scientific matters. There was a particularly difficult problem in astronomy, he added, which had baffled the scientists of all three universities for three years. So far no one had been able to provide a satisfactory explanation.

> It was not until late Shabbat afternoon, during the Third Meal, that R. Yaacov Tzvi approached the Gaon and conveyed the professor's

request to speak with him. He remarked that, in his opinion, the great *mitzvah* of sanctifying God's Name and engendering respect for the Jewish people was at stake here. The Gaon agreed.

The professor arrived just as the Shabbat ended and the *Havdalah* ceremony was performed. With the aid of an interpreter he presented his question to the sage. In response, the Gaon proceeded to draw a number of diagrams and notations related to the question. Along with these he presented a lengthy explanation. The professor was overjoyed with what he heard, expressed his profound thanks and took his leave. As R. Yaacov Tzvi escorted him down the stairs and to the door, the professor, his face radiant with awe, exclaimed, "Do not think that this guest of yours is of the human species. He is an angel of God who is at home in the farthest reaches of the heavens. With just a few words he has opened my eyes and given me the solution to a problem which I was convinced could not be solved."

The professor could not sleep that night and went instead to share his experience with his colleagues in the academy. Since it was their custom to grant honorary degrees to great scholars, they all agreed that they would gather immediately the next morning and, together with the entire student body of the university, go to the Gaon and formally express their appreciation. When they arrived at R. Yaacov Tzvi's home, however, the Gaon was already gone and although they attempted to catch up with him he was nowhere to be found.

[3] Fishman, David E., *Russia's First Modern Jews — The Jews of Shklov,* New York, 1995. "Taken together, the circle of devotees and disciples of the Gaon of Vilna in Shklov was one of the most intensive and creative centers of rabbinic learning in Eastern Europe in the late eighteenth and early nineteenth centuries" (p. 104).

[4] He is the author of *G'viah HaKesef* (novella on Torah and Talmud) and *Mass'at Benyamin* (sermons concerning Torah and redemption). It was R. Benyamin's descendants who formed the branch of the Rivlins who became the *Perushim* ("separatists") or *Mitnagdim* (Opponents of the Hasidic movement) in Lithuania (Byelorussia) and Jerusalem, and followed the customs and system of learning of the Gaon. R. Benyamin's brother, R. Eliyahu Riveles (or Platkes), on the other hand, was a disciple of R. Shneur Zalman of Lyady, and his descendants were Chabad Hasidim. With the immigration of his grandson, R. Eliyahu Yoseph Rivlin, to the Holy Land in 1847, the Chabad members of the Rivlin family joined their relatives and settled in such places as Jerusalem, Hebron and Tiberius, where the major Chabad communities existed at the time.

[5] The unconventional personality of R. Benyamin is also apparent in his dietary habits. "He never ate bread or meat, nor did he drink wine or any other drink, even on the Shabbat and Yom Tov... he ate only whole grains and fruit, and on rare occasions a bit of fish with potatoes dipped in olive oil. His favorite drink, for thirst or with which to honor his guests, was the strong coffee we jokingly call "black bitter." *Kiryah Ne'emanah,* quoted in

Benyamin Rivlin, HaRav Moshe Rivkash and his Descendants (Jerusalem, 1971) pp. 26-27.

[6] R. Yehoshua Zietlin (1742-1822) was a scholar and *shtadlan* (representative of the Jewish community to the government authorities with access to high dignitaries and legislative bodies). He was a student of R. Aryeh Leib Gunzberg (author of *Sha'agat Aryeh* and, after the Gaon, considered one of the greatest Talmudists of his time). He wrote *Haggahot Chadashot* ("New Glosses") on the *Sefer Mitzvot Katan*. Together with R. Benyamin Rivlin he headed a large pharmaceutical company (Rivlin-Zietlin) that supplied medicinal herbs to all of White Russia. It was partly due to their business connections that they had influence on the government. He was also one of the wealthiest merchants in the area and owned estates with over 900 serfs. He built a palace for himself to the east of Shklov that housed a vast library. Many scholars were invited to make use of this library, including R. Benyamin Rivlin and R. Mendel Lapin (Lefin) of Satanov who wrote on education, science, medicine and hygiene. Lapin's famous ethical work *Cheshbon HaNefesh* (Spiritual Accounting) was patterned on Benjamin Franklin's Poor Richard's Almanac. It is likely that he gained access to this work in English from R. Yehoshua Zietlin's extensive library. R. Dr. Baruch Schick of Shklov (also see below *Sha'ar Be'er Sheva* and Part II, Chapter 3) also frequented the estate and Zietlin saw to it that there was a chemistry lab on the premises for the doctor to perform his experiments, *Chazon Tziyon,* p. 19.

[7] *Chazon Tziyon,* p. 14.

[8] Other sources indicate the Gaon's abortive travel to the Land of Israel occurred in 1772 or in 1781.

[9] *Chazon Tziyon,* p. 4. Also, see below, the Approbation to the 1968 edition, "We, the descendants and the grandchildren of the family, have received the tradition, from one to another, that our grandfather, the sage and mystic, Rabbi Hillel, may his merit protect us, merited to stand before his master, the Gra z"l, many years."

[10] Actually, the first settlement outside of the Old City was *Mishkenot Sha'ananim,* founded by the endeavors of another disciple of the Gaon, R. Shmuel Salant, who led the Jerusalem community for over 80 years and who considered it his primary mission in life to settle the Land of Israel in such a way that the redemption would be hastened. The enormous success that he had in this mission, against tremendous odds, shows in the fact that when he arrived in the beginning of the 19th-century the Jewish population of Palestine was minuscule, while when he died years later, the population had grown significantly. It was due to R. Shmuel's efforts that the famous English philanthropist, Sir Moses Montefiore, supported the building of numerous settlements. Mishkenot Sha'ananim was later named Yemin Moshe in his honor.

[11] The manuscript has recently been published in Hebrew by R. Yoseph Rivlin's great grandson, Prof. Yoseph Rivlin of Bar Ilan University in Israel, with extensive notes and references to *Kol HaTor* and other related material.

[12] Published under the title *Shirei Shlomo,* (1933). Continuing in the family

tradition that began with R. Benyamin Rivlin of attaining proficiency in a number of languages, he also co-edited a Hebrew-Yiddish-English dictionary with J.C. Epstein (1924).

[13] The fact that there were originally seven complete chapters is clear from R. Shlomo Zalman Rivlin's introduction (printed in the 1968 B'nei B'rak and subsequent editions) and references found in the existing five chapters. In addition, scattered quotations appear from the two missing chapters in R. Shlomo Zalman's other writings. In the continuing mystery of *Kol HaTor* the entire missing sixth chapter along with the listing of the contents of the final seventh chapter was discovered and printed for the first time in the Jerusalem 1994 edition of *Kol HaTor*. (This new edition also included the last page of the 5th chapter that was already discovered earlier in the 1980's and printed as a "missing" page from *Kol HaTor* in "*Nitzaney Aretz*," a journal of Yeshivat Mercaz HaRav who received the document from the Organization for the Dissemination of *Kol HaTor,* B'nai B'rak. This page did not appear in either of the two editions published in 1968). The editor of this new edition, Prof. Yoseph Rivlin, writes that he found these lost sections together with the remaining manuscript already in our hands in the house of his father, Shmuel Rivlin, the son of Shlomo Zalman Rivlin, who had published the first partial edition. The missing sections of the handwritten manuscript had been copied by Shlomo Zalman Rivlin from the original *Kol HaTor,* never having been published, due to lack of funding as explained above.

[14] They included R. Chaim Friedlander z"l, Rosh Yeshivah and well-known scholar of Kabbalah (who was instrumental in publishing many of the works of the Ramchal); R. Shmuel Devir z"l, *Dayan* (Judge) and member of the Rabbinical Court of B'nei B'rak; R. Shalom Ulman, author of kabbalistic works on the Ramchal and the Gaon.

[15] Both editions include written appeals in search of anyone knowing the whereabouts of the original manuscript of *Kol HaTor* or the missing last two and a half chapters from R. Shlomo Zalman's 1946-47 edition.

[16] See Part I, Chapter 4, *Sha'ar Be'er Sheva,* par. 8 and corresponding note.

[17] Originally published in *Nitzanei Aretz,* referred to here above. This passage is from the end of the first section of the fifth chapter of *Kol HaTor* and mentions specific "end times" for the events through which the Redemption is to unfold. I have also translated this passage with notes in Part I, Chapter 3.

[18] This phenomenon should not surprise us. R Hillel implies in *Kol HaTor* that, as was the case with himself, one must have a direct connection with the inner soul of *Kol HaTor,* and with the soul of the Gaon himself, to be drawn into the Secret Doctrine of Mashiach ben Yoseph and hear its voice calling.

[19] See especially the Gaon's extensive commentaries to *Tikkuney Zohar, Tikkuney Zohar Chadash, Sifra DeTzeniuta* and his commentary to Habakkuk. See also *Likutei HaGra* (with commentary of *Be'er Yitzchak)* where the unification of the Two Messiahs is discussed (pp. 80, 81, 125, 175).

[20] R. Yoseph Spinner, who worked closely with the members of the Organization for the Dissemination of *Kol HaTor* in B'nei B'rak, heard from R.

Aaron Abraham Slotki, who was the former head of the Kabbalah Yeshivah Sha'ar HaShamayim and who lived well past the age of 100 and died in 1976, that during that time R. Hillel's original manuscript of *Kol HaTor* was known and circulated in Torah circles. On the other hand, when R. Zussman, a second-generation disciple of Rav Avraham Yitzchak Kook, was asked if Rav Kook was familiar with *Kol HaTor*, the answer was negative.

R. Yaacov Moshe Charlap, outstanding disciple of Rav Kook, however, does refer to *Kol HaTor* (*Mosadei Aretz*, appended to the end of *Chazon Tziyon*, 1946), and R. Zussman, a student of R. Charlap, said that when he was serving under his teacher as a young man, he witnessed R. Shlomo Zalman inquiring of R. Charlap concerning the kabbalistic material in *Kol HaTor* on numerous occasions. Still, there is no source that indicates that Rav Kook had access to *Kol HaTor*, despite the fact that it is assumed he was in contact with all the sages and kabbalists of his generation and that his system of thought often appears as a commentary and elucidation of many principles found throughout *Kol HaTor*. Apparently this is another one of the enigmas surrounding *Kol HaTor*.

[21] The Gaon himself studied the works of the Ramchal, praised him with the highest regard, and is known for his statement that, if the Ramchal were still alive in his time, he would have walked barefoot from Vilna, Lithuania to Padua, Italy in order to sit at his feet and study with him. In this sense the Gaon did have contact with the Ramchal, although there is no indication anywhere in the writings of the Gaon that he was influenced by the Ramchal, certainly not his kabbalistic writings. In fact, most of the Ramchal's Kabbalah works were not accessible till much later.

[22] Part II, Chapter 1 is devoted to Mashiach ben Yoseph and the *Trein M'shechin.*

[23] Traditionally, the universe in its present form is to exist for 6000 years (as we currently experience time following the collapse of Adamic consciousness) followed by a seventh millennium (Talmud, *Rosh HaShanah* 31a; Talmud, *Sanhedrin* 97a; Talmud, *Avodah Zarah* 9a; Gaon's commentary to *Sifra DeTzeniuta* 5, p. 66 (33b)). This macro-time scale parallels, in exact ratio, the micro-time scale of the week of Genesis, i.e., six days followed by the Shabbat, in accord with the verse, "A thousand years in Your sight are like a day gone by..." (Psalm 90:4). Thus, by dividing every 1000 year period (1 "day") into 24 parts we can calculate that every 42 years and 8 months equals 1 "hour" on the cosmic clock. Similarly, every 250 years is 6 "hours" and every 500 years is 12 "hours". According to this principle, and taking into account that a day in Genesis always begins at the onset of night, the year 5000 (1240 C.E.) was "nightfall" or the beginning of the "sixth day" of creation. The year 5500 (1740) heralded the "dawn" or "sunrise," and the year, 5750 (1990), corresponds to "high-noon" of the "sixth day". The year 5750 brings us 750 years or 3/4 into the sixth millennial day with a remaining 250 years or one quarter until its completion. According to the Gaon the first 250 year period from 5500 to 5750 is the messianic age of Mashiach ben Yoseph; the second and final period from 5750 to 6000 is the messianic age of Mashiach ben David. The demarcation between these two eras is, however, not absolute, and there is a definite period of overlap during which the two processes operate simultaneously. See the Gaon's

commentary to *Sifra DeTzeniuta* 1, p. 20 (10b); R. Shlomo Eliyashiv, *Leshem Sh'vo V'Achlamah, Sefer Hakdamot VeSh'arim*, p. 172; R. Rafael Shochat, *Torat HaGeulah B'Mishnat Rabbeinu HaGadol HaGaon MiVilna* (unpublished manuscript; note of Leshem at end).

[24] *Leshem Sh'vo V'Achlamah, Sefer De'ah* 1:5:4 (p. 76).

[25] The principle of a parallelism between the historical development of science and Kabbalah is also advanced by the contemporary Torah master, R. Dr. Chaim Zimmerman, z"l: "According to the sages, Knowledge (whether it is Torah knowledge or secular knowledge) comes from Heaven. This means that the sum total of all knowledge that flows into the world during any one period or generation is determined by *hashgachah* [Divine Providence] in direct correlation to the merit of the generation and of those individuals who discover it. According to this principle [of parallelism], we can verify that in a period when knowledge is revealed in the non-Torah world, the same quality of knowledge is revealed in the Torah world. When the non-Torah world had a Newton and a Leibnitz, the Torah world had the Gaon of Vilna and the *Sha'agat Aryeh*. In a generation of Einstein and Planck, the Torah world had a R. Chaim Soloveitchik and R. Abraham of Sochotchov.... In short, the more science progressively reveals the secrets of our physical world, the more the secrets of the Kabbalah become indispensable in understanding the real meaning of the Torah. The *hashgachah* has determined that these two categories of knowledge develop and progress in parallel lines." (R. Dr. Chaim Zimmerman, *Torah and Reason*, Hed Press, Jerusalem 1979, pp. 287, 291).

R. Yoseph ber Soloveitchik, illustrious philosopher of U.S. Orthodox Judaism, has similarly written:

> "R. Shneur Zalman of Lyady, the founder of Chabad Hasidism, that great luminary of *halachah* and mysticism, sensed that the fundamental method of *halachah* (Jewish Law) is that act of quantification which is so integral a part of the mystery of the *Tzimtzum* (Constriction). This wondrous principle expresses itself in two parallel dimensions: in the real world, empirical reality, and in the ideal world, *halachic* constructions. The supernal will clothes itself in these two creations and becomes embodied through them in the attribute of *Gevurah* (Justice) and *Tzimtzum* (Constriction). Moreover, "God has set each one of these against the other" (Ecclesiastes 7:14), i.e., God has introduced a parallelism; for just as the quantitative reality to which our senses are exposed lends itself to quantification by cognitive man, who turns qualities into quantities, percepts into equations, so too the supernal illumination, "which may be perceived by means of the many mighty contractions, which it undergoes as the different levels of reality emanate from one another," is placed within and under the dominion of the delimited, "contracted," quantitative act. The "movement" from quality to quantity, from experience to equations, which takes place in the real, empirical world, also finds its expression in the ideal realm of *halachah* (Jewish Law).... The statement of Galileo that "the great book which ever lies before our eyes, I mean the Universe, is written in mathematical language and

the characters are triangles, circles and other geometrical figures" applies as well to the *halachah*. And not for naught did the Gaon of Vilna tell the translator [R. Dr. Baruch Schick of Shklov] of Euclid's Geometry in Hebrew that, "to the degree that a man is lacking in the wisdom of mathematics he will lack one hundred-fold in the wisdom of the Torah." This statement is not just a pretty rhetorical conceit that testifies to the broad-mindedness of the Gaon but a firmly established truth of *halachic* epistemology.... The supernal will is reflected both in the mirror of reality and the mirror of the ideal *halachah* (Jewish Law), through the medium of objective, quantitative measurements. (R. Yoseph ber Soloveitchik, *Halachic Man*, JPS, 1983, pp. 56-57)

[26] The Hasidic movement also takes note of this passage from the *Zohar* and agrees that it is heralding new revelations in Jewish mysticism, albeit with a different venue. It is well known in the Chabad tradition that the mystic revelations of the "wisdom from above" refer to the emergence of the Hasidic movement and to the publication of classic Hasidic (Chabad) literature, which occurred at the end of the 18th and beginning of the 19th centuries; see Rabbi M. M. Shneerson, *On the Essence of Chassidus*, Kehot Pub., 1974, p. 91.

A direct tradition from the Ba'al Shem Tov himself is quoted by R. Aaron Marcus (1843-1916), a German Torah scholar who wrote on Kabbalah and Hasidut. He became a strong adherent of Hasidic teachings and maintained close relations with many Hasidic leaders in Poland and Galicia, in particular with R. Shlomo Rabinowitz of Radamsk. In his *Keset HaSofer* he writes what is almost a commentary on the Gaon's view of the revelations of science during the period preceding the Final Redemption: We now know with certainty that the prophecy of the *Zohar* in *Parashat VaYeira* has been fulfilled in our generation. Thus, throughout the first 6 centuries of the sixth millennium (5000-5600 = 1240-1840), the spiritual quality of *Malchut*-Kingdom, which is also known as the "Lower Wisdom," would ascend slowly. Then in the six hundredth year of the sixth millennium (5600 = 1840), "the gates of wisdom above and the wellsprings of wisdom below" began to open. This is also the prophecy of our master R. Yisrael Ba'al Shem Tov concerning the *kavanot* (meditations) while reciting Psalm 107 [during the Minchah prayer immediately preceding the onset of the Sabbath]. He interpreted the verse homiletically, "In His hand are (*mech'karei aretz*) the deep secrets of the earth and the heights of the mountains are His" (Psalm 95:4). Instead of reading *mech'karei aretz*, "deep secrets of the earth," read *me'chakrei aretz*, "investigators of the earth." The "Hand of God" represents here the aspect of *Malchut*-Kingdom, the last [and most manifest spiritual] level that is now operative. It is in this Hand of God that all the progress and success of the gentile investigators lies; *Keset HaSofer*, Bereshit 2, p. 8.

[27] R. Shlomo Eliyashiv states: "What was forbidden to investigate and expound upon just yesterday becomes permissible today. Every true exegete is aware of this. Numerous matters whose awesome nature repelled one from even approaching in previous generations, behold, they are easily grasped today. This is because the gates of human understanding below have been opened up as a result of the steadily increasing flow of Divine revelations above;" (*Leshem Sh'vo V'Achlamah, Chelek HaBi'urim*, p. 21d)

8 For a thorough discussion of traditional, as well as, some contemporary views of Torah and Science, see *Challenge - Torah Views on Science and its Problems*, Aryeh Carmell and Cyril Domb, editors (Association of Orthodox Jewish Scientists and Feldheim Publishers, 1978). It should be noted that in the first volume of this otherwise comprehensive work only one short paragraph is quoted from *Kol HaTor*, and then almost in passing.

It is only in the second companion volume that a short summary of *Kol HaTor's* position on science is presented. *Encounter - Essays on Torah and Modern Life*, H. Chaim Schimmel and Aryeh Carmell, editors (Association of Orthodox Jewish Scientists/Feldheim Publishers, 1989, no longer in print). The essay is entitled "*Tora im Derech Eretz:* A Fresh Approach" by Rabbi A. H. Rabinowitz. This source is quoted here in full to corroborate the assertion that what *Kol HaTor's Sha'ar Be'er Sheva* is advocating in the name of the Gaon, regarding the necessary messianic role of science, is virtually unparalleled and unprecedented throughout the entire spectrum of rabbinic and kabbalistic literature:

> In a little-known volume compiled by a disciple of the Gaon of Vilna, *Kol HaTor*, this subject [of the relationship between Torah and secular study] is treated in depth. The views of the Gaon, as presented by his disciples in that volume, shed a fresh perspective on *Tora im Derech Eretz*, one for which even the opinions of Rav Shor and Rav Kook [previously discussed in the essay and both representing among the most extreme views on the subject] have only slightly prepared us. As far as I am aware, there is not even an inkling of it in Rabbi S. R. Hirsch's original approach. R. Hillel ben R. Binyamin of Shklov, expounds there the Gaon's view on the messianic process until the final redemption of Israel. Part II of the fifth chapter, called *Sha'ar Be'er Sheva*, is devoted to a detailed presentation of the Gaon's attitude towards the seven wisdoms, their study, and their part in the messianic scheme.

Still, the editors of R. Rabinowitz's posthumously published essay were compelled to add the bracketed note, "It must be noted however that this work [*Kol HaTor*] is not universally accepted as an authentic presentation of the views of the Gaon of Vilna."

29 Maharal of Prague, *Netivot Olam, Netiv Torah*, Chapter 14, pp. 60-61. See the Gaon's statement quoted in *Sha'ar Be'er Sheva*, par. #10: "It is impossible to climb a ladder whose top reaches towards the heavens without first stepping on the rungs of that ladder that are stationed near the earth."

30 Based on the *Zohar*, the Ramchal states that there are four categories of knowledge that one is required to know as deeply as possible: 1) to know and perceive the mystery of how God brought the universes into existence and how His light permeates the totality of creation; 2) to know how the human body is a microcosm of the entire universe (in particular of the *Sefirot*) and to know how man's actions affect the upper universes; 3) to know the mystery of transmigration of all the souls that have ever been born and how each soul is brought to its perfection through this process; and 4) to know the mystery of the material universe. See *Zohar Chadash Shir HaShirim* on Song of Songs 1:7 and next note.

52
The Living Legacy of *Kol HaTor*

---

[31] Two parallel texts (with slight variations) appear in the Ramchal's introduction to *Adir BaMarom* and at the end of *Milchemet Moshe* (printed as an appendix to *Da'at Tevunot*, B'nei B'rak, 1975). After explaining the *Zohar's* first three categories, he writes:

> The fourth category of knowledge is to know the mystery of this world, as the *Zohar* states, "To look into the world." This means that there is an obligation to know that everything in this world operates according to the mystery of the *Sefirot*, that is, to know the internal design that is immanent in nature. This is the intention of the numerical equivalence between the word Nature (*HaTeva* = 86) and God (E-lohim = 86). This is in contrast to the opinion of the philosophers [who apprehend the world solely as it appears to their senses]. The truth is, however, that the laws governing the existence of every creature in the world can only be understood in terms of the *Sefirot*. The knowledge of natural science as well as all other knowledge is predicated upon this principle, i.e., the mystery of the *Sefirot* according to their true supernal function. One must then know the root of all this above.
>
> "Concerning the [second category of] knowledge of the human body we have explained the principle that "From my [microcosmic] flesh I will behold [the macrocosmic] God" (Job 19:26). This same principle is to be applied to the knowledge of nature and its laws. Thus there are things that can only be understood about the *Sefirot* via knowledge of the human body, while there are other things that can only be understood about the *Sefirot* via knowledge of the world. Although both of these really constitute one unified system, certain things are revealed in man and others are revealed in the world. It follows that the world must be understood in two [complementary] ways: First, in its manifestation here below. This can only be done, however, if one concentrates on the deeper *sefirotic* design that is inherent in the world, as opposed to the cynicism of the philosophers. It is around this principle that the majority of the *aggadic* and *midrashic* statements of the sages revolve when they speak about *Ma'aseh Bereshit* (Work of Creation) and other matters relating to all the details of heaven and earth. This knowledge is also exceedingly great and precious. Second, after a proper understanding of the laws of nature has been established below, their mystery and their root must be ascertained above in the *Sefirot*. Only then can we understand the why of things. Lastly, we must understand all of this in the secrets of the Torah, for all of these matters are contained within its teachings."

In his *Ma'amar HaAggadot* (printed at the beginning of all editions of *Ain Yaacov*) the Ramchal further clarifies how the talmudic sages related to the "external" wisdom of the world:

> "The sages encoded much of the esoteric tradition that they had received in matters relating to nature or astronomy. In other words, they utilized the knowledge of nature and astronomy that was accepted among gentile scholars of their time in order to transmit something else. Thus, they never intended to teach the physical

"facts" concerning these phenomena, but rather, to utilize these facts as vehicles for kabbalistic secrets. One should therefore not think that they were wrong because a particular model, which they used, is no longer accepted. Their intention was to clothe the hidden tradition in the accepted knowledge of their generation. That very tradition itself could have been clothed in a different garment according to what was accepted [as scientific fact] in other generations. And, in fact, the originator of that particular *aggadic* statement would have done so himself if he would have stated it in those other generations."

In *Adir BaMarom* (p. 66b), the Ramchal writes further:

"All the *aggadic* statements that you find in the teachings of the sages concerning the sun and the other stars that are no longer accepted [according to current scientific belief] are referring to the inner dimension of Divine Providence. One who is not familiar with the Paths of Wisdom [the Kabbalah] can only grasp the external structure of reality in accord with its physical description... The essence of the matter is that the sages are referring to the inner structure of reality. This is the knowledge of the Torah, which encompasses all wisdom. It is, however, all in the mystery of the internal design and not in the external form."

[32] It would appear that another important exception to this rule is to be found in Hasidic literature, particularly that of Chabad Lubavitch. This branch of Hasidut (which is often considered by both camps to be mystically antithetical to the school of the Gaon of Vilna) also maintains the belief that science has to play a prophetic role in helping to usher in the Messianic Era via the usage of its models and metaphors to better understand Judaism's own esoteric traditions. Commenting on the same passage from the *Zohar*, the previous Lubavitcher Rebbe said, "The truest unification between science and Torah is such that from its theoretical models it is possible to perceive matters pertaining to the innermost aspects of the Torah." ("Concerning the Development of Science in Our Present Time," printed in Hebrew translation from the Yiddish original in *B'Or HaTorah* 2, p. 8.) In this article based on the Rebbe's statements, however, the role of science is downplayed. There, the text reads, "The *Zohar* plainly means that the gates to the wisdoms, or the sciences in general, *and of more essential import* [italics mine], the gates to the wisdom of the Torah in particular, will be opened at that time." The non-equivalence of science and Torah is emphasized, despite the fact that the *Zohar* places equal emphasis on both. On the other hand, the Rebbe points out in the same article that "The fact that the *Zohar* mentions both matters (the development of Torah and Science) in one context proves that both are intimately connected and that a development in the area of the Torah draws after it a [corresponding] development in the sciences." It does appear, however, that in the Chabad system, the ultimate fulfillment of science "is such that from its theoretical models it is possible to perceive matters pertaining to the innermost aspects of the Torah," i.e., in order for an educated person to better grasp mystical concepts already known and well developed in Hasidic thought. Yet, in the Gaon's system, the messianic fulfillment of science is decidedly different. In *Sha'ar Be'er Sheva*, par. #6, R. Hillel writes: "The Wisdom of the Torah (Kabbalah) is contained in the light of

the Supernal Wisdom. In order to understand and grasp this Wisdom, however, it is also necessary to learn the Seven Sciences that are hidden in external reality," i.e., in order for the scholar/kabbalist to actually decode heretofore inaccessible knowledge hidden in cryptic passages of the Talmud, the *Zohar* and in the writings of the Ari and the Gaon. Furthermore, it appears that, according to Chabad Hasidut, the revelation of the inner teachings of the Torah (Hasidut) stimulates the growth of the Seven Sciences, but not vice versa. In the Gaon's system, on the other hand, the development of science actually awakens the inner teachings of the Kabbalah. In any event, we see that a mystical relationship between Torah and science and the Torah scholar's obligation to master and integrate the "Seven Sciences" is maintained by both the non-Hasidic as well as the Hasidic mystics, and from this perspective, can certainly be considered a traditional Jewish belief.

[33] Ramchal, *Derech Chochmah, Kitvey HaRamchal,* Jerusalem.

[34] This is the actual term that R. Hillel uses to describe *Kol HaTor* in Chapter 3, par. 1.

Chapter 2

The Messianic Mission
of the Gaon of Vilna

- The Gaon of Vilna
- "There Is No One Like Him"
- The Chamber of the Gaon
- The Censored Mystic
- The Revelations of Eliyahu
- Gematria, Transmigration, and Divination
- The Messiah from the House of Yoseph
- Master of the Seven Sciences
- The Extraordinary Letter
- The Call of the Turtledove

Chapter 2

The Messianic Mission
of the Gaon of Vilna

The Gaon of Vilna Rabbi Eliyahu ben Shlomo Zalman (1720-1797) was a legendary figure in his own lifetime. In the Jewish world of the 18th-century there were numerous phenomenal Torah geniuses from both the Hasidic and *Mitnaggid* (non-Hasidic) communities, as well as, charismatic *tzadikim,* whose divine-like qualities shone forth like the brightest stars of the night sky. Yet, even among these, the Gaon of Vilna stood out like the blinding light of the stellar explosion of a super-nova. A being of such magnitude does not easily fit into any of the known categories of human experience, certainly not within the last few hundred years of history.[1]

Even familiarity with comparative mysticism, and the philosophy of human thought throughout the ages, can only begin to prepare us for an understanding of the Gaon's system of cosmology and the role he envisioned for himself within that cosmology.

Although there are a number of biographical works and articles on the Gaon in Hebrew, until recently little of substance had been rendered into English.[2] Even of that which is now available it is the Gaon's intense mystical life that is often excluded.[3] Even in the standard Hebrew works on the Gaon, the passionate messianic mission that directed his life has been met with disbelief, low esteem, and censorship.

The major problem one encounters when attempting to achieve an understanding of the Gaon is that the closer one becomes acquainted with his personality, the more one feels distanced. This is due to the sheer magnitude and incomprehensible superhuman powers of his mind and otherworldly manner of conduct. His most renowned and illustrious disciple, R. Chaim of Volozhin, himself a recognized superlative Torah master and kabbalist, publicly admitted, "How can I not be embarrassed to be called his disciple in view of my not having attained even a fraction of his splendor".[4]

All of the Gaon's followers, of which he had many, spoke about him with such rapture and extravagant respect that it rivals the attitudes of the Hasidim to their wonder-working *rebbes* and *tzadikim*. (In fact, the Gaon was originally referred to by his communities as the Gaon and *Hasid* – the Pious One — from Vilna). As will be apparent from their own words, his followers were intoxicated, as it were, with their teacher's charismatic personality and saintliness. Likewise, from the texts quoted, it will be evident that the wonders performed by the Hasidic masters, and the revelations received by them, were by no means limited to their own class.

An acute awareness of a student's spiritual and intellectual distance to his teacher is true with regard to many of the great Torah masters. Yet, with the other spiritual leaders of the Gaon's generation (and thereafter) there is usually some way of approaching and connecting with their teachings. Often, they themselves would intentionally "bring down" their revelatory insights to the level of the average Torah scholar and layperson. This was particularly the case with the Hasidic masters, who translated a number of esoteric truths into a profound form of "therapy of the soul" for the Jewish people.

The feeling with the Gaon, however, is that he simply cannot be approached. For all of the vast writings that the Gaon left us, they do not include a specific manual or overview of what, with the entire Torah in his hands, he expected of us (other than mastering the entire Written and Oral Traditions, exoteric and esoteric). He apparently left no practical system that is spelled out in a simple and methodical manner. His practical teachings, as well as his personality, remain as hidden and inaccessible as a secret chamber within a mighty and impenetrable fortress. It will be apparent, however, that the virtually impenetrable enigma of the Gaon is, in fact, accessible to one who possesses the keys supplied by *Kol HaTor*.

The view being presented in this introductory material about the Gaon — and throughout the present work — is predicated upon the fact that there are many unusual characteristics, statements, and actions of the Gaon that can only be fully understood and placed into a coherent context with the aid of the lost teachings of *Kol HaTor*. As will become evident, the author of this "secret text" *(megilat setarim* — his own term), R. Hillel Rivlin of Shklov, claims that he — and he alone — received directly from the master himself the missing key that unlocks crucial elements in the otherwise bizarre personality of the Gaon of Vilna. In so doing, R. Hillel also reveals an astonishing underground messianic mission for global evolution and redemption that the Gaon was masterminding.

The purpose of this short biography of the Gaon, however, is not only intended to serve as added testimony to his phenomenal genius, and to report the generally unknown mystical aspects of his life, even with the usage of the new information supplied from *Kol HaTor*. This introduction to the Gaon is, in effect, an introduction to *Kol HaTor* itself. Only to the extent that one appreciates the highly unconventional and singularly unique nature of the Gaon, is one able to appreciate the highly unconventional and singularly unique nature of *Kol HaTor*.

Even if *Kol HaTor* did not claim its authority from the Gaon of Vilna, it would stand on its own merit as a fascinating system of spiritual thought — especially with regard to the prophetic confluence between science and Kabbalah. Yet, *Kol HaTor* was never intended to be studied alone. It is the interfacing of *Kol HaTor* with the other extensive esoteric teachings of the Gaon that reveal its hidden depth and a crucial cosmological map and guide for the present generation. Therefore, it is important to develop a working image of the Gaon, especially as the ultimate synthesis of the scientist and kabbalist. And it is precisely R. Hillel's portrayal of his teacher in *Kol HaTor*, together with numerous other sources from the Gaon himself, which offers us the missing key, unlocking this personal connection with Rabbi Eliyahu, the Gaon of Vilna.

"There Is No One Like Him" Although the Gaon lived in the 18th-century, he has been compared to the level of a *Rishon* — a Torah sage who had lived some six hundred years earlier[5] — even to the *Ramban* (Nachmanides) himself.[6] Other Torah masters declared further that the Gaon was a spiritual throwback to the period of the *Geonim*. [7] One of the masters of Kabbalah from the last generation responded to the question of why the scholars considered the Gaon of Vilna so unique among all the other great sages of his time by answering:[8]

> Know, my son, there are unique individuals in each generation, but not all excel in all branches of knowledge. One may be gifted with penetrating knowledge, but not have an encyclopedic mind and vice versa. And if you find an individual who is endowed with both of these gifts, he may not excel in linguistics, astronomy, engineering and other disciplines where others will show their superiority. But to be an acknowledged leader in every field — the exoteric and esoteric teachings of the Torah, together with the highest levels of piety, sanctity, and purity, and every science and discipline — linguistics, astronomy, engineering, etc. — a prodigious genius such as this, was unheard of even in previous generations. Only our great teacher, the Gaon of Vilna achieved this level.

The prestige held by the Gaon, even in the eyes of the gentiles, was also legendary in its time. His face radiant with awe, a leading German professor and head of Berlin's three universities exclaimed after a brief encounter with the Gaon:

> Do not think that this guest of yours is of the human species. He is an angel of God who is at home in the farthest reaches of the heavens. With just a few words he has opened my eyes

and given me the solution to a problem which I was convinced could not be solved.[9]

Overly extravagant praises? Religious "hero worship"? The reader must bear in mind that these, and the following statements, all of which were based upon eye witness accounts, were made and recorded by a very serious elite circle of Jewish leaders from Lithuania ("*Litvaks*"), who are known for their no-nonsense and matter-of-fact way of life. One such sage wrote:

> All those who stood before him saw the great signs and wonders which God bestowed upon him from above and which he himself did not even intend. One thousand sheets of paper would not be sufficient to express his praise of which there is no exaggeration because our very own eyes merited witnessing these interactions with him.[10]

Another wrote:

> I once heard R. Chaim Volozhin say in public: "Some people believe that if my brother R. Zalman [a close disciple of the Gaon who recognized him as an unusual Torah genius but died at a young age] would have lived a lengthy life, he too would have reached the spiritual level attained by the Gaon, yet I must tell you they are mistaken. My brother totally discarded the encumbrances of this physical and material world to the point where he attained the level of an angel, who was merely disguised as a man. The Gaon, on the other hand, continued to conduct himself as a mortal, while at the same time purified his being to the level of an angelic being... That is the purpose of the creation, to conduct oneself as a man, and at the same time, purify the physical and material reality of this world to a sacred state."[11]

Even an avowed Jewish heretic by the name of Abraham Abba of Glussk who, after ingeniously conniving a private audience with the Gaon through deceit, declared in a private letter to his friend Moses Mendelssohn — the father of German Enlightenment, "Behold, in spite of all the evil that befell me and what I endured because of him [the Gaon], nevertheless, my heart stands firm in informing you of the truth as I honestly believe it: Of all the wise men throughout the world, there is no one like him."[12]

Any attempt to portray the Gaon must include an episode told by R. Isaac, the son of R. Chaim of Volozhin, one of the closest disciples of the Gaon of Vilna:

> Once Father [R. Chaim of Volozhin] prepared to travel to the Gaon. I said to Father, "I too want to journey to the Rabbi." Father was overwhelmed, and said whilst trembling, "You too want to travel to the Rabbi?" I too became frightened, but nevertheless I kept to my wishes and stated, "Yes, I wish to do so". Father hesitated, but finally he agreed, and we went off. As we were on our way, I noticed Father's face, and behold, he turned pale because of fear and trembling. As the wagon drew closer to Vilna, Father's face became even more pale. By the time we came to Vilna, it was difficult to recognize him. Again he turned to me and inquired, trembling, "You too want to go to the Rabbi?" I gathered myself together and said, "Yes." As we were standing at the door of the chamber of the Gaon, his knees actually quaked out of awe for his teacher...and once more he inquired of me, "You too want to go in?"... Thus did we enter the chamber of the Gaon.[13]

Attempting to describe an image of the Gaon, especially in the space of a few pages, appears to be an impossible task. Yet, if we are to fully appreciate the Secret Doctrine of *Kol HaTor* and the world view that it presents in the name of the Gaon, we are obligated to attempt to enter —

even if only a bit — into the Chamber of the Gaon.

**The Chamber
of the Gaon**

The Gaon was the synthesis of the true *chacham-m'kubal* (sage-mystic). Yet, he was first and foremost the mystic. In fact, for all that the Gaon accomplished for Torah and the Jewish people during his seventy-seven years the greatest legacy he left was the new levels he revealed of the inner Torah — the Kabbalah. The Gaon's son, R. Avraham, wrote:[14]

> The Gaon's knowledge of exoteric Torah was surpassed by his mastery of the esoteric Torah. All the gates of knowledge were opened to him in order that he should learn, and consequently teach, to the Jewish people [the kabbalistic works of] the *Zohar, Tikkunei HaZohar, Sifra DiTzniuta, Ra'aya Meheimna, Sefer Yetzira, Ma'aseh Bereshit,* and *Ma'aseh Merkavah.*

Along with his absolute allegiance to the Talmud and to the minutiae of *halachah* (Jewish Law), everything that he analyzed or assessed was also simultaneously perceived from the perspective of the *Zohar* that he held as sacred as the Talmud itself. Everything he wrote or said was done based upon a clearly defined system of Kabbalah.

R. Menachem Mendel of Shklov, one of the Gaon's most outstanding disciples (he transcribed the Gaon's dictation to his commentary on Proverbs) wrote:[15]

> I heard from my Master on numerous occasions that every one of his explanations of the simple meaning (*pshat*) of the Torah concealed an even deeper significance (*sod*). "Without the *sod*," he said, "the simple meaning is simply not true."

> I am obligated to proclaim that which I heard explicitly from his holy mouth, namely, that he

never explained the simple *pshat* of a single verse if he did not know its inner *sod*. Only then did he dress the *sod* in the *pshat*.

In a note to the text of the Gaon's commentary he also wrote:[16]

> When one will clearly understand the *sod* then everything will be clear to him – the *pshat*, the *remez*, *drush* and *sod* [all four dimensions of the Torah, known as the acronym *Pardes*]. Until then, even the *pshat* will elude him, as it is written in *Zohar Mishpatim* [99a]. This is what I have heard from my mentor, my teacher and *rebbe* — for whom I would offer myself numerous times as ransom in place of his death. Understand this.

R. Yisrael of Shklov, another outstanding disciple of the Gaon, wrote:[17]

> His entire methodology in the revealed Torah was permeated by kabbalistic knowledge. No mystery eluded him. I heard this from the one for whom my soul longs, the great Rav and saint, the recognized kabbalist, our teacher and master, Menachem Mendel z"l [of Shklov]. While transcribing the Gaon's commentary on the *mishnaic* order of *Taharot* the Gaon told him that he never drew any novel conclusion or explanation on that order unless he understood the connection between the external *pshat* and the internal *sod*.

In his introduction to *Hadrat Kodesh* (Sacred Beauty), the Gaon's esoteric commentary on *Midrash Ruth*, R. Avraham Simcha, R. Chaim of Volozhin's nephew, wrote:

> It is impossible that the esoteric portion of the Torah could ever be at variance with its exoteric portion. How could the Torah ever contradict itself? Seeming divergences between

halachic decisions [based on one or another of
the two systems] arise only because we do not
understand the true explanation of the text in
question. In dealing with any text, whether it
was Scripture, *Mishnah*, Talmud or *Zohar*, he
united their exoteric and esoteric
understandings. They became one in his hand,
with a perfect and absolute unity. One who is
accustomed to study his holy words in *Aderet
Eliyahu* [the Gaon's commentary on *Chumash*]
will witness in numerous places that this was,
in fact, his method of analysis, namely, to
securely unite the revealed with the concealed.
I have seen this in numerous instances in his
manuscripts, and such is also the case
regarding his *halachic* decisions in the
Talmud... I also heard directly from my uncle
the *gaon*, our teacher, R Chaim z"l [of
Volozhin], that this was the entire *modus
operandi* of our master in Torah.[18]

These and other similar statements by the Gaon's
disciples[19] revolve around their master's emphatic insistence
that the Torah cannot be understood without recourse to its
s*od* (esoteric meaning). Actually, this is a precept that is
axiomatic in the *Zohar* and followed by all sage-kabbalists.

A related esoteric precept that was fundamental to the
Gaon was his transcendent view of Scripture itself, as well as
of all historical events. His view of history and of events
destined to unfold in the future also followed the most
rigorous esoteric cosmology. This all-encompassing and
holistic world view of the Gaon is succinctly spelled out in his
commentary to the portion of the *Zohar* known as the Book of
Concealment (*Sifra DiTzniuta*), where he writes: [20]

The general principle is that all that has existed, all
that now exists and all that will exist until eternity, is
all contained in the [Written] Torah from [the first
word] "In the beginning" until [the last words] "in the
eyes of all Israel." This refers not only to generalities,
but also to the particulars of every single species and

of every single human being, including everything that will transpire in his lifetime, from the day of birth until the day of death, as well as, all of his transmigrations and all of their particulars and minute details. This is likewise true with regard to every species of animal and every living creature in the world, as well as, every plant and mineral. All of the particulars and minute details of each and every form and sub-species, including everything that they and their roots will undergo, [is included in the Torah].

Similarly, all that is written concerning the Patriarchs, Moses and the Nation of Israel in every generation [is encoded in the Torah]. For the fractal sparks (*nitzotzot*) of these souls transmigrate in every generation, as is known. This extends to include the entire history of mankind, from Adam until the end of the Torah. All that occurred to them is repeated in every generation and in the life of every individual, as is known to one who understands.

In a general way all of this is also included in the first chapter of the Torah, from "In the beginning" until "Noah found favor in God's eyes" (Genesis 6:8). More generally, all of this is included in the account of the first seven days of creation (Genesis 1:1 – 2:3). Moreover, all of this is included in the seven words of the first verse of the Torah... And finally, all of this is included in the letters of the first word of the Torah and in the *dagesh* (phonetic point) inside the first letter.[21]

The Censored Mystic   Ironically, it is the Gaon's stature, as possibly the greatest mystic in modern history, and his extensive Secret Doctrine of Redemption, that has been censored from the world at large. From the beginning, the secular Jewish historians wrote that he knew nothing of Kabbalah, and even great Hasidic leaders claimed that the Gaon treated the *Zohar* lightly and that the teachings of the holy Ari — R. Yitzchak

Luria — were not considered worthy in his eyes.[22]

On the other hand, the Gaon has been the victim of self-censorship from among his very own disciples and admirers. In the interest of the Gaon, many of his own writings and those concerning personal encounters with the Gaon have been hidden, or chipped away, by the different schools of thought, who associated themselves with the Gaon. After the Gaon passed away, the Rabbis of Vilna considered, and understandably so, his extensive kabbalistic writings to be too awesome and dangerous for the public at large, and caused them to be withheld from publication. Even when his "non-Kabbalah" works were published, e.g., his commentary on Proverbs, most of the references to esoteric concepts were deleted. (They have since been reinstated in the more recent editions). On the other hand, when the *maskilim* — members of the broad-based movement for the integration of secular learning into Jewish education — published his works, they also censored from the public the "mystical" side of the Gaon. In this case, however, the intent was in order to emphasize the Gaon's devotion to rationalism and Hebrew grammar, which was of prime import in their system of thought.

As explained in the introduction the doctrine of *Kol HaTor* – and the unique image of the Gaon that it reveals — was itself kept hidden for some two hundred years. When *Kol HaTor* first went public in 1968, chapters six and seven were providentially missing. And even then one of the those two editions self-censored a crucial chapter of *Kol HaTor* which contains, in many ways, the key to the Gaon's entire system of thought (*Sha'ar Beer Sheva*, the main subject of the present work). To date, a missing last page from Section I of Chapter 5 has been published along with the entire chapter six and the content listing of chapter seven. Even so, the *Kol HaTor* we have today, although still true to the original, was edited and condensed in 1947 by R. Shlomo Zalman Rivlin upon the advice of sages in order to make it understandable to the average Torah scholar and educated layperson. The *Kol HaTor* in our hands is only a "reader's digest" version of R. Hillel's original manuscript. The whereabouts of the much larger original work, and whatever additional information it may contain about the Gaon of Vilna, is unknown.

The attempt at the "re-making" of the Gaon also struck his famous commentary on the *Shulchan Aruch* (Code of Jewish Law), which was tampered with in order to protect, in the opinion of the editor, the honor of the Gaon. It was here where the Gaon had vehemently criticized Maimonides' attitude towards basic mystical concepts of Judaism found throughout the a*ggadic* portions of the Talmud and had accused him of being influenced by an over-rational Aristotelian philosophy. The righteous anger reflected in the language of the Gaon so astonished some of the sages that they originally doubted its authenticity, and therefore deleted the offensive language. The true and original text has since been confirmed and reinstated.[23]

Protecting the honor of the Gaon from appearing as a legendary, wonder-working *"Ba'al Shem"* — Master of the [mystical] Name of God — is also the reason the following event, and a few others, are not known outside of a small society. Even the master kabbalist, R. Shlomo Eliyashiv, considered the greatest exponent of the esoteric teachings of the Gaon, refrained from referring to the details of this event and wrote, "It is not fitting to write down what I heard in this case."[24] The reference is to the Gaon's supra-natural mastery over material forces, which was related in a first-hand account by his close disciple, R. Menachem Mendel of Shklov (in his introduction to the Gaon's commentary on *Pirkei Avot* and *Mesechtot Ketanot*):

> Once, when I was sitting with [the Gaon], the conversation touched upon the subject of the philosopher Aristotle. Our master the Gaon said, "It is clear that Aristotle thoroughly rejected the belief in creation *ex nihilo*. If he were to appear before me now, however, I would show him the orbits of the planets around the sun together with the stars shining right here on this table, just as they light up the firmament of the heavens [i.e., create an actual microcosmic fractal of the universe]. Could he continue to believe that the world is

run solely in accord with natural laws? And was it impossible for Shimon HaTzadik [last of the Men of the Great Assembly, 3rd-century B.C.E.] who lived at that time to show him the many great wonders of the Creator? Rather, Aristotle was not interested in the truth; therefore he never made the effort to clarify this issue with Shimon." I recoiled backwards when I heard these things from his pure mouth. He noticed this and said to me, "Why should this shock you? With one esoteric formula I could do the same thing. The *Gaonim* after the time of the Talmud also knew this."

Whereas this type of episode was thrived upon by the Hasidic movement, this side of the Gaon was suppressed, especially by Lithuanian Jewry and its legacy. Another example of the censored teachings of the Gaon is found regarding his attitude of the role of the study of Kabbalah in the overall process of redemption. He wrote on the *Zohar*.[25]

In every generation a fractal spark (*nitzotz*) of our Teacher Moses emanates into a single individual. From this individual it continues to emanate out to all the disciples of the Torah of that generation. All novel understandings of Torah are thus revealed in the world via the emanating light of our Teacher Moses...

There are times when no worthy individual can be found through whom the emanating light of Moses is to spread out to the generation. Due to our many transgressions, therefore, such a generation does not receive an illumination of that light... It is for this reason that the period of our exile is lengthened. Our exodus from the [present] exile is therefore dependent upon the study of the Kabbalah for this is the [essence of the] Torah of Moses.

Yet, when this teaching was popularized in a small anthology of the Gaon's aphorisms called *Even Shleimah* it was reworded to state:

> The [final] redemption will come only as a
> result of Torah study, chiefly the study of
> Kabbalah.[26]

It must be born in mind that the Gaon was writing his
commentaries for an elite society of Torah scholars, who
more than understood that the study of the Kabbalah does
not exist without the interdependency of the other areas of
the Torah. Yet, it is also these little qualifications of under-
emphasizing the full intensity of the Gaon's supreme
redemptive role of the Kabbalah that collectively have altered
his deeper truth and the extreme passion of his mission. *Kol
HaTor*, on the other hand, leaves us no doubt as to the full
intensity of his intent in the above passage. Even more so,
Kol HaTor once again recasts the Gaon's understanding of
the relationship between the study of Kabbalah and the
redemption into a very real agenda for global evolution
centered in Jerusalem, Israel. R. Hillel writes:[27]

> Our master has written much stressing that
> the redemption is dependent upon the study of
> Kabbalah. Through this the Torah of our
> righteous Mashiach will be revealed little by
> little. This is the Torah of the Land of Israel.
>
> Our master descended from the heavens to
> reveal the formulas of the Torah in the period
> of *Ikveta DiM'shecha* (Heels of the Messiah) in
> the mystery of *Tzafenat Pa'aneach* — The
> Revealer of Hidden Things — and to instruct us
> according to these formulas in the practical
> path that is to be followed in this final era.

R. Hillel writes further:[28]

> The revelation of the [previously hidden]
> formulas within the Torah will proceed and
> increase together with the Advent of the
> Mashiach in our Holy Land until all of the
> mysteries of the Torah will be revealed in the

Last Generation. This is the Torah of Mashiach our *Tzadik*, as the verse (Isaiah 2:3) intimates, "The Torah will emanate from Zion" [*Tzadik* and *Tziyon* are both equated with Yoseph]. The Torah that will "emanate from Zion" refers to the revelations of its hidden treasures and mysteries, may they be revealed speedily in our day.

The *mitzvah* and sacred responsibility grows [for every *talmid chacham*] to occupy himself with the study of Kabbalah. [It is specifically through the learning of the Kabbalah] that the mysteries of the Torah will be revealed. This is part of the sacred mission of the Messiah of the Beginning, Mashiach ben Yoseph. The ingathering of the exiles will occur through him, and it is through the study of Kabbalah that this Redemption will be accelerated until it will reach its final completion through Mashiach ben David and our Teacher Moses, speedily in our day, amen.

The Revelations of Eliyahu
Born into a distinguished rabbinic family, Eliyahu ben Shlomo Zalman was a descendant of the great Lithuanian talmudist, R. Moshe Rivkes (died c. 1671), the author of *Be'er HaGolah* (Fountain of the Exile) on the *Shulchan Aruch* (Code of Jewish Law).

From the beginning, R. Eliyahu showed signs of being a child prodigy. While still a youth, he mastered all branches of the Written and Oral Torah — an ocean of knowledge. At the age of seven he was already giving public lectures and sermons that astounded his listeners. By thirteen no teacher could be found for him in all of Europe, and he subsequently studied on his own. His study methods were rigorous. It is said that he would study twenty-two hours a day, sleeping in only half hour intervals at any one time.[29] From a relatively young age, he was recognized as the leader of Lithuanian Jewry. Many flocked to his door seeking guidance and advice.

Initially he would spend long hours studying and contemplating in a secret spot in the woods. Only his wife knew of his location, which was revealed to her only in order that she would be able to bring him food.[30] Later in life, however, even though he seldom left his study, little happened in the Jewish community without his knowledge and approval.[31]

In their introduction to his commentary on the *Shulchan Aruch* (Code of Jewish Law), the Gaon's sons write that at the age of nine their father began the study of Kabbalah, and that within half a year, he had completely learned all the teachings of R. Yitzchak Luria, the Holy Ari, the most complex and profoundly influential mystical system up to that time.[32] R. Chaim Volozhin, one of the Gaon's most illustrious disciples, writes that the Gaon applied his mastery of practical Kabbalah to the construction of a *golem*, a form of artificial intelligence brought to life with divine formulas. He stopped when he saw a heavenly apparition, a sign that he was judged too young for such a project. He was not yet thirteen at the time.[33] Momentarily we will see, according to *Kol HaTor*, what was really at stake in this unusual experimentation.

With over seventy books and commentaries written by the Gaon, there is virtually no area of Torah knowledge he left untouched.[34] Applying his mastery of the entire Torah he was able to correct all major texts whose readings had become uncertain over time, as well as clarifying the sources for numerous Jewish laws and customs. His esoteric works include lengthy commentaries on the Torah (*Aderet Eliyahu*), Song of Songs, *Sefer Yetzirah* (*Book of Formation*), *Sifra DiTzniuta* (*Book of Concealment*), *Zohar and Tikkuney Zohar* (*Book of Splendor*), *Sefer HaBahir* (Book of Illumination), *Aggadot HaShas* (homiletic sections of the Talmud) and various other works that were lost. The Gaon's son, R. Avraham, writes,[35]

> "Our master, my father the Gaon, may his memory be a blessing, composed close to thirty large volumes on the entire *Zohar* and he stated with a full heart that he would not be

ashamed to expound these novella even in the presence of Rabbi Shimon bar Yochai [the author of the *Zohar*]."

By the close of the 19th-century, however, the Jerusalem kabbalist, R. Yitzchak Kahana, adds, "Our generation was not worthy of receiving these writings. As a result, the majority of [the Gaon's] words regarding concealed matters, which constituted ten-fold what he wrote on revealed matters, have been lost."[36] One modern scholar estimates that, altogether, the Gaon's kabbalistic writings exceeded in volume those of all his Hasidic contemporaries combined.[37]

All this he did before the age of forty. For, according to a number of sources, he was in such an intensely illumined state from that time on that the ever-increasing flow of knowledge was technically impossible to commit to writing. Even his closest disciples, responsible for spreading his teachings, could not record them all, as he never paused in his lessons to allow time for notes.[38]

One of the Gaon's master disciples wrote:[39]

There were esoteric secrets that the Gaon would not reveal to any of his disciples. The secret of "[the two Jewish heretics] Sasson and Simcha" (Talmud, *Succah* 48b) was one of these. Concerning this passage we heard from his holy mouth that one of the earlier masters *(gedolay harishonim)* fasted numerous fasts in order to be worthy of having the mystery of this passage revealed to him from above. His request was not granted. Our holy Rabbi, his soul be in Eden, confided that the secret of Sasson and Simcha had been revealed to him and that if he had been created only in order to grasp this matter, it would have been sufficient for him.[40]

While expounding his teachings to his disciples the Gaon would experience non-ordinary states of consciousness.

Both R. Chaim of Volozhin as well as R. Hillel, who was one of the Gaon's closest students and a regular guest in his house, report that they witnessed a radiant light emanating from the Gaon's face.[41] R. Hillel writes that it then became clear to him that the Gaon was experiencing a specific state of consciousness known since ancient times as *Gilui Eliyahu*, revelation via the prophet Elijah. Both sources testify that the Gaon had regular visitations from members of the "Heavenly Academy" who revealed the secrets of the Torah to him. These included the Patriarch Jacob, Moses our Teacher, Elijah the Prophet, Rabbi Shimon bar Yochai (the author of the *Zohar*), the holy Ari himself as well as numerous *maggidim* (angelic entities).[42]

During the first day of the Succot festival, the father of the Gaon noticed that his son, our master, was in an extraordinary state of joy. When asked by his father to explain the reason for his overwhelming joy, the Gaon initially refused to comply with his father's request. Yet, after being commanded by his father to reveal the truth, and for the sake of the mitzvah to "Honor thy father and mother", he said the following: "Only because I am obligated to comply with your wishes do I tell you this: The Patriarch Jacob revealed himself to me today in the Succah". I also saw in our master's original notes the following comment: "Elijah the Prophet himself revealed to me the secret of the talmudic formula "These and these are both the words of the living God."[43]

R. Chaim Volozhin again relates another event in the life of the Gaon that transcends our normal categories of experience.[44]

> Once in Vilna in the courtyard of the synagogue adjacent to the study of the Gaon a *dybbuk (ruach ra'ah)* entered and possessed a certain man. A great commotion entailed with crowds of onlookers rushing in to behold the strange phenomenon. Our master opened the window of his study to see what all the noise was about. Immediately, upon beholding the face of our master the possessed person began

to scream. "Rebbe, you are the one for whom they proclaim Above, 'Beware of Eliyahu and his Torah.' If you were to decree upon me even with only the words of your mouth (i.e., without the usage of esoteric formulas) to leave this man I would have no choice but to go". Our master answered him, "I have never wanted to have any dealing with your [legions] and also now I will not speak with any of you at all."

Gematria, Transmigration, and Divination

Three other relatively unknown characteristics of the Gaon were his strict adherence to the theosophy of transmigration, his extensive and systematic usage of *gematria* and his reliance upon a system he utilized for divination. Each one of these practices by itself would appear a bit unusual for a genius the stature of the Gaon — a master of logic and science. It is *Kol HaTor*, however, that reveals not only the centrality of all three of these concepts in the teachings of the Gaon, but their interconnection with each other as well.

Gematria is the correspondence of words based upon their similar numerical value. Although appearing on the surface as simply "numerology", *gematria* is considered a sacred science, and has been a universally accepted practice by all traditional rabbinic schools (exoteric as well as esoteric) since ancient times. It is utilized extensively in the Talmud and by Rashi, and all the major commentaries make references to it. Correlating words and verses with each other, via their common value, is allowed for in the Hebrew language, because there are no numerals; rather each letter also has a numerical value and can thus be read as an equation, as well as a word. Just as in mathematics there are numerous systems with specific rules, so also with *gematria*, which is the Torah's corresponding mathematical-like system of representation.

On the surface, the use of *gematria* can seem trite and superfluous. The Gaon himself points this out in his commentary on the portion of the *Zohar*,[45] which states: "The reapers of the field are few, and even they work only at the edge of the vineyard." The Gaon comments, "This refers to those who do not master the wisdom [of Kabbalah], but rather occupy themselves with *gematria* which is 'at the edge of the vineyard.'" Even in this respect, however, they fail to clearly grasp the real intent." Similarly, upon the prophetic verse (Isaiah 40:4), "Every valley will be elevated....", the Gaon commented that the [concept of the valley] refers here to the wisdom of *gematria,* which now appears to be lowly, but will be shown to be of great importance in the Messianic Future".[46] He also said that, "Every Israelite's name and mission is encoded in the Torah in allusions and *gematrias.*[47]

It was left to R. Hillel to instruct us as to the "real intent" of *gematria* and to show us its great importance in the present period of the Advent of the Mashiach, as we will see presently.

Another esoteric facet of the Gaon, which has also been all but concealed from the public eye, is his strict adherence to the belief in *Gilgul* — the Doctrine of the Transmigration of Souls. The Gaon writes, for example, in his commentary on Proverbs[48] (which is not considered to be among his kabbalistic writings):

> The Holy One created man in order that, in the end, He will bestow upon him goodness. And even if man will sin, the Holy One will bring him back to this world two, three and even four times until he will rectify that which he has corrupted [during his previous lifetimes].

Transmigration is a vast field of thought that plays a recurring role in the Kabbalah writings of the Gaon, as it also does in the Kabbalah of the Ari. *Gilgul* has little to do with the popular conceptions of reincarnation. The true study of *gilgul* is considered to be one of the most advanced areas of kabbalistic specialization (e.g., *The Gate of Transmigration* is the last of *The Eight Gates* of Lurianic Kabbalah). Although there have been, and there still are today, some scholars who reject this doctrine, and many more who are indifferent to its tenets, this was not the case with the Gaon of Vilna. In the

Gaon's commentaries on the *Zohar* and other works, the details of this highly complex science are taken as a matter of fact and central to his advanced understanding of biblical events, the cosmological principles of reward and punishment, and world history in general.

This is readily seen in the above quote of the Gaon from the *Sifra DiTzniuta* where he wrote:

> The general principle is that all that has existed, all that now exists, and all that will exist until eternity, is all contained in the Written Torah... This refers not only to generalities, but to all the particulars of every single species and of every single human being, including everything that will transpire in his lifetime, from the day of birth until the day of death, as well as all of his transmigrations and all of their particulars and minute details.
>
> Similarly, all that is written concerning the Patriarchs, Moses, and the Nation of Israel in every generation [is encoded in the Torah]. For the fractal sparks (*nitzotzot*) of these souls reincarnate in every generation, as is known.

For the Gaon, transmigration was a daily reality. In fact, there was a tradition circulating about the Gaon that claimed he was an incarnation of Moses himself: [49]

> I heard directly from our teacher and master, the gaon Menashe Elya z"l [a disciple of the Gaon], the head of the religious court of Kalish, that it was clear to him from specific events and from certain manuscripts that the Gaon, his soul be in Eden, was a fractal spark (*nitzotz*) of Moses our Teacher, peace be upon him, and it was for this reason that the Gaon was not granted permission from Heaven to enter into the Land of Israel [just as Moses was not permitted to enter]".

The assertion that the Gaon was an incarnation of an aspect of Moses was, similar to other eccentric phenomena associated with the Gaon, not easily accepted even by all of those who associated themselves with the Gaon's school of thought and, in fact, this assertion was rejected by at least two authorities.[50] Yet, as we will see momentarily, R. Hillel had the inside story directly from the Gaon himself.

Concerning divination there is a fairly well known tradition of what is called the *Goral* of the Gaon. This is a handed down methodology revealed by the Gaon for using Scripture as an oracle.[51] The text of the entire Bible (the Tanach) becomes the means of divination. Based on the sacred number seven, as alluded to in the verse, "Upon one stone are seven facets" (Zechariah 3:9), the practitioner holds a special edition of the Tanach that is printed with two columns on each page and silently meditates on the question he wishes to ask. He then (1) opens randomly to any page; (2) turns seven additional pages; (3) counts seven columns; (4) counts seven open paragraphs; (5) counts seven lines down; (6) seven sentences; and then (7) seven words.

The *Goral* of the Gaon gained public notoriety due to an amazing event that took place in Jerusalem following Israel's War of Independence that involved the famous Tzadik and Jerusalemite Rabbi Aryeh Levin. The chief rabbi of Jerusalem, R. Tzvi Pesach Frank, had called upon Reb Aryeh to use the *Goral*, originated from the Gaon and handed down to the elders of the city. It was the last resort that was used to identify the bodies of twelve men who were martyred defending the settlements of Gush Etz Tziyon in the war. They knew who the twelve were but it was no longer possible to identify who each one was.

The actual process was reported by a journalist, who was present at this rare and solemn event. The Hebrew Bible that was used was printed in Amsterdam in 1701 and had the required two columns on each page. As the twelve candles, lit for the twelve souls, flickered away, Reb Aryeh opened the Bible at random and then turned in batches haphazardly seven times. Then going forward, he turned over seven single leaves; after that, seven pages; then seven columns; then seven verses; then seven words; and finally seven single letters. Thus it was "seven times seven, following the formula, "Upon one stone are seven facets". Whatever the seventh letter was, Reb Aryeh now looked for the next verse, which began with that letter. By the verse of Scripture found in this way, he would assign a name, body by body, to each of the twelve unidentified soldiers. To the astonishment of everyone who was there, each verse at which they arrived clearly indicated, out of the twelve possible names, which name went with each body. The identification of the twelve men was regarded as definite, and the ruling accepted as binding.[52]

Yet, it is R. Hillel who places the Gaon's *Goral*, together with transmigration and *gematria*, into a larger perspective. He writes:

> We now stand upon the threshold of the present phase of redemption — the "Call of the Turtledove" [the phrase alludes to a time table] yet we are engulfed in darkness. There is no priest, nor prophet; there is no Oracle (*Urim V'Tumim*) to guide us along the essential path. Certainly [we lack the means to deal] with the details and the fine *minutiae* of this path. Therefore, the Lord has sent us ...our master the Gaon. He has descended from heaven in order to reveal the formulas of the Torah in the period of the Advent of the Mashiach and the mechanisms of revelation in the mystery of "a predicament and its numerical formula [for a solution]," as explained in the writings of our master. [From these formulas] we can learn much concerning our work in the advent of the redemption. They will be for us as an Oracle and as a "Code of Law" *(Shulchan Aruch)* in the period of the "Last Generation," in the mystery of "the End of Days", with the help of God. This is the inner meaning of the verse, "In order that they will tell it over in the last generation." "To tell" is the same root [in Hebrew] as "to calculate, that is, "In order that they will

calculate in the last generation."[53]

Everything is encoded within the Scriptures (Tanach) and the Oral Tradition. This includes every creature, spiritual or physical, as well as its purpose, whether holy or profane. ...Similarly, all of the details and minutiae of every creation and of every individual, according to his lineage, as well as according to the common name by which he is known, are encoded in Scripture and the Oral Tradition.[54]

Every individual among the community of Israel has a spiritual source encoded into his name, according to the root of his soul and according to the merit of his ancestors. As is known, the name given to a child at birth is not accidental; rather the name is placed in the mouth of the parents by heavenly design, according to the root-soul of the child. Furthermore, each individual has no less than seven name-formulas. Each of them is encoded in Scripture or Talmud (*Chazal*) or both. This is in accord with the mystery of "the practical application of Torah formulas" according to our master's explanation on the *Zohar*.[55]

Our master knew where every Jew, and his mission involved with the process of redemption, was encoded within the holy Torah.[56] Many of the sages of our community in Shklov, as well as those from other cities, came to our master, the Gaon, in order to request his advice in this matter [of which field of science to study]. The Gaon would determine the area of study that was suitable for each and every individual, based on his particular aptitude and inclination. In addition, with his divine inspiration (*ruach hakodesh*), he would reveal where each individual's name and mission was alluded to in certain verses of the Bible. At times he would do this by means of

82
The Messianic Mission of the Gaon of Vilna

the *Goral*.[57]

The means by which to attain this knowledge [of one's mission] is first indicated through one's actions themselves, etc., and then through the application of the *Goral* of the Gaon in the mystery of "the practical application of Torah formulas" (*Ma'aseh VeCheshbon*).[58]

In *Kol HaTor*, R. Hillel actually outlines the manner in which it is possible to discover, within biblical verses and rabbinical formulas, each one's specific role and mission in the messianic process of redemption. He then emphasizes:

Everyone who deciphers the formulas of his name and mission is obligated to gird himself with all of his strength and desire, for this is the purpose of creation. This is the very reason why his soul has come into this world, the world of mission (*Asiyah*).[59]

The Gaon's follower's among the scholars of Shklov and their descendants, who inherited the legacy of *Kol HaTor,* made regular use of *gematria* in their sermons and writings. These calculations served as a channel of divine inspiration to aid them in directing their business affairs, social interaction, and marriages, as well as in strengthening their belief in their individual, and collective, missions.[60] Along with the systematic usage of *gematria,* the scholars of Shklov and the leaders of the new settlement in Israel also employed the *Goral* of the Gaon.[61]

Yet, the systematic discipline of *gematria* and Torah formulas was not generally accepted by the Torah world and public at large:

"The Wisdom of the Decoders Will Be Despised." One of the items that the sages listed that would occur in the period of the Advent of the Mashiach (Talmud, *Sotah* 49) is that, "The wisdom of the decoders will be despised." In his commentary on the *Zohar*, our master explains that this is referring to the wisdom of codes and *gematrias*, as well as to "the practical application of Torah formulas" that are revealed through Mashiach ben Yoseph. These are all part of the mission of our master the Gaon.... Therefore, he descended from heaven to reveal the codes of the Torah in the Advent of the Messiah. Yet, as is known, he suffered much from those who mocked this matter [of the science of *gematria*.][62]

Even up until the 20th-century, R. Hillel's great grandson and leader of the Ashkenazi community of Jerusalem, R. Yitzchak Tzvi Rivlin, would publicly declare in his sermons, even in the face of mockery, that the *Yishuv* (new Jewish settlement) was built upon *gematria*.[63]

In addition to the well known *Goral* of the Gaon, R. Hillel Rivlin and the leaders of the new settlement appear to have received from their spiritual mentor yet another type of formula of divine power. This was the great *Secret Goral* of the Gaon: [64]

Only regarding a difficult question, whose solution is vital for the needs of the new settlement, is it permissible for those initiated into the esoteric truth to also use the great *Secret Goral* that was revealed by the Gaon. ... It is not permitted, however, to use this secret formula, except in a dire emergency, in order to save the public and the holy community. All the more so is it permissible to prevent a desecration of God's Name (*Chillul HaShem*). Even then it must only be performed via *The Rectifications of the Revealer of Hidden Things* and with not less than three righteous men...

The role of transmigration in the doctrine of the *Kol HaTor* also plays a pivotal role:

Everyone is obligated to know the Torah

formulas and *gematria* of their name. If one does not, then one will be prone to transmigrate anew in order to rectify what was lacking in the present incarnation. This is what the *Zohar* (with the Gaon's commentary) is referring to when it states, "The one who does not know his *gematria* and formulas, wherein are encoded into his name, will in the future, descend into the netherworld [i.e., they will be forced to reincarnate, because they did not clearly understand what their role and mission was in their previous lifetime].[65]

Yet, in order to understand the tradition quoted above, that the Gaon was an incarnation of Moses our Teacher, we must now turn to what is certainly the most astonishing and well-kept secret about the Gaon of Vilna.

The Messiah from the House of Yoseph

It is within the context of the higher root of the soul, and its corresponding formulas in the Torah, that another dimension of the Gaon will now be discussed, a dimension which is virtually unknown outside of a few very small groups. It is a concept that some would normally expect to be associated with certain Hasidic *rebbes*. For this reason, as discussed above, those who do know about this aspect of the Gaon do not share this information easily. Nonetheless, according to R. Hillel, this secret lies at the essence of the Gaon's personality and is the source of the hidden power behind the doctrine of *Kol HaTor*. The most hidden and mystical aspect of the Gaon was who he understood himself to be, and the destiny he was fulfilling. R. Hillel claimed that the Gaon was the Mashiach ben Yoseph - the Messiah from the House of Joseph.

A third generation disciple of the Gaon, and one of the leading Kabbalists of Jerusalem wrote:[66]

"Mashiach ben Yoseph comes in each generation in order to reveal the secrets of the

Torah to those who are worthy. And my heart tells me that it is for this purpose that a holy angel descended from the heavens — the great teacher, the Gaon, our master Eliyahu of blessed memory. His task was to reveal both the exoteric and the esoteric Torah to us. Only due to our great sins were we not considered worthy of this privilege. Therefore, the majority of his writings concerning concealed matters, which comprised ten-fold more than his writings on revealed matters, have been lost".

For R. Hillel, it was not only his heart that told him who the Gaon really was, but also his spiritual mentor, the Gaon himself. In numerous places throughout *Kol HaTor*, the Gaon is revealed as the embodiment of the Illumination of Mashiach ben Yoseph.

Our master began [his mission] with the revelation of the secret formulas of the Torah when he was twenty years old, in the year 5500 (1740).... It was then that the Godly spirit, the soul of the Messiah, began to move his divine inspiration (*ruach hakodesh*)[67] to reveal the formulas of the Torah, little by little, in his mission as the First Messiah. These formulas reveal the arcane mysteries and the concealed secrets in the period of the Advent of the Mashiach, of which none were hidden from him.[68]

In this last generation, our master, the Gaon, is also an illumination of the light of Mashiach ben Yoseph, and his guiding light will continue to increase and to ascend before us until the height of the [sixth millennial] day [5750/1990]. Specific individuals, from among his disciples who fulfilled his commandments regarding the Vision of Zion, also merited to receive, and to become extensions of, his spirit and great light in this capacity [of Mashiach ben Yoseph].[69]

Our master, who was the illumination of Mashiach ben Yoseph, would daily recite the prayer "Yoseph Lives On" [i.e., that his mission should succeed].[70]

Mashiach ben Yoseph is discussed at length in Part II, *Messianic Conspiracy*, Chapter 1, Mashiach ben Yoseph. For now, however, with this information regarding the Gaon's identity, supplied from the secret text of *Kol HaTor*, we are prepared to understand the contested tradition concerning the Gaon that claimed he was an incarnation of Moses. In 1786, leaving his wife and children, possessions and holy books, behind (all to be brought later) the Gaon set out to journey to the Holy Land. (It was during this journey that the Gaon wrote his famous ethical epistle to his wife and children, known as *Alim L'trufa — Leaves for Healing —* which has been reprinted numerous times). He was forced to return without succeeding in his intended mission, yet he never revealed the reason.

Although recording different theories, the Gaon's chroniclers did not know the reason for his aborted trip, nor did his own children. His sons asked him many times why he did not complete his journey, but he would not answer them. Once, however, after they had repeatedly implored him he answered, "Heaven did not grant me permission."[71] Based upon evidence, as quoted above, one of the Gaon's students came to the conclusion that the reason that the Gaon suddenly turned back was that he was an incarnation of Moses. Yet, only R. Hillel was privy to the inner meaning of the Gaon's statement, as well as to substantiating the other evidence, while placing both within the context of the Gaon's larger messianic mission.

"The time of singing has arrived, and the call of the turtledove is heard in our land." The *call* of the turtledove refers to [the aspect of Mashiach ben Yoseph known as] Joshua. The *turtledove* itself refers to [the aspect of Mashiach ben Yoseph known as] Moses. Initially, our master saw that he was the aspect of Joshua [who

entered the Land of Israel and initiated its
settlement] as was indicated [by various verses
in the Torah where the Gaon's name was
encoded]. ...This was the mission of Mashiach
ben Yoseph (as the Gaon comments on the
Zohar).[72] Now, since at that time our master
was incarnating the aspect of Joshua, i.e., the
aspect of Mashiach ben Yoseph, he set out for
the Holy Land. In the middle of the journey,
however, he ascended to the level of [the *sefirah*
of] *Tiferet*, which is the elevated state of Moses
our Teacher. He then realized that he no longer
had permission to enter the Land of Israel,
rather he was to hand over the matter to his
disciples, who were from the aspect of Joshua,
and it is they who would begin the ingathering
of the exiles.... One of his disciples [i.e., the
author R. Hillel] received from him an amazing
scriptural formula [indicating this mission]
where his name was encoded, going back three
generations... [Hillel ben Benyamin ben
Zalman].[73]

Rabbi Eliyahu, the Gaon of Vilna, was the Messiah —
more specifically a Mashiach ben Yoseph of his generation. It
is part of the mission of this Messiah, the First Messiah, to
gather the exiled Jews back to their homeland. It was only
that during his journey to the Land of Israel that the Gaon
saw that he had ascended to the aspect of Moses, and like
Moses, he was not granted Heavenly permission to enter the
Land of Israel.[74]

The concept of Mashiach ben Yoseph, in general, and
its relationship to Moses, in particular, is discussed at length
in Part II, *Messianic Conspiracy*, Chapter 1, Mashiach ben
Yoseph. For now let us conclude this unexpected portrayal of
the Gaon as the Mashiach ben Yoseph with another aspect of
the life of the Gaon that *Kol HaTor* once again places within a
very unexpected context. R. Hillel writes:[75]

It is well known that there was a period when
our master, the Gaon, placed himself in

voluntary exile and would travel from place to place, etc... His intention, however, has never been properly explained. The essential goal of our master, the Gaon, was to examine the human activity among our people and their ethical self conduct. This accords with our master's writing that the purpose of man's creation is in order to subdue his bad character traits, to rectify himself, and to rectify others, according to the values of our sacred Torah.[76] However, in every place our master came he did not reveal his identity to anyone; he concealed himself so as to appear as one of the common people. Yet, just before he left each locality, he revealed a little of himself to the rabbi of that congregation and to select individuals who resided there, in order to point out to them the rectifications (*tikkunim*) that that congregation required. These *tikkunim* included character traits, *halachic* observance, and community service. Together with this he would emphasize to them and rouse them to the importance of preparing for the ingathering of the exiles. This he would go into at great length, because, "It is time to favor her, because the appointed time has arrived."

Master of the Seven Sciences It is well known that the Gaon was a scientist *par excellence* and the acclaimed master of essentially all the known secular wisdom of his time. This has neither been contested by his most religious admirers, nor by his anti-religious detractors. Yet, what was the Gaon *doing* with his encyclopedic knowledge of theoretical and practical science? With the Gaon now firmly revealed as the mystic *par excellence,* and one who saw himself with an extraordinary role to play in the destiny of the Jewish people and in the development of the world at large, we are now prepared to look at the Gaon as the scientist from a very different perspective. We will see that, for the Gaon, even secular science was to play a pivotal role in his mission as

Mashiach ben Yoseph. Since this topic is the central theme of the present work, and the translation of *Sha'ar Beer Sheva,* below in Chapter 4, speaks for itself, it will be dealt with here only briefly.

For the Gaon, the study of Torah included all knowledge, from the most recondite secrets of heaven to the most mundane concerns of earth. Indeed, he saw the study of the natural sciences as necessary for understanding the Torah in its entirety. In the introduction to his translation of Euclid, which was done at the Gaon's behest, R. Dr. Baruch Schick of Shklov records a now well-known dictum of his master: "To the extent that one lacks knowledge of the properties of the natural forces, he will lack one hundred-fold in the wisdom of the Torah."[77]

On the surface, this statement sounds like a precursor to half of Albert Einstein's observation that, "Science without religion is blind, and religion without science is lame."[78] And, in fact, from the time of its publication, this statement of the Gaon has been well used by the advocates of the *Haskalah* (Enlightenment) movement, as well as by the religious proponents of *Torah Im Derech Eretz* (lit. *Torah with the Way of the World),* to bolster each one's view that Judaism requires integration of secular knowledge into the religious life style and mind set. On the other hand, once again, there are other Torah scholars who, although identifying strongly with the Gaon in all other areas, reject this side of the Gaon and do not believe that the statement recorded by R. Dr. Schick issued from him.[79] (This school of the Gaon, although claiming allegiance to him in all other areas, rejects the philosophy, as well as the authority of *Kol HaTor.)*

But once again, it is only the doctrine of *Kol HaTor,* together with the Kabbalah writings of the Gaon, which reveal the inner meaning of this statement. Viewed from this perspective, both the proponents of secular wisdom, and its adversaries, have misinterpreted the Gaon's intention. It is here where it becomes apparent that, in the Gaon's view of Judaism, there can *never* be a real confluence between science and Judaism. Rather, there can only exist a confluence between science and the *inner* teachings of Judaism — the Kabbalah. The Gaon's usage of science can only be appreciated and understood from his view as the kabbalist *par excellence*. It is *Kol HaTor* that begins to recast even the image of the Gaon as the scientist *par excellence* into a totally new light. His science and technology was the scientific and technological mission of Mashiach ben Yoseph.

The clarification of the Gaon's definition of Torah and science explains a number of apparently contradictory statements of the Gaon, where in some instances, he appears to strongly oppose secular learning and in other cases, such as here, he appears to strongly support secular learning. The answer is that a simple person only needs to learn from the secular world what is necessary in order to understand Torah and its applications. A Torah scholar, however, especially one who is learning Kabbalah, must learn the Seven Sciences for the purpose of messianic redemption and global transformation... and the Gaon would require that in the time we are living now *all* students of Torah must be engaged in the Kabbalah.

The Gaon mastered all the "Seven Wisdoms" of science, which included mathematics, astronomy, physics, chemistry, engineering, pharmacology, medicine, musicology, parapsychology, and the brain sciences.[80] This also included the knowledge of occult wisdom.[81] The Gaon composed works on mathematics (*Ayil Meshullash*, 1833), on geography (*Tzurat HaAretz*, 1822), on astronomical calculations and on the seasons and planetary motions (in manuscript). He wrote another work containing treatises on trigonometry, geometry, and algebra (published as *Eliah Wilna und Sein Elementargeome Trisches Compendium*, 1903). The Gaon was also a strong advocate of Hebrew grammar, which had essentially been abandoned among the religious world, and he composed a number of treatises on the subject (e.g., *Dikduk Eliyahu*).

His home in Vilna was frequented by non-Jewish scholars and scientists seeking answers to perplexing questions. Although his original solutions to their problems won him the title of the *Gaon of Vilna* ("Genius of Vilna"), even among the non-Jewish population, his main intention was to sanctify the Name of God in the eyes of the nations, and also to hasten the final redemption. To this effect, he encouraged his students to master the Seven Sciences as well, so that they, too, could apply them wherever and whenever possible, to sanctify the Name of Heaven and to accelerate the redemption process.

Without recourse to any further research or even contemplation, the Gaon was known to solve "on the spot" vexing scientific problems presented to him by numerous doctors and specialists. One such documented case was mentioned above, involving a leading German professor. Other inquiries the Gaon directed to his master disciples in Shklov where, along with a private yeshiva, an actual laboratory for experimentation was maintained.[82] The inventions of the scholars of Skhlov were likewise even known among the non-Jewish professionals of that time and era. R. Hillel writes:[83]

> Our master's knowledge of the Seven Wisdoms was not limited to theory; it was notably practical. There are many well-known examples of this. Our master authored a number of ingenious inventions in the fields of engineering, natural pharmacology and medicine, music theory, and others.

R. Hillel further points out that the Gaon attained complete mastery over the Seven Sciences, at least in part, through investigating the forces of nature — "the fountains of wisdom from below." Yet, even here, R. Hillel begins to reveal the Gaon's real intent:[84]

> Already from his youth, our master, the Gaon, developed an interest in, and began to investigate, the forces and properties of natural [phenomena], in order to grasp their [inner] purpose. With his great powers of analysis, he found the [corresponding] spiritual principles for all of these [properties] in the secret teachings of the Torah and of the sages... [By

mastering this wisdom] he also hoped to achieve an even greater understanding of the secrets of the Torah. [Yet], he used to say that all that had been revealed [in previous generations] was no more than a drop in the ocean compared to what was concealed in the wisdom of the Torah, and which will be revealed in the future, together with the teachings of the righteous Messiah.

Yet, even beyond the Gaon's esoteric understanding of the natural laws of creation, was the messianic mission to which this great understanding was being directed. Jerusalem was to be the meeting place of the heights of mysticism, the depths of science and the new "Vision of Zion." He continues:

Our master knew how to unlock the wondrous forces and properties of natural phenomena hidden in the Torah. No mystery eluded him; the pathways of the heavens were lit up for him like the pathways of the entire Torah. On a number of occasions our master told us that the most opportune place for attaining the "gates of wisdom above [Kabbalah]" and the "wellsprings of wisdom below [science]" is the holy city of Jerusalem, may it be rebuilt and established.

The Gaon of Vilna's goal towards the confluence between the secrets of science and the secrets of Kabbalah was nothing less than a global revolution. For those initiated into his doctrine, both together were essential for the implementation of the Gaon's messianic vision of world redemption. Before a group of his followers from Shklov, and a young R. Hillel (he was eighteen years old at the time), the Gaon revealed his plan:[85]

The question is how, and under what circumstances, will the gentiles recognize the wisdom of Israel, as stated in the verse, "She is your wisdom and your understanding in the eyes of the nations." (Deuteronomy 4:6)?

There is no other way to explain the intention of the verse except as follows: First the gentiles will recognize Israel's superior wisdom in the worldly sciences. Then they will realize that this wisdom is derived solely from the esoteric secrets of the wisdom of the Torah. Only then will the verse be fulfilled, "She is your wisdom and your understanding in the eyes of the nations." And they will exclaim [the concluding words of the verse], "This great nation is surely a wise and understanding people," i.e., great in wisdom (chochmah) and understanding (binah). Only thus will the verse be fulfilled, 'God will grant you ascendancy above all the nations He has made, for praise, fame and beauty."

There is no other avenue to attain this ascendancy except through extensive, and well-founded, training in both extremities, i.e., from the depths of the earth [science] to the heights of the heavens [Kabbalah]. This is the intention of the verse, "[Yours O God is the greatness and the power, the harmony, the eternity, the splendor and] all that binds heaven and earth" (I Chronicles 29:11). We must be well versed in the secrets of our Torah that derive from the Supernal Wisdom. And we must be equally well versed in the secret depths of the laws of nature that derive from the wisdom of the Torah. These [two extremities] are interdependent, as indicated in the statement of the holy Zohar, "In the six hundredth year of the sixth millennium, the gates of wisdom above together with the wellsprings of wisdom below will be opened up, and the world will prepare to usher in the seventh millennium."

It is impossible to climb a ladder whose top reaches towards the heavens without first stepping on the rungs of the ladder that are stationed near the earth. [In the same way it is impossible to grasp the full implications of spiritual truth without understanding its relationship to scientific fact.] This is the essential idea that was conveyed to our father Jacob in his vision of the ladder. There is no greater way to sanctify God's Name and save the honor of Israel in the eyes of the nations than to achieve this great end.

Most interestingly, the Gaon's messianic synthesis of mysticism, science, and a Jewish Jerusalem as an international world center of knowledge, coalesces in his experimentation with a *golem*. As mentioned above, along with the episode concerning Aristotle, the Gaon's mastery over the hidden mechanics of the force of life itself was revealed by R. Chaim of Volozhin. In his introduction to the Gaon's commentary on the *Sifra DiTzniuta* he writes:[86]

> The Gaon claimed that his version of the *Sefer Yetzirah* was faultless. In response I said to him that it should now be simple to create a *golem*. He answered, "Once I actually began to create a *golem*. Before I was able to complete it, however, I saw an apparition above my head and I desisted, saying to myself that, in all probability, Heaven was preventing me because of my youth." When I asked him how old he was at the time, he replied that he had not yet reached his thirteenth year.

R. Hillel also records this tradition, but begins to place the Gaon's early experimentation with supernatural forces within a specific context. He writes:[87]

> [As a result of his high level of divine inspiration] he also knew how to operate an esoteric formula of Divine Names, which he used to identify the essence of all spiritual and material properties. Finally, with his great and awesome power he also knew how to create a living *golem*.

Still further, *Kol HaTor* recasts the Gaon's involvement with the creation of a *golem* as an intrinsic part of his mission as the Mashiach ben Yoseph. He writes:[88]

> While still in his youth, after he had mastered all of the Talmud and the codes, etc., as is known, our master began his involvement with the esoteric teachings of the Kabbalah. From then on he was involved, to an amazing depth, revealing the formulas of the Torah (as explained above). When he was yet a boy of about fourteen years old, he received much [initiation] into the inner teachings of the Torah from the leaders of our congregation in Shklov, the relatives of the Gaon's father, my grandfather HaRav Shlomo Zalman [first cousin to the Gaon's father], the son of HaRav Zvi Hirsh [the Gaon's grandfather's brother], and HaRav Eli Zeitlis. He was especially involved in the secret of the permutations of the [Hebrew] letters in the science of artificial creation. And as we heard from him directly, his intention was also in order to achieve understanding, and thereby, to successfully create an artificial life form ... [here a word or a number of words were deleted by the original editor] in order to crush the external forces [lit. *Samael*] at the Gates of Jerusalem. It was for this purpose that, while still in his youth, he began experimenting with the awesome formation of artificial life (*golem*), as is known.

The Extraordinary Letter

There is yet another little known phenomenon about the Gaon that, once again supports, together with the many other highly unusual characteristics of his life, the claim of R. Hillel that the Gaon was a Mashiach ben Yoseph. The doctrine of *Kol HaTor* maintains, in fact, that the Gaon was instigating and spearheading a messianic conspiracy for the rebirth of

Jerusalem as the world center for scientific and spiritual wisdom.

This last piece of unusual evidence is known as the Extraordinary Letter of the Gaon.[89] According to the accepted tradition, the Gaon composed and sealed a short letter that he commanded only to be opened after one hundred years. In accord with his will, one hundred years later, the Torah scholars of Vilna opened the Gaon's letter, only to discover that it was encoded in anagrams and cryptic formulas, and no one was able to decipher its contents. Consequently, copies of the letter were sent to all the important Jewish communities, including Jerusalem, where there resided kabbalists, yet, as one of sages proclaimed, "There is no human being on earth that is capable of explaining this letter; only in the future will Elijah the prophet decipher it."

Once again, it is only *Kol HaTor* that places even this bizarre letter, and the Gaon's command as to its opening, into a specific context — a context that is woven together with the other messianic missions of the Gaon. R. Hillel Rivlin writes:[90]

> In the beginning of the seven hundredth year of the sixth millennium, that is, at the beginning of the year 5,600 (1840) and from there onward, begins the messianic revelation of the secret of Higher Wisdom (the source of the Kabbalah) together with the Lower Wisdom (the source of science). ... From this year and onwards, begins the [period of] *Kol HaTor* — the Call of the Turtledove — via the illumination of our master, the Gaon, that will "shine ever more brightly until the height of noonday" [5,750-1990].[91]
>
> This matter [of the gradual unfolding of specific "end times"] is also alluded to in the secret of the letter of our master. At his behest, this letter was sealed, and not to be opened until one hundred years had passed, i.e., until the year of *eit l'chenena* — "A time to favor her [for

her set time has arrived]".

The phrase "A time to favor her" (Psalms 102-14) has the numerical value of 613, i.e., the year 5,613 or 1853.[92] The phrase is here being used as a code for one of the key "end times" referred to in *Kol HaTor*. An "end time" refers to any one of a number of specific dates in a time table when, all factors being equal, it is more opportune for us to "stimulate" the cosmic order and actually accelerate the process of our own evolution. In this case, although the details of how this was to occur are not clear, it is apparent from *Kol HaTor* that the Gaon's Extraordinary Letter was intentionally "planted" and ordered to be released at a specific time co-ordinate in the future — the "time to favor her." The intent was to stimulate a key juncture on the map of time, even long after his own physical death. In the capacity of the Illumination of Mashiach ben Yoseph, the Extraordinary Letter was, for the Gaon, another mission in his far-reaching messianic conspiracy. Yet, there were even other "messianic seeds" that the Gaon planted in his lifetime that were to extend still further the light of his great mission.

The Call of the Turtledove

From *Kol HaTor* it is evident, from the otherwise strange and inexplicable Extraordinary Letter of the Gaon, that he saw himself as fulfilling a messianic mission that even extended well beyond his own immediate generation. In fact, it is the Gaon who quite literally "planted" the seeds of his chosen disciples in the Land of Israel and in the Holy City of Jerusalem, in order to begin to usher in the mystery of the Final End, the End of Days. R. Hillel writes:[93]

> I am obligated to proclaim, but only a small fraction — as much as we have permission to reveal. This is the matter of the Awesome Vision, the extraordinary and sacred vision which our master, the Gaon, beheld shortly after he returned from his [attempted] journey to the Holy Land in 5542 (1782). Consequently, our master was gripped by a deep concern and personal quandary, which is difficult to

describe. On the one hand, he saw, through his divine inspiration (*ruach hakodesh*), the great mission which was placed upon him from Heaven to awaken and initiate the actual ingathering of the exiles. On the other hand, he saw the great dangers inherent in this obligation, both in the traveling to the Holy Land, and in the conditions of the settlement. From a practical perspective there was a great responsibility, because the Land of Israel was a desolate wilderness — infectious disease reigned, and the land was filled with wild marauders. There were severe shortages of basic necessities, and there was no source of income. He was so immersed in this quandary that we had never seen him in such a state. He constantly prayed, in fasting and in tears, in order to receive clear guidance from Heaven. He also did what he did with secret formulas, etc....

And behold, he was answered with a great and sacred vision with supernal revelations — the Patriarch Jacob was revealed to him in the mystery of, "The End of Days", etc.... In that sacred vision they revealed to him numerous verses, which speak of the extraordinary guarantees concerning the resettlement of the Land of Israel, and encoded within those verses was his name. Among them was the verse, "Do not fear, My servant Jacob, for I have chosen Jeshurun [another appellation for Israel]" and the words "I have chosen Jeshurun" have the numerical value of our master's three generations — Eliyahu ben Shlomo Zalman ben Yisachar Dov. This was the first time he beheld his mission in the great role of the Messiah of the Beginning, as indicated in the word Jeshurun, which has the numerical value of Mashiach ben Yoseph.[94] This awesome vision greatly encouraged and strengthened the resolve of our master, and from that time onward, the difficult problems and natural dangers ceased to plague him as they had previously.

...Our master was given the power to lay the foundations for the *At'chalta* in the ingathering of the exiles, in order to complete the *At'chalta*, in accord with the verse, "Behold, I am sending to you Elijah the Prophet" (Malachi 3:23). This mission of our master was also revealed to him in the verse (Deuteronomy 25:15), "A complete and just weight," in which his name is encoded — Eliyahu ben Shlomo.

After our master returned from his journey to the Land of Israel, because permission was not granted to him from Heaven, as is known, he transferred his authority to one of his disciples, who was hewn from his soul-root [and whose name's numerical value (i.e., "Hillel"), was also encoded and revealed in the Gaon's vision].

Elsewhere in *Kol HaTor*, R. Hillel reveals more about himself:[95]

In this last generation, our master, the Gaon, is also an illumination of the light of Mashiach ben Yoseph, and his guiding light will continue to increase and to ascend before us until the height of the [sixth millennial] day. Specific individuals from among his disciples, who fulfilled his commandments regarding the Vision of Zion, also merited to receive, and to become, extensions of his spirit and great light in this capacity [of Mashiach ben Yoseph].

R. Hillel again writes:[96]

In his commentary to the *Sifra DiTzniuta*, our master speaks about the great secret of the Final End, the End of Days. His words there are extremely veiled. Nevertheless, he adjures the reader in the Name of the God of Israel not to divulge this secret [even if he is able to decipher the meaning on his own]. It was only to a select few of his disciples, who promised him that they would travel to the Holy Land and engage in the ingathering of the exiles, that he revealed a small fragment of what he knew. And only to one who was a branch of his higher soul-root did he openly transmit the mystery of the Wondrous End of Days.

R. Hillel is making it clear, however humbly, that there are secrets involved in the redemption process that he alone received from the Gaon. This was due, not only to the common blood relationship they shared (they shared the same ancestor — Eliyahu Hasid), but more so, to a strong soul connection in accord with the spiritual laws of transmigration that existed between the two. Apparently, unique even among the disciples of the Gaon whom he sent to the Land of Israel, R. Hillel was the primary extension of the Gaon's mission of redemption. This includes the doctrine for the implementation of the messianic confluence of science and Kabbalah, which is not recorded by any other of his disciples outside of R. Hillel. (This explains why there is no specific mention of a codified doctrine called *Kol HaTor* in the writings of the Gaon and from among all of his other disciples, although virtually all the components of the doctrine are found in the Gaon's writings and in those of his other students).

In conclusion, it has been shown that concerning the Gaon of Vilna, we are, in fact, dealing with a type of being who does not fit into any of the known categories of human experience. Beyond the mastery of any single branch of knowledge, be it religious or secular, mystical or scientific, was the Gaon's vision of their unique confluence as integral to the process of the advent of the Messianic Era, the final redemption of the Jewish people, and global evolution into a higher dimension. Only with the return to the Land of Israel, and the reestablishment of the physical and spiritual center of the Jewish people, could the vision of total unification come to fruition. The Gaon transmitted this vision to R. Hillel ben Benyamin Rivlin, and it is contained in the body of *Kol HaTor*. And as we saw above, it was R. Hillel, who, with the Gaon's secret doctrine of *Kol HaTor* in hand, led the first caravan of seventy Jews to Jerusalem to begin to initiate its material and spiritual rebirth.

---

[1] See introduction to the Gaon's commentary on *Midrash Ruth,* J.H. Lewin, *Aliyot Eliyahu* (Ascents of Elijah), (Vilna, 1856; Jerusalem,1989), p.268.

[2] Since 1990, when the manuscript for this publication was written, there has been a new and growing interest in the Gaon of Vilna and related subjects. Some of this interest has been concurrent with the fact that the year 1997 was the 200th anniversary of the passing of the Gaon. That year was marked by the International Conference on "The Gra and His Historical Influence," held in Jerusalem. In spite of this academic activity, however, there has been almost nothing printed concerning the Gaon's *Kol HaTor* doctrine. ArtScroll Publications has now translated into English a modern classic Hebrew biography of the Gaon, *The Gaon of Vilna - The Life and Teachings of Rabbi Eliyahu, the Gaon of Vilna (HaGaon HaChasid MeVilna)* by R. Betzalel Landau, New York, 1994 (no mention *of Kol HaTor*); *The Hasidic Movement and the Gaon of Vilna* by Elijah Judah Schochet, Jason Aronson, 1994 (two indirect quotes from *Kol HaTor*); *Russia's First Modern Jews, The Jews of Shklov*, David E. Fishman, New York University Press, 1995 (no mention of *Kol HaTor*); *The Gaon of Vilna, The Man and His Image*, by Immanuel Etkes, University of California Press, 2002 (no mention of *Kol HaTor*); *The Gaon of Vilna - The Story of Rabbi Eliyahu Kramer*, by Yaacov Dovid Shulman, CIS Publishers, 1994 (a dramatized biography, with one reference to *Kol HaTor*); "An Attempt to Hasten the Redemption," by Arie Morgenstern, an article in *Jewish Action* magazine, Fall 1997 (no mention of *Kol HaTor*); *Hastening Redemption – Messianism and the Resettlement of the Land of Israel* by Arie Morgenstern, Oxford University Press, 2006 (no mention of *Kol HaTor*); *Torah Umadda - The Encounter of Religious Learning and Worldly Knowledge in the Jewish Tradition*, Norman Lamm, 1990 (no mention of *Kol HaTor*). An important exception to these other works is the collection of essays, *HaGra u'Bet Midrasho* (The Gaon of Vilna and his Disciples), editors Hallamish, Rivlin, and Shuchat, Bar-Ilan University Press, Ramat Gan, Israel 2003 (Hebrew, with 3 of the 16 essays in English). This volume references *Kol HaTor,* see especially Yoseph Rivlin's article, "The Influence of Kabbalah and *Zoharic* Literature on the Gaon's Writings and Commentaries" (Hebrew).

[3] Of note, however, is Prof. Zvi Werblowsky's partial translation of R. Chaim Volozhin's introduction to the Gaon's commentary on the *Sifra DiTzniuta* in his *Joseph Karo – Lawyer and Mystic* (JPS, Philadelphia, 1977). It has also been reprinted in *Jewish Mystical Testimonies* (Jacobs, 1976). A complete translated version is included here in the Appendix.

[4] Norman Lamm, *Torah Lishmah - Torah for Torah's Sake in the Works of Rabbi Chaim of Volozhin and His Contemporaries*, (New York, 1989), note 12, p. 33.

[5] Statement of the *Chazon Ish*, quoted by Lamm, note 20, p. 34.

[6] Moses M. Yoshor, *The Chafetz Chaim*, (New York, 1984) Introduction, p. xx. Similarly, the Hasidic master, R. Yitzchak Izik of Komarno, wrote that from the days of Maimonides, no one compared with the Gaon in his depth and breadth of knowledge. (Landau, Hebrew edition, p. 340).

[7] *Aliyot Eliyahu*, Introduction to *Hadrat Kodesh*, R. Abraham Simcha, nephew of R. Chaim of Volozhin.

[8] R. Shlomo Eliyashiv quoted by R. Tzvi Hirsch Ferber of London. *Talpiyot* 5711, p.359 quoted by R. Shraya Deblitzki in the Forward to *The Gaon of Vilna Views Life*, Singer-Ackerman (1974, Jerusalem).

[9] *Aliyot Eliyahu*, p. 77, note 31. See above, Chapter 1, The Living Legacy of the Gaon of Vilna, Section Messianic Synthesis, for the full text.

[10] R. Eliyahu Ragoler, *Yad Eliyahu,* Siman 25.

[11] *Aliyot Eliyahu*, p.75, note 20.

[12] *Aliyot Eliyahu*, p. 79, note 34. The account was personally related to Lewin by R. Yaacov Tzvi Mecklenburg (d. 1865), the Rabbi of Koenigsberg, Germany, and author of *HaKetav VHaKabbalah.* Following is the full translation:

> In a private letter to his friend Moses Mendelsohn of Berlin, the *maskil*, grammarian and preacher, Abraham Abba of Glussk (whose works were burned for heresy in the courtyard of the Vilna synagogue) wrote what he had heard about the Gaon: "... He is also an amazing scholar in all the wisdoms and sciences, including metaphysics, physics, and music. Nothing is hidden from him. He is proficient in the rules and grammar of the Hebrew language — a subject that is alien to most people." Abraham Abba continues and writes that he could not believe that a traditional rabbi was living in his time who had actually mastered all branches of secular knowledge. Yet, upon entering Vilna he repeatedly heard such reports from a number of colleagues and scholars. As a result of this, he was consumed by a desire to speak with the Gaon. His peers laughed at him, however, saying that such a thing was not simple, especially for someone who had no beard, no *peyot*, and whose style of dress was decidedly non-Jewish. But, he continued to Mendelsohn, he had thought about it and devised a plan. He would masquerade as the "Rabbi of Padua, Italy."
>
> He cleverly forged fifteen letters from fifteen "rabbis of Italy," which stated that they had sent the "Rabbi of Padua" to the Gaon as their emissary. The false letters explained that all the Jews of Italy were being threatened with expulsion. If, however, they could satisfactorily answer a list of challenging heretical questions, they would be spared. As they had heard that the Gaon was a true

master of all wisdom, they were now turning to him in their hour of despair.

Abraham Abba of Glussk then approached the Gaon's secretary with the fifteen forged letters in hand. After about a quarter of an hour, the doors to the Gaon's study opened and, "Behold, a man with awesome features appeared, crowned with *tallit* and *tefillin*, holding the letters in his hand. He remained standing in the doorway and did not enter the adjoining room where I stood. He did not greet me, nor did he raise his eyes to look at my face." The Gaon then spoke in Hebrew and asked him about the heretical questions. He presented the first of the questions, and after a moment, was asked to proceed with the following question without having received an answer to the first.

This continued without any explanation until all the questions were presented. The Gaon then responded and said that, although he had heard 73 questions, in truth there were only 15, because the 1st and 7th were essentially the same, the 25th and the 47th were identical, and so on. "Can you imagine the level of his mind?" he writes, "Such a feat is almost beyond human ability! He surveyed such deep matters as these and arranged them in their respective categories, according to the rules of logic, all in a single glance!"

At one point in the course of their meeting, however, the Gaon addressed a question to the "Rabbi of Padua." In his reply, Abraham Abba of Glussk forgot himself for a moment and declared that neither Rashi (Rabbi Shlomo Yitzchaki, 1040-1105) nor the sages of the Midrash had understood the true meaning of a scriptural term in question. Abruptly, the Gaon broke off the conversation and returned to his study. Upon returning to his inn Abraham Abba of Glussk was met by a number of men who asked him to accompany them. He was to be brought before the Vilna *Beit Din* (rabbinic court). The *Beit Din* tried him and found him guilty of insulting Torah scholars. The penalty for this according to the *halachah* (Jewish Law) was forty lashes. After this, he was to be bound and chained to the wall of the main synagogue with a sign above his head reading, "This one is being punished for mocking the words of our holy rabbis." Everyone who passed by him on their way to pray the afternoon *minchah* service yelled, "sinner of Israel" and spat in his face until [as he later related] "a stream of saliva like the Jordan River flowed in front of me, for Vilna is not like Berlin; the population of Vilna is very large and all of them, from young to old, come to pray the *minchah* service."

The following day Abraham Abba of Glussk was happy to be sent on his way. Yet, he concludes his personal account to Mendelssohn by affirming that, "Behold, in spite of all the evil that befell me and what I endured because of him [the Gaon], nevertheless, my heart stands firm in informing you of the truth as I honestly believe it: Of all the wise men throughout the world, there is no one like him."

[13] R. Moshe Zvi Neriah, "*Pirkei Volozhin*", *Shanah be'Shanah*, 5723 (1962-63),

p. 535. R. Neriah heard this story from R. Yaakov Moshe Charlap, who reported it as told by R. Isaac to his pupil R. Shmuel Salanter, (as quoted from *Torah Lishmah*, p.5, note 16).

[14] R. Abraham, son of the Gaon, Introduction to *Shenot Eliyahu*.

[15] Introduction to Gaon's commentary on Proverbs. See further quotes in *Ma'alot HaSulam* (*Aliyot Eliyahu*), p. 47, note 7.

[16] Proverbs 2:9. See also Gaon's commentary on Proverbs 25:11 and note from R. Menachem Mendel to Proverbs 10:26.

[17] Introduction to *Takleen Chadateen*, reprinted in the new edition of *Aliyot Eliyahu*, p. 47. Similarly, "We were told by our master that, God forbid, one should say that the esoteric level of a subject contradicts the *halachic* decisions about that topic". *Magen V'Tzina*, R. Yitzchak Izik Chaver (second generation disciple of the Gaon).

[18] See *Keter Rosh*, oral traditions from R. Chaim of Volozhin, end, #15.

[19] R. Hillel himself writes, in Chapter 3, par. #12 (Kasher, p. 515), "A great axiom of our master was that an interpretation of the Torah on the level of its simple meaning (*pshat*) cannot be correct if it is not completely consistent with the inner level of meaning (*sod*). Still, the instruction of the inner teachings must be carried out discreetly and with humility. This is alluded to in the verse, "Bow down before God with holy trembling" (Psalm 29:2). The initials of each [Hebrew] word spell *Kabbalah*."

[20] *Sifra DiTzniuta,* Chapter 5, p. 34a.

[21] This same idea is expounded by R. Yitzchak Izik Chaver in his *Pitchey Sh'arim, Netiv Seder HaPartzufim*, par. #7, p. 82b (164): Concerning this it was said, "All that was, will be; and all that has been done, will be done; there is nothing new under the sun" (Ecclesiastes 1:9). Every single detail of creation is an expression of that which originally existed during the first six days of creation. This is like a tree whose seeds contain [all the information for] all the trees that will evolve from them until the end of time. The same principle applies to all plants and animals. Within the brain of Adam [the first being], too, were contained all of his future progeny.

[22] See Introduction to *Sifra DiTzniuta* in the Appendix, "...that is a preposterous claim made by ignorant and vain men from distant towns, who did not merit to see the light of our master's Torah, irresponsible people who speak against the saintly, who are like flies that hover over carcasses, that wish to cause our great master's fragrant ointment to give off a sickly odor — that our master, within whom dwelled the spirit of God, did not value the teachings of the Ari, God forbid. There are those who add that even the *Zohar* was in low esteem in our master's eyes, that he did not study it regularly, and did not see it fit to do so". See Lamm, pp. 19-22 and notes. "In principle, one should not be surprised if the Gaon explains a subject in the esoteric Torah differently than the Ari, for his opinions contain much power and strength. This is not a new idea, for we find in numerous places in *Sifra DiTzniuta* where the Gaon's explanations differ with those of the Ari, yet shed a shining light upon previously hidden secrets. Furthermore, in the *Eight Gates* (which the Gaon never saw) the Ari digresses from some of the

principles that he elucidated in his other works, and explains in the same manner as the Gaon... Certainly they are both the words of the living God, for it is well known that there are various aspects and perspectives in any one particular subject". R. Shlomo Eliyashiv, unpublished letters.

[23] *Aliyot Eliyahu,* new ed., p. 44. Lamm, p. 45, note 98.

[24] *Leshem Sh'vo V'Achlamah, Sefer HaK'lallim,* p. 42a.

[25] *Even Shleima,* 11:7, note 5, p. 103 (52a), from the Gaon's commentary to *Tikkuney Zohar* 42c, and *Ra'aya Mehemna* 1:77a, 1:82b.

[26] *Even Shleimah,* 11:3, p. 100 (50b), drawn from the Gaon's original commentaries on the books of the *Zohar, Ra'aya Mehemna* 1:82b, *Tikkuney Zohar* 64d, *Tikkuney Zohar Chadash* 36c.

[27] *Kol HaTor,* Chapter 1, pars. #6 and #7. (Kasher, pp. 473-474).

[28] Ibid. Chapter 3, par. #12. (Kasher, p. 515).

[29] *Aliyot Eliyahu,* p.83.

[30] Landau, p. 36 (English).

[31] *Aliyot Eliyahu,* p. 87.

[32] R. Chayim Volozhin, Introduction *to Sifra DiTzniuta.*

[33] Ibid. and *Sha'ar Be'er Sheva,* par. #14.

[34] R. Yisrael of Shklov, Introduction to *Pe'at HaShulchan.*

[35] *Rav Pa'alim,* Yaacov Landau Pub., Tel Aviv, p. 58.

[36] *Toldot Yitzchak,* Section 2, pp. 140-141.

[37] Professor Zvi Werblowsky, *Joseph Karo - Lawyer and Mystic* (JPS, 1980), p. 311.

[38] *Pe'at HaShulchan,* Introduction; R. Itzele of Volozhin, introduction to his father's *Nefesh HaChaim.*

[39] R. Menachem Mendel of Shklov, Introduction to the Gaon's commentary on *Pirkey Avot.*

[40] The Gaon's secret of Sasson and Simcha is explained in Part II, Chap. 4.

[41] R. Chayim Volozhin, Introduction *to Sifra DiTzeniuta. Chazon Tzion,* p. 41.

[42] Ibid.; Introduction to Gaon's glosses to *Shulchan Aruch.*

[43] Talmud, *Eruvin* 13. The *Rosh* from Amtzislow heard this from R. Chaim Volozhin.

[44] Introduction to *Hadrat Kodesh,* as told to his nephew R. Abraham Simcha.

[45] *Idra Rabba,* 3:127b. This can also be found at the beginning of the Gaon's commentary to *Tikkuney Zohar.*

[46] Gaon's commentary on *Tikunei HaZohar, Tikun* 70, p. 139b and *Tikunim from Zohar Chadash,* p. 5b.

[47] *Brit Avot B'Se'arat Eliyahu* (*Covenant of the Forefathers in the Storm Wind of Elijah*), R. Yoseph Rivlin, Chap. 35, unpublished manuscript and see further below.

[48] *Even Shliemah*, chapter 10, #31, note 29.

[49] *Aliyot Eliyahu*, p. 100.

[50] Ibid.

[51] The term *Goral* is borrowed from the Yom Kippur service in line with the verse, "Aaron shall place two lots (*goralot*) on the two goats, one lot (*goral*) marked 'for God,' and one lot (*goral*) marked 'for Azazel'" (Leviticus 16:8). Since there is no concept of "chance" in Judaism, these lots were a bona fide way of "divining" God's will in any particular situation. According to the elders of Jerusalem (see following note) this tradition of drawing lots traced its origins back to the ancient rule, that when there is a great need, to go the Kohen Gadol in the Sanctuary, and consult the *Urim* and *Tumim* — the breastplate that he wore on his chest which consisted of an array of precious and semi-precious stones.

[52] Simcha Raz, *A Tzadik in our Time*, pp. 162-170 (1977, Feldheim, Jerusalem).

[53] Chapter 3, par. #1, (Kasher, p. 507).

[54] Chapter 3, par. #9, (Kasher, p. 513).

[55] *Tikkunei HaZohar,* based on Ecclesiastes 9:10.

[56] Chapter 3, par. #1, (Kasher, p. 507).

[57] *Kol HaTor, Sha'ar Be'er Sheva*, par. #11.

[58] Chapter 3, par. #3, (Kasher, p. 509).

[59] Chapter 3, par. #3, (Kasher, p. 510).

[60] *Chazon Tziyon*, p. 16.

[61] Ibid.

[62] Chapter 2, Aspect #50 (Kasher, p. 486).

[63] *Chazon Tziyon,* p. 21, note 23.

[64] Chapter 3, par. #11, (Kasher, p. 515).

[65] Chapter 3, par #3 (Kasher, p. 509).

[66] R. Yitzchak Kahana, *Toldot Yitzchak*, section #2, pp. 140-141.

[67] Based on Judges 13:25, "The spirit of the Lord began to move in him...".

[68] Chapter 1, par. # 4.

[69] Chapter 1, par. #23, (Kasher, p. 478).

[70] Chapter 2, Aspect #108 (Kasher, p. 493). This prayer is found at the end of

Chapter 5, Section 1, (Kasher, p. 530).

[71] Introduction to *Biurey HaGra* by the Gaon's sons on *Shulchan Aruch* (*Orach Chayim*). *Aliyot Eliyahu*, p. 100, note 86.

[72] *Tikkuney Zohar Chadash,* page 27 on the verse, "His left hand is beneath my head."

[73] Chapter 3, par. #8, (Kasher, p. 512).

[74] The Gaon's commentary on the *Zohar, Yahel Or, Mishpatim,* p. 18.

[75] Chapter 3, near the end, (Kasher, p. 517).

[76] *Even Sheliema* 1a and 1b and the Gaon's comments on Proverbs 4:13.

[77] Quoted in introduction to *Pe'at HaShulchan,* and in R. Shlomo Zalman Rivlin's introduction to the 1947 edition of *Kol HaTor* (printed in the 1968 B'nei B'rak edition).

[78] *Science, Philosophy, and Religion: a Symposium, 1941*

[79] The first half of this statement was recorded by R. Dr. Baruch Schick of Shklov in the introduction to his Hebrew translation of Euclid (which, he writes, was undertaken, along with other scientific works, at the encouragement of the Gaon). The statement of Schick, in the name of the Gaon and with the implication of a necessary confluence between Torah and science, has been challenged, e.g., R. Betzalel Landau, *HaGaon HaChasid MeVilna,* p. 117 and notes (English edition, p. 153). However, Schick's Euclid was published eighteen years before the Gaon passed away and thus was certainly known to him. In addition, a similar quote appears in the introduction to *Pe'at HaShulchan* by another of the Gaon's disciples, R. Yisrael of Shklov, "All the wisdoms (natural sciences) are necessary to understand our holy Torah and they are all included within it [the Torah]. To what degree this statement of the Gaon is or is not echoing R. Schick's quote and R. Hillel's is a matter of controversy. The quotation here from R. Hillel Rivlin is thus a third independent source. It should be noted that the second part of the Gaon's statement quoted in *Kol HaTor* is not found in the other sources. See also Part I, Chapter 4, *Sha'ar Be'er Sheva,* par. #12 and Volume II Chapter 3 Leviathan for more about the R. Schick controversy.

[80] As outlined in *Sha'ar Be'er Sheva.*

[81] Introduction to *Pe'at HaShulchan,* "The Gaon's father also instructed him to study the occult sciences which were known to the members of the Sanhedrin and the *tannaic* sages [of the Mishnaic period in order to cross-examine witnesses and suspects], as explained in the talmudic episode of R. Shimon ben Shetach."

[82] Part I, Chapter 1, *The Living Legacy of Kol HaTor,* notes in Section: "The History of *Kol HaTor* and the Rivlin Family."

[83] *Kol HaTor, Sha'ar Be'er Sheva,* pars. #10 and #14.

[84] Ibid, par. #14.

[85] Ibid, par. #10.

[86] The Gaon's experimentation with a *golem* — an artificially created automaton — is also reported by R. Chaim of Volozhin, the Gaon's most famous disciple. See, here below, Chapter 4, *Sha'ar Be'er Sheva*, par. #14, note, and Appendix.

[87] *Sha'ar Be'er Sheva*, par. #14.

[88] Chapter 3, par. #12, (Kasher, p. 516).

[89] It has been reprinted in *HaGaon HeChasid M'Vilna*, p. 321, and more recently in *Arba'at HaRoim - HaTekufah HaGedolah*, Part II, p. 55.

[90] The "Missing Page" from *Kol HaTor*, very end of Chapter 5, Section I.

[91] Based on Proverbs 4:18 and alluding to the sixth hour of the sixth day.

[92] This would place the time of the writing in 1753, when the Gaon was 33 years old.

[93] Chapter 3, following par. #12, (Kasher, p. 516).

[94] This would appear to contradict the statement above that the Gaon began his role as Mashiach ben Yoseph when he was 20 years old, rather than 62 years old, as in this report. Yet, R. Hillel also stated above that even when he was very young, the Gaon's experiment with a *golem* was "in order to crush the external forces (lit. *Samael*) at the Gates of Jerusalem." Thus, the Gaon knew that he was an aspect of the Mashiach even then. The answer is that there are different aspects and phases of Mashiach ben Yoseph, and the Gaon himself was evolving through these different phases. This is clearly evident from the tradition brought above and restated in *Kol HaTor* that "Only during his journey to the Land of Israel he saw that he had ascended to the aspect of the Faithful Shepherd (Moses)", i.e., he had now evolved even beyond the particular aspect of Mashiach ben Yoseph, whose special mission was the actual resettlement of the Land of Israel.

[95] Chapter 1, par. 23. (Kasher, p. 478).

[96] Chapter 3, last paragraph. (Kasher, pp. 517-518).

Chapter 3

Contents of *Kol HaTor*

•Approbation to 1968 B'nei B'rak Edition of *Kol HaTor*

•Contents of the Seven Chapters of *Kol HaTor*

    1.   Fundamentals of the Dawn of Redemption

    2a. The 156 Aspects of Mashiach ben Yoseph

    2b. Two Generational Messiahs

    3.   Sacred Formulas in the Dawn of Redemption

    4.   Three-Fold Preparation for the Advent of the Mashiach: Signs, Times, and Agents

    5a. Seven Rectifications of the Decoder in Preparation for Redemption

    5b. *Sha'ar Be'er Sheva* -The Gate of the Well of Seven [Sciences]

    6.   The Essentials of Service and Their Implementation in Accord with the Dawn of Redemption

    7.   Through *Tzedaka* You Will Be Established

•Overview of *Kol HaTor*

  • The Seven Point Agenda for Redemption

  • The Seven Characteristics of Redemption

  • The Seven Practical Paths to Redemption

  • The Seven Rectifications of the Decoder in Preparation for Redemption

Approbation

[Translation of the Approbation
to the 1968 B'nei B'rak Edition of *Kol HaTor*]

A Letter from the venerable sage, Rabbi Chaim Shraga Feivel Frank, rabbinic judge and spiritual leader in the Holy City of Jerusalem and Rav of the neighborhood of Yemin Moshe, Jerusalem, author of Toldot Ze'ev on the laws of Shabbat in two volumes.

Let us look into the work of the holy book *Kol HaTor* [Call of the Turtledove] by my master and ancestor, the sage and mystic, our teacher Rabbi Hillel, son of the sage and saint, Rabbi Benyamin Rivlis [Rivlin] from Shklov, z"l. It illuminates, with perfect clarity, the paths of redemption and the wells of salvation, which were revealed to the world by his teacher, the Master, who was the likeness of an "angel of God," our master the Gra, z"l.

Our teacher, the Gra, merited to spread his wings over all the branches and hidden treasures of the Torah, in breadth and in depth, including *gematria*, allusions, and the hidden and recondite secrets, which no eye has glimpsed, and whose depths have not been plumbed in generations before or since. Especially, concerning the subject of the return to the land of our desire, resettling in the land of our glory, and rebuilding in the land of our holiness, there was revealed the divine spirit [*ruach hakodesh*] within the study hall of the Gra.

We, the descendants and the grandchildren of the family, have received the tradition, from one to another, that our grandfather, the sage and mystic, Rabbi Hillel, may his merit protect us, merited to stand before his master, the Gra z"l, many years. He received from him hidden secrets concerning the resettlement of the Land of Israel, and was commanded by him to awaken the slumbering love for "a dwelling place for the eternal God" [Deuteronomy 33:27] — that is, Zion and Jerusalem. [He was commanded] to return her to her former stature and to restore her as in days of old, to magnify her glory and let honor dwell within her, because when Jerusalem is rebuilt, the son of David [the Mashiach] comes (Talmud, *Megilla* 17b). Rabbi Hillel condensed the essentials of what he heard directly from the Gra in the book *Kol HaTor*.

It is a tragedy that, due to our many transgressions, this book is incomplete and that many pieces have been hidden from us. However, it is, nevertheless, incumbent upon us to praise the Master of All for [blessing us with] the descendants and grandchildren of the sage, the author of *Kol HaTor*, specifically: my grandfather, the leader, the Rav, the Light of the Redemption, our teacher Rav Zalman Chaim Rivlin, z"l, who raised the standard of Torah in Jerusalem with the Torah academy *Etz Chaim* in the year 5594 [1834]; and my uncle, the leader, the Rav, the great light, our teacher Rav Yoseph ("Yosha") Rivlin, z"l, who founded the new neighborhoods in the new city of Jerusalem, outside the walls of the Old City; and their cousin, the Rav, the recognized sage, Rabbi Yitzchak Tzvi Rivlin, z"l, the first Rav of the neighborhood Zichron Moshe in Jerusalem. They are the ones who guarded the remnants of the manuscript, preventing its loss. The sage, Rabbi Yitzchak Tzvi, mentioned above, collected, selected, and arranged specific chapters and passed them on to his cousin, Rabbi Shlomo Zalman, the son of Rabbi Yoseph ("Yosha") Rivlin, mentioned above. It was he who published (for an unknown reason) [only] a limited edition of approximately one hundred copies, and distributed them among family members and a few friends. Now, even these, are not to be found.

Therefore, a great debt of gratitude is owed to the "Committee for the Dissemination of *Kol HaTor*," which has recognized the value of this book, and has had the initiative to spread its light in every Jewish home, in order that they should know how to proceed and what they must do in the days of the Messianic Era.

Especially at this time, when the Lord, let His Name be blessed, in His great mercy and kindness, in the month of Ziv, in the year 5727 [June 1967], has bequeathed to us all of the Holy Land of Israel, and our glorious Holy City of

Jerusalem, as it is said (Zechariah 2:16), "and the Lord will bequeath Yehuda his portion on the holy earth, and He will again choose Jerusalem."

Who will insure that the *Kol HaTor* will penetrate the ears of all Jews, so that they will realize that in the final period of the Era of Redemption, the obligation is upon us to begin with the "reawakening from below," in order to bring about the "reawakening from above," in order to bring upon us the paragon of peace, with the building of the Chosen House, and the Lord will be an everlasting light for us? Amen, may this be His will.

A soul constantly seeking for the kindness of Heaven in mercy, and looking forward to the salvation of the Lord quickly and in the near future,

Chaim Shraga Feivel, son of the sage Rav Zalman Frank, z"l

Contents of *Kol HaTor's* Seven Chapters

(The original editor of *Kol HaTor*, R. Shlomo Zalman Rivlin, provided the seven chapters with a summary of contents)

Chapter Headings of *Kol HaTor*

Chapter 1
Fundamentals of the Dawn of Redemption

In the period of the Last Generation, our mission is that of our master, the Gaon, the Emanation of Mashiach ben Yoseph. According to our master, R. Eliyahu, all the phases of the *At'chalta* — the ingathering of the exiles and resettlement of the Holy Land — in general and in particular up until the final End Period are within the mission of the first Messiah — Mashiach ben Yoseph. This process originates from the "left side"- the attribute of *din* — which is stimulated from "below" in a natural manner. This is similar to the events at the beginning of the second Temple, in the days of Cyrus. Afterwards, the redemption will be completed from the "right side" – the attribute of *Chesed* — which is the mission of Mashiach ben David.

The fundamental doctrine of our master is: "Yoseph lives on." As we now stand upon the threshold of the *At'chalta*, it is incumbent upon us to learn well all of the 156 characteristics, aspects, appellations, and properties of Mashiach ben Yoseph, as well as the mysteries of the *At'chalta,* which are alluded to in the sacred works of our master. This is in order that we may know the path before us and what action to take, guided by the light of our master that continues to illuminate our path through high noon [of the sixth day, i.e., 1990].

Chapter 2 Section I
The 156 Aspects of
Mashiach ben Yoseph

It is a commandment and a grave obligation for every Jew, and especially for those involved with the ingathering of the exiles, to learn, to know, and to understand well, in depth and breadth, all of the 156 aspects and characteristics of the Messiah of the Beginning. This is all the more so with anyone who carries the burden of responsibility for any aspect of public affairs in the Holy Land. How much more so is it crucial for those actual leading the holy resettlement! Arousal from below is through Mashiach ben Yoseph, the ingathering of the exiles, and all events of the *At'chalta*/Beginning.

Chapter 2 Section II
Two Generational
Messiahs

It is incumbent upon us to act with all of our strength in order to unite the Two Messiahs, Mashiach ben Yoseph and Mashiach ben David — the Branch of Yoseph and the Branch of Judah [the progenitor of the Davidic line] in total unity. This is the fundamental principle in order to unite the Holy One and His Shechina in total restoration. We must come to the Lord's aid in strength. "The redeemers will ascend upon Mt. Zion." The redeemers are the

Two Messiahs in their battle for Jerusalem against the alliance between *Seir* and his uncle [Esav, the rabbinic archetype for Christendom and Yishmael, the rabbinic archetype for Islam, respectively].

This will occur through our efforts to gather the exiles, rebuild Jerusalem, and through the establishment of Inner Circles. The general process of redemption is initiated through the first messiah — Mashiach ben Yoseph — and is completed by Mashiach ben David. Similarly, in every action, whether collective or individual, throughout the advent of the *At'chalta* via the natural process, the first intercessor is Mashiach ben Yoseph and the concluding intercessor is Mashiach ben David. This relationship parallels that of the Two Generational Messiahs following the motif of "Judah saves Yoseph."

Chapter 3
Sacred Formulas in the
Dawn of Redemption

Sacred formulas [are revealed] in the advent of the messianic era. Everything is alluded to in the Written Torah, and everything is alluded to in the Oral Torah. Likewise, everything concerning the advent of the messianic era is alluded to in the Secret Doctrine of our master. We now stand upon the threshold of the present phase of redemption, of the "Call of the Turtledove," yet we are engulfed in darkness. There is no priest or prophet; there is no Oracle (*Urim V'tumim*) to guide us along the essential path. Certainly this is the case with the details and the fine minutiae of this path. Therefore, the Lord has sent us the Emanation of Mashiach ben Yoseph, who is our master, the Gaon. He has descended from heaven in order to reveal the formulas of the Torah, in the advent of the Mashiach, and the mechanisms of revelation in the mystery of "a predicament and its numerical formula [for a solution]," as explained in the writings of our master.

[Here will be explained] the reason our master was forced to return from his attempted immigration to the Land of Israel and his instructions to his disciples in light of sublime formulas. [Also] according to our master the Gaon, the acceleration of the redemptive process is dependent upon the study of the esoteric teachings of the Kabbalah.

Chapter 4
Three-Fold Preparation for
The Advent of the Mashiach -
Signs, Times, and Agents

Here will be explained the purpose of redemption, the redemption of the truth, and the sanctification of God's Name, until the ultimate rectification of God's Kingdom. The thrice-woven cord of "Signs," "Designated Times," and "Appointed Agents" appear simultaneously in a three-pronged campaign. The agents react to the signs and thus can help accelerate the arrival of the designated times.[3] These are alluded to in the verses (Song of Songs 2:12), "The blossoms have appeared in the land; the time of singing has arrived, and the call of the turtledove is heard in the land" and (Psalms 102:14, 15), "For it is time to favor her; for the fixed time is come. For your servants hold her stones dear, and cherish her very dust."

It is incumbent upon us to learn, and to understand, the interface between these three fundamental principles. To the degree that we actively anticipate the countenance of the redemption, "For your servants hold her stones dear, and cherish her very dust," the redemption will draw closer to us, in the mystery of "for the designated time is come," and as it is written, "Return to Me and I will return to you." In this regard, there are revealed to us several formulas for the appointed times and the Revealed End in the Last Generation. This will continue until the Final End — the Wondrous End.

Chapter 5 Section I
Seven Rectifications of the Decoder in Preparation for Redemption

All the essential principles of the *At'chalta* and its advent, its ways and means, are interfaced with the three foundations of Signs, Times, and Agents. All phenomena that occur via action and calculation are interdependent and intertwined with the Seven Rectifications of the Revealer of the Hidden in the mystery of Formula 999 in *Yesod*. This is the level of Mashiach ben Yoseph and the Two Armies of God — *Netzach* and *Hod* — that are the divine manifestations of the *Trein M'shechin* — Mashiach ben Yoseph and Mashiach ben David.

It is our practical obligation to attain the ultimate level of "arousal from below," which is Formula 999 in *Yesod* — One Thousand Minus One — that are the 999 phases of the Mashiach. Here will be explained the supra-natural assistance within every constructive action which is performed in a natural manner, and thus through its power, together they will ascend to the thousandth level, in accord with the verse [Isaiah 60:22], "the small one will become a thousand," which is the level of *tov* ("good") in the mission of our master, the Gaon.

"To everything there is a season, and a time for everything [under the heaven]" (Ecclesiastes 3:1) [refers to] recondite allusions in the paths of the Redemption, in the secret of the "Revealer of Hidden Things" (Genesis 41:45); [Messianic] end times, in the secret of a "time for singing" (Song of Songs 2:12) and a "time to favor her... [for the designated time is come]" (Psalms 102:14) are within the context of the seven commands, from the first hour (5500/1740) of the light of day till the sixth millennium in the era of the End of Days, during the Final Generation, until the final end, the period of the Wondrous (or Hidden) End.

Chapter 5 Section II
The Gate of the Well
of Seven [Sciences]

The obligation to study the Seven Natural Sciences, according to the Gaon, Rabbeinu Eliyahu, is in order to perceive the wisdom of the Torah, sanctify the Name of God and to accelerate the Redemption.

Chapter 6
The Essentials of Service and
Their Implementation in Accord
with the Dawn of Redemption

The stipulations and manner of the essentials of service, to be performed at the Dawn of Redemption, will all be similar to those of the period [leading up to the rebuilding] of the Second Temple, in accord with the mission of Mashiach ben Yoseph. These are the Seven Hewn Pillars of the period of the Revealed End: 1) ingathering of the exiles; 2) rebuilding Jerusalem; 3) removing the impure spirit from the Land [of Israel] by replanting the holy earth and the fulfillment of the [agricultural] commandments related to it; 4) establishing inner circles (lit. people of truth), in order to redeem the truth and sanctify the name of God; 5) [promoting the spread of] Torah from Zion; 6) waging war against Amalek; 7) healing Zion. We, the emissaries of the Most High, are obligated, with all of the strength of our hands, to fulfill these [essentials of service] in the secret of "human actions together with numerical calculations."

Chapter 7
Through *Tzedaka* You Will
Be Established

Jerusalem is only redeemed with *tzedaka*/righteousness (charity), as it is written: "Zion will be redeemed with justice;

and those who return to her, with *tzedaka*/righteousness [Isaiah 1:27]. It also says: "You will be established with *tzedaka*/righteousness and your children's peace will be abundant" [Isaiah 54:14]. "You will be established with *tzedaka*/charity" is both a decree and an act of grace. The Holy One desired to bring merit to all of Israel — to the ones close and to the ones far away — with the commandment to rebuild Jerusalem. Therefore He decreed that Jerusalem would be rebuilt with *tzedaka*/charity. Everyone of Israel must participate in the building and expansion of the Heritage of God [as written] "Expand the site of your dwelling place, etc." [Isaiah 54:2]. This is all the more so during those days, and with those commandments, that have a connection and essential affinity with Jerusalem and her reconstruction.

Supporting the rebuilding of Jerusalem is an obligatory reciprocity for what all Israel, individually and collectively, receives from Jerusalem. Our Jewish brothers, who still dwell in the exile, receive from their brothers, who dwell in Jerusalem and are rebuilding it, thousands and even tens of thousands more than what they donate to Jerusalem, even when the contribution is generous. For all the spiritual radiance of salvation, blessing, redemption, loving kindness and mercy, success, health, etc., of Jews, wherever they are, comes only from Jerusalem and her reconstruction.

Overview of *Kol HaTor*

The Seven Point Agenda
for Redemption
(From Chapter 1 of *Kol HaTor*)

According to our master, the Gaon Rabbi Eliyahu, these are the seven fundamental messianic principles of the *Ikveta DiM'shecha,* in accord with the verse, "Upon one foundation stone there are seven facets" (Zechariah 3:9).

1. "Od Yoseph Chai - Yoseph Lives On" (Genesis 45:28). The underlying doctrine of our master was that the messianic process continues unabated to function on every level. The beginning of the redemption — in general and in particular — is dependent upon the First Messiah, the messiah of the redemption — Mashiach ben Yoseph. In theory, due to the lack of our merit, the Mashiach was destined to die and his mission was to fail. However, because of the elongation of the exile and the suffering he endures by carrying our afflictions, the decree was annulled and his mission is succeeding, albeit through a slow and tortuous path. These are the pangs of the Mashiach in the Last Generation, as the prophet declares: "He suffers for our sins" [see Isaiah, end of chapter 52 and chapter 53].

2. "He Acted and Succeeded" (II Chronicles 31:21) "And the Lord brought success to everything that he [Yoseph] touched" (Genesis 39:23). It is well known the statement of our master that, 'There are two *mitzvot* that one enters into literally with his entire body — the Sukka and the Land of Israel" — and both must be constructed by hand, as stated in the Talmud (Megilah17), "Once Jerusalem is rebuilt [via Mashiach ben Yoseph] then [Mashiach] ben David will come."

3. "In Its Due Time I [God] Will Accelerate It" (Isaiah 60:22). Even the divinely appointed "End Periods" can, and will, be accelerated to unfold before their predetermined times, via specific acts of human stimulation known as the "arousal from below".

4. "Acquisition and Conquest in the Final Era." These two aspects of Mashiach ben Yoseph refer to 1) Building and planting as in the time of Ezra and Nehemiah, and 2) Military conquest as in the time of Joshua. Ezra and Nehemiah, as well as Joshua, were historical manifestations of Mashiach ben Yoseph in their respective times.

5. "A Refuge in Zion" (Joel 3:5, Obadiah 1:7). "Almost every day our master spoke to us with great emotion, and the deepest concern, that Zion [the Land of Israel] and Jerusalem will be a place of refuge and that we cannot loose the moment." Every mention of Zion is a reference to Mashiach ben Yoseph in accordance with the *midrash* (Tanchuma), "What happens to Yoseph also happens to Zion."

6. "Esoteric Teachings from Zion" from the verse, "From out of Zion will go Torah [lit. Teachings]" (Isaiah 2:3). This refers to the learning of the Kabbalah, which will be revealed in the Land of Israel, primarily in the capital of Jerusalem.

7. "Revealer of the Hidden" (*Tzafenat-Pa'aneach* Genesis 41:45). In the beginning of the Redemption, crucial formulas hidden in the Torah and in the words of the talmudic sages begin to be revealed.

The Seven Characteristics of Redemption
(From Chapter 1 of *Kol HaTor*)

1. Suffering and Respite. One must know from the start that the messianic process alternates between suffering and respite, as alluded to in the two verses: (Ezekiel 47:13) "Yoseph will have two [alternating] portions" and (Psalms 16:6) "Sufferings have befallen me [together] with pleasantness." The messianic process unfolds through suffering and often through a circuitous fashion. Mashiach ben Yoseph must blaze a trail through a labyrinth of difficulties. He will succeed, however, in the end with the help of Mashiach ben David, as it is depicted (Genesis 37): "Judah [the progenitor of the Davidic line] saves Yoseph."[1]

2. Working Undercover. The process of messianic revelation must take place in a subtle manner, such as in a conspiracy. One of the formulas taught by the Gaon was that the very word *sod*/secret, as in the verse (Psalms 25:14), "The *sod*/secret of God is [revealed] to those who revere Him", is equal to the numerical value of Mashiach ben Yoseph [i.e., written out in full. The three letters of *samech* (120) + the two letters of *vav* (12) + the three letters of *dalet* (434) = 566 which equals Mashiach ben Yoseph (566)].

3. Gradual Development. This is what the sages formulated in their statement (Jerusalem Talmud, *Berachot* 5b): "The redemption of Israel is a gradual process like onto the awakening of the dawn." A key principle, according to our master, is that all the events that will occur on the path to complete redemption will begin through gradual development. Such is the case with the ingathering of the exiles and the rebuilding of Jerusalem, both of which begin very slowly.[2]

4. Beggar on a Donkey. If the Redemption is not merited, the process manifests itself through natural events, as opposed to miraculous ones. This entails poverty and material shortage, as personified by a poor person slowly approaching, riding a lowly beast.

5. Inner Circles. One of the central factors in the success of our work is the establishment of spiritual fraternities, especially in Jerusalem, for the purpose of implementing the Agenda for Redemption. This is expressed by the sages (Talmud, *Shabbat* 119): "Jerusalem was only destroyed because the Inner Circles ceased to exist."

6. Economic Equality. The resettlement of the Holy Land in general, and especially the rebuilding of Jerusalem, must be based upon the principle of equality, as the sages formulated (Talmud, *Sanhedrin* 98): "The Son of David will not come until the principle of equality is established"; and [ibid.]: "The Son of David will not come until economic equality is achieved."

7. With Justice You Will Be Established (Isaiah 54:13).

There are two implications to the term justice/*tzedaka*: 1) Justice, in the sense of equalization, and 2) Justice, in the sense of charitable donations. The Land of Israel must be resettled through *tzedaka*, in both senses, because the Holy One desired to give to each individual near and far the opportunity to participate.

The Seven Practical Paths to Redemption
(From Chapter 4 of *Kol HaTor*)

1. Ingathering of the Exiled. In reference to the ingathering of the exiled the verse states (Zephaniah 3:20): "At that time I will make you a name and praise among all the people of the earth, when I restore your captivity before your eyes, says the Lord." Here, "a name and praise" refers to the wisdom of Israel, which will be revealed before the eyes of the entire world. This developmental process occurs in stages, together with the ingathering of the exiles.

2. Rebuilding of Jerusalem. In reference to Jerusalem the verse states (Isaiah 62:7): "Don't allow Him to be silent until He will establish, until He makes Jerusalem a [source of] praise in the earth." This is referring to the acknowledgement and praise of Israel's wisdom, whose center will be in rebuilt Jerusalem.

3. Removal of Contamination from the Land. This is achieved through the cultivation of the land and through the fulfillment of the numerous agricultural *mitzvot*. This accords with the verse (Ezekiel 36:8): "But you, mountains of Israel — you will shoot forth your branches and bear your fruit for my people Israel, when they are about to come." The Talmud explains (*Sanhedrin* 98a): "There is no more obvious sign of the Redemption than the successful cultivation of the Land of Israel". [i.e., "When the Land of Israel will generate an abundance of produce" — Rashi, ibid.]

4. Redemption of the Truth via Inner Circles. All the work involved with the ingathering of the exiled is a preparation for the establishment and the continued existence of the Inner

Circles [of Truth], in order to attain the level of the Redemption of Truth, the Sanctification of God's Name, and the Ultimate Rectification of God's Kingdom. Without the establishment of the Inner Circles there is no hope, God forbid, to all of the work of the Beginning of the Redemption.

5. Sanctification of God's Name. Sanctification of God's Name in the eyes of the nations, via the unification of scientific wisdom together with the esoteric wisdom of Israel, will cause the sinners of Israel to return from their ways. When they will see that even the gentiles recognize the power of God to His people, they will then be ashamed and return to God, and a *Kiddush HaShem* will be affected. Sanctification of God's Name is also achieved through the military victories of Israel during the final battles of Gog and Magog, via the providence of Mashiach ben Yoseph. This will occur after the initial redemption from the subjugation to foreign powers.

6. Revelation of the Secrets of the Torah. In reference to the revelation of the inner teachings of Torah it is written: "She is your wisdom and your understanding *(Chochmah* and *Binah)...*" — these are the secrets of the Torah, as it is known to those initiated into the esoteric wisdom. The teachings of the Kabbalah themselves are the very source of Israel's ascendancy and the means through which Israel can achieve the most elevated status. This is the intention of the verse, "to grant you ascendancy beyond all the nations..." for Israel's praise in the eyes of the world is her esoteric wisdom.

7. The Ultimate Rectification of God's Kingdom. The previous six paths culminate in the final *tikkun* of God's Kingdom on earth, which is the final union between the forces of the *Trein M'shechin.*

The Seven Rectifications of the Decoder in Preparation for Redemption
(From Chapter 5 of *Kol HaTor*)

1. Egalitarianism. This *tikkun* refers to the equalization of the values of the Two Armies (*Y-HVH Tzevaot* and *E-lohim Tzevaot*] as in: "Their feet were a singular foot" (Ezekiel 1:7).

[These are the *trei palgei gufa* — the two halves of the singular body of the messianic process] 499½ from the right side and 499½ from the left side, etc. Practically speaking, between colleagues this same aspect of egalitarianism is necessary to establish equanimity (*kav hamashveh*) within the Inner Circles.

On the simple level (*al derech p'shat*), Egalitarianism refers to the personal and ethical conduct of each individual; particularly in overcoming pride and arrogance, both on the material and spiritual plane.

2. Transcendence. The *tikkun* of Transcendence refers to a state of higher consciousness released through the power of Metatron who is the collective Oversoul of Mashiach ben Yoseph, in the mystery of Formula 999 in *Yesod*. This relationship is reflected in that *Metatron* [314] *Sar* [500] *HaPanim* [185] (Prince of the Countenance) has the numerical value of 999.

On the simple level, Transcendence refers to the obligation for everyone to insure that he is on a path of continual spiritual growth. If one does not ascend from the purely physical then one remains comparable to a lowly beast.

3. Holism. The *tikkun* of Holism refers to the *sefirah* and divine attribute of *yesod,* which characteristically contains all the other *sefirot* and divine attributes in the secret of "Zion [*yesod*] is the containment of beauty."

On the simple level, Holism refers to the principle: "All of Israel are responsible for each other." Each individual is an integral part of the community and "Jerusalem was destroyed only because individuals did not reprove each other."

4. Sanctification. The *tikkun* of Sanctification refers to the supernal seminal essence, the Dew of Light, which is the highest root and source of divine purity emanating in the *da'at*, the middle brain. From there, it is drawn down through a subtle channel within the spinal column, which is represented by the letter *vav* of God's Name, in order to unite with its final destination, represented by the final letter *hey* of God's Name. In this manner a sacred passage way is prepared for the souls to enter into this world.

On the simple level, Sanctification refers to purification from all desires that are harmful to body and soul. One must actively seek a spirit of purity which leads to divine transmission (*ruach hakodesh*).

5. Creativity. The *tikkun* of Creativity is the revelation of new aspects in both the revealed and concealed teachings of Torah, specifically in the secret of Formula 999 in *Yesod*, which, little by little, arouses and activates the "New Light" of Zion (*ohr chadash b'yesod*) as it is written: "From out of Zion [*yesod*] goes forth [the inner] Torah."

On the simple level, Creativity means that after one has achieved the prerequisite levels of growth, every one must produce new Torah understandings, as well as perform community service. Everyone has a unique mission in the world, which includes revealing new concepts in Torah and creating and producing that which benefits the community.

6. Power. The *tikkun* of Power is the overpowering of the Amalakite spirit, according to the process exemplified by: "When Moses raised his hands" he was supported by the *Trein M'shechin* of his generation — Aaron and Hur.

On the simple level, Power refers to prevailing over the collective source of spiritual impurity. One who has attained to all the previous levels now has the power not only to fight a defensive war, but to actually launch an offensive against the very spirit of impurity and moral decay that hides within the community of Israel.

7. Fusion. The *tikkun* of Fusion refers to the fusion of the masculine and feminine aspects of Divinity in the secret of three digits 999. After the two branches — *Etz Yehuda* and *Etz Yoseph* — will first become one in the hand of mankind, then they will both become one in the Hand of God. This is the ultimate redemption of truth and the completion of the messianic process; this is the level described by the prophets as "The groom rejoicing with his bride."

On the simple level, Fusion refers to the process of fusing with God's Presence. After one has ascended through the six levels just outlined above, it is possible to attain to the level of re-uniting the Holy One together with His Divine Presence, to experience the return of the Shechina to Zion and the fulfillment of Redemption. Amen, so be His Will.

---

[1] See Gra *Tikkunay Zohar Chadash* p. 53, *Yamin Mekarevet.* Also see *Torat HaGeulah,* p16.

[2] See *Midrash Rabba Esther*, section 10:12.

[3] The Hebrew term for signs, *yi'udim* (singular - *yi'ud*), is usually translated as missions, appointments, designations or assignments. In the framework that R. Hillel is defining, however, the implication of *yi'udim* is that of the "signs", the actions or the events (the people, places and things), which alert the agents to translate those signs into "assignments". Throughout Chapter Four of *Kol HaTor*, where this triune application is expanded upon, R. Hillel does not indicate whether the *yi'udim*/signs are manifested from external sources or from the agents themselves. This ambiguity appears to be intentional because it does not matter how and why the signs of the new respective missions are revealed. Regardless, the agents must know how to interpret them and respond to them in order to stimulate the designated times. The *yi'udim* are the "signs of the times" which the agents recognize as their assignments to help trigger the "time of the sign".

Chapter 4

- *Sha'ar Be'er Sheva*
- A "Missing Page" from *Kol HaTor*

Kol HaTor

Translation of
Chapter 5, Section II

Sha'ar Be'er Sheva
Gate of the Well of Seven [Sciences]

Content: The obligation to study the Seven
Natural Sciences[1] according to the Gaon in
order to grasp the wisdom of the Torah,
sanctify God's Name and accelerate the
redemption.

1. It is well known that our teacher, the Genius (*gaon*) of
Israel, our master, Eliyahu, his soul be in Eden, was much
involved in investigating the properties of physical reality [in
line with the concept], "the deep secrets of the earth [are in
God's hand]" (Psalm 95:4).[2] This was in order to grasp the
[inner] wisdom of Torah [that is embedded in nature], to
sanctify the Name of God in the eyes of the nations *(Kiddush
HaShem)* and to accelerate the Redemption.

Already, from his youth, he exhibited wondrous
knowledge in all aspects of the Seven Sciences, and he
strongly urged and, in some cases, commanded his disciples
to acquire as much expertise as possible in these Seven
Sciences [in order to probe] "the deep secrets of the earth."
This would [ultimately] lead to the recognition that Israel's
wisdom is [none other than] the wisdom of its Torah, in
accord with the verse: "She [the Torah] is your wisdom and
your understanding in the eyes of the nations" (Deuteronomy
4:6). Israel would thus achieve its highest spiritual
superiority, in accord with the verse: "[God] will grant you
ascendancy above all the nations that He has made, for
praise, fame, and glory" (ibid. 26:19).

In accord with that which is stated in the holy *Zohar*
[see below], our master directed all of his efforts toward
preparing for this goal as the six hundredth year of the

present (sixth) millennium [5600 = 1840 C.E.] approached.[3]

2. The principle source for our master, the Gaon's doctrine, concerning the acquisition of the Seven Sciences as a preparation for the approaching six hundredth year of the sixth millennium, was in the words of the holy *Zohar* (*VaYeira* 117a):

> In the six hundredth year of the sixth millennium, the gates of wisdom above, together with the wellsprings of wisdom below, will be opened up, and the world will prepare to usher in the seventh millennium. This is symbolized by a man who begins preparations for ushering in the Sabbath on the afternoon of the sixth day. In the same way [toward the end of the sixth millennium] preparations are made for entering the seventh. The hint for this is: "In the six hundredth year of Noah's life... all the wellsprings of the great deep burst forth and the floodgates of the heavens were opened" (Genesis 7:11).

Our master, the Gaon, often spoke with us concerning these words from the *Zohar* in conjunction with the profound calculations that they involve. He emphasized that the Beginning of the Redemption (*At'chalta D'Geulah*) would be co-terminus with the ingathering of the exiles and with the opening of the wellsprings of wisdom. [This entire process would require our] "stimulation from below," which in turn revolved around [the people of] Israel being [re-centered] in Jerusalem, as will be explained. Our master also saw recondite allusions concerning his own mission in [the unfolding of] these events, for, as known, he was an illumination of [the light of] Mashiach ben Yoseph, the Messiah of the Beginning.[4]

Our master, the Gaon, studied the Seven Sciences (*Sheva Chochmot*) hidden in the Torah in the mystery of the "Seven Books."[5] This was in accord with the [inner] meaning of the verse, "Wisdoms (*Chochmot*) have built her house; her hewn pillars are seven" (Proverbs 9:1).[6] Our master thus told us: It is incumbent upon us to bring about the sanctification of God's Name during the [impending] period of the *Ikveta DiM'shecha*[7] in the following areas:

1. The rebuilding of Jerusalem

2. The ingathering of the exiles

3. The re-flourishing of the Land of Israel

4. The improvement of character traits[8]

5. The revelation of the hidden aspects of the Torah[9]

6. The study of the Seven Sciences

3. As stated in [the seventh chapter of the book of Deuteronomy] *Ki Tavo*, the highest level of blessing that can be bestowed upon the people of Israel and the Land of Israel is, "[God] will grant you ascendancy above all the nations that He has made, for praise, fame, and beauty" (26:19). Mankind will only acknowledge the ascendancy of Israel's [wisdom], however, when it will become known that that wisdom is none other than the wisdom of the Torah, in accord with the verse: "She [the Torah] is your wisdom and your understanding in the eyes of the nations. When they appreciate the entire system [of the Torah], they will say, 'This great nation is surely a wise and understanding people'" (4:6).

And when will mankind recognize Israel's wisdom?— when Israel will dwell upon its land. Only then will they be blessed with all the blessings and benefits that are enumerated there [in *Ki Tavo*]. As long as Israel is exiled from the Land, however, they are scorned and persecuted. All of their wisdom is in the category of "the wisdom of the wretched man is despised and his words go unheeded" (Ecclesiastes 9:15). [If this is not enough], they are also plundered because of [gentile] envy and jealousy.

4. With regard to the superiority of Israel's wisdom, our master, the Gaon, explained: Whenever the terms "praise and fame" or "praise" [alone] are mentioned [in the Bible] in conjunction with Israel or the Land of Israel, they refer specifically to Israel's wisdom as [it will be] seen by the entire

world. For example:

a. Regarding Jerusalem, the verse states: "O Jerusalem, I have set watchmen on your walls. They will never be silent day or night. [They say:] 'You who make mention of God, take no rest. And give Him no rest until He establishes and makes Jerusalem a praise on earth'" (Isaiah 62:6-7). A literal interpretation of this verse indicates that the rebuilding of Jerusalem will evoke admiration and praise. According to what we have said, however, the verse is also referring to the praise that Israel's wisdom will evoke when it is re-centered in a rebuilt Jerusalem.

b. Regarding the ingathering of the exiles the verse states: "'At that time I will make your fame and praise [known] among all the peoples of the world, when I restore your captivity before your eyes,' says the Lord" (Zephaniah 3:20). "Fame and praise" refers to the wisdom of Israel that will be revealed before the eyes of the entire world. As explained above, this will occur in conjunction with the ingathering of the exiles.

c. Regarding the re-flourishing of the Land of Israel, it is written: "For as the land brings forth its growth, and the garden causes its seeds to spring forth, so the Lord will cause [Israel's] righteousness and praise to spring forth before all the nations" (Isaiah 61:11). As the context of this verse indicates, the recognition and praise of Israel's wisdom is intimately bound up with the re-flourishing of the Land of Israel.[10]

d. Regarding the revelation of the inner teachings of the Torah, the verse states: "She [the Torah] is your wisdom and your understanding." Wisdom (Chochmah) and Understanding (Binah) refer specifically to the secrets of the Torah, as is known to those initiated into the esoteric wisdom. The inner teachings of the Torah are the very source of Israel's excellence and [the means by which they can achieve] their most elevated status. Again, this is the intention of the verse: "[God] will grant you ascendancy above all the nations that He has made, for praise, fame, and glory." As explained, it is Israel's wisdom that will be praised and elevated in the eyes of the nations. In connection with this, our master added a fitting allusion: [the phrase] "for praise and fame" (*LeTehilla U'leShem* = 846) is numerically equivalent to [the phrase] "Seven Sciences" (*Sheva Chochmot* = 846).[11]

e. Regarding the learning of the Seven Sciences, our master told us: The messianic revelation will unfold slowly, and in small increments, in conjunction with the [progressive] revelation of the wisdom of the Torah. This refers, in particular, to the revelation of the secret wisdom of the Torah and the [parallel] opening of the seven wisdoms above by virtue of [our] stimulation from below. This is the meaning of the *Zohar's* statement (*VaYeira* 117a): "In the six hundredth year of the sixth millennium the gates of wisdom above and the wellsprings of wisdom below will be opened." The intention is that this will take place slowly in conjunction with the revelation of the messianic [light].

All of these are included in the destiny of our master, the Gaon, the illumination of Mashiach ben Yoseph.

5. Who can utter, and who can estimate, the great concern that our master had for elevating the honor of the Torah and its study amongst the multitudes of the House of Israel? Who is the scribe, and who is the poet, who can depict the great need he felt for sanctifying [the Name of] God in the eyes of the nations? [How] many times did he say, amidst heavy sighing, "Why is it said among the nations, 'Where is the wisdom of Israel?'" Time and again he would confide in us [saying], "Are the bearers of our Torah working for the

sanctification of God's [Name], as did Israel's great leaders of the past? Many of them sanctified the Name of Heaven with their extensive knowledge in the investigation of the mysteries of nature, of the wonders of the Blessed Creator's [wisdom]. As a result, many righteous gentiles publicly extolled the wisdom of Israel and its Torah sages. [Among these sages were] the members of the Sanhedrin, the *Tanaim*,[12] the *Amoraim*, etc. In later generations, [these were followed by] our master, Maimonides, and the author of the *Tosafot Yom Tov*,[13] as well as others, who continually sanctified the Name of Heaven in the eyes of the Nations by [applying] their wisdom to probing 'the deep secrets of the earth' (Psalm 95:4)."

From all that has been stated, regarding the aforementioned verses from the Torah and the Prophets, and regarding the words of the holy *Zohar*, we can conclude with the following principles:

a. The study of the Seven Sciences through "stimulation from below" aids in grasping the mysteries of the wisdom of the Torah, in elevating the wisdom of Israel, in sanctifying [the Name of] God in the eyes of the Nations, and in hastening the redemption.

b. The revelation of the wisdom of Israel will coincide with the ingathering of the exiles.

c. The source and center for the revelation of Israel's wisdom will be in [rebuilt] Jerusalem.

d. The revelation of the wisdom of Israel in the eyes of the Nations will be concurrent with the re-flourishing of the entire Land of Israel.

All of these [principles] are similarly to be found in the statement of our sages (Talmud, *Sanhedrin* 98a): regarding the Revealed End as preparation for the Final Redemption[14] and in the mystery of "it will be revealed to all nations."[15]

6. The Light of Supernal Wisdom is the foundation principle

of the entire creation. It is the supernal light of Divine Wisdom itself. All the upper and lower universes and all that are in them [emanate from this Light and are included in it]. As this transcendent aspect of God's Wisdom flows through the universe of Emanation (*Atzilut*), all the spiritual and material properties of the entire universe that are potentially contained within it begin to manifest.

All of these [properties] are encoded in the Torah in the form of "divine formulas." [It is with these formulas that the Torah is able to contain] not only the general character of these properties, but all their details and fine minutiae in all generations.

According to the great principle of our master the Gaon in his commentary to *Sifra DiTzniuta*[16], all the unique properties of the supernal lights flow from the transcendent and holy power of the Light of Supernal Wisdom. It is their fractal sparks (*nitzotzin*) that descend from above to below until reaching the dimension of Action (*Asiyah*), where they become materialized in the lower world. This is true of every single property, in general and in particular, each according to its respective source and line of connection. All natural phenomena of the external world thus derive from the power of the Light of Supernal Wisdom. Their essential properties descend from above to below and are concentrated into seven compartments. This is the meaning of the verse, "Wisdoms have built her house; her hewn pillars are seven" (Proverbs 9:1). This is referring to the Seven Sciences that interpenetrate [and flow through] the Seven Pillars of the world, as is known.[17]

All of these — [the Seven Sciences and the Seven Pillars], all of creation, all the upper and lower universes and all that is in them — are connected to the Light of Supernal Wisdom through a subtle channel (*tzinor*). This is the mystery of [the verse], "He suspends the world upon no-thingness (*beli-mah*)" (Job 26:7). This [channel in Ezekiel's vision] is the mystery of the thread of Radiance (*Nogah*) and the appearance of the Electrum (*Chashmal*). [*Chashmal* is thus] an acronym for **Chochmah Shel Ma'alah** (Wisdom from above). All of these [levels in turn] derive from their original root in the blessed light of the Infinite One (*Ohr Ain Sof, Barukh Hu*).[18]

All of these [levels] are contained in the mysteries of the Torah because, "There is nothing that is not alluded to in the Torah."[19] The Torah, in its entirety, derives from the [Light of] Supernal Wisdom, as the Midrash states: "The distillation of Supernal Wisdom is Torah."[20] To this our master added: "The distillations of Torah are the seven lower sciences of the external world."

It is to these seven wisdoms that the *Zohar* refers when it speaks of [the opening of] "the wellsprings of wisdom below," in accord with the verse, "all the wellsprings of the great deep burst forth [and the floodgates of the heavens were opened]" (Genesis 7:11). This is also the mystery of Jacob's blessing to Yoseph in his capacity as Mashiach ben Yoseph:[21] "The God of your father will help you and the Almighty will bless you with the blessings of heaven above and the blessings of the deep that crouch below" (Genesis 49:25). This means that the "blessings of the deep below" flow from the "blessings of heaven above."[22]

In order to understand and grasp the wisdom of the Torah contained in the light of the upper wisdom, it is necessary to learn the Seven Sciences hidden in the lower world of nature.[23] This is the mystery of [the verse that refers to Israel's receiving the Torah at Mt. Sinai] "...they stood on the bottom side of the mountain" (Exodus 19:17).[24] Our master said that [the usage of patterns and examples found in the bottom side of reality] is analogous to a teacher of children who is able to explain numerous matters in the Torah [that his young pupils might not otherwise understand] by using toy models and similar devices, as well as simple diagrams.[25]

7. The Torah of our righteous Mashiach derives from the level

of the Light of Supernal Wisdom. This Torah will be revealed at the end of days by our master, Moses, with the arrival of Mashiach ben David. Still, to the degree that we are drawn ever closer to the complete Redemption (*geulah shlemah*) during [the preparatory period of] the Beginning of the Redemption, the Torah of our righteous Mashiach will be revealed little by little to select individuals by the Messiah of the Beginning (*M'shecha d'At'chalta*), Mashiach ben Yoseph. His mission thus includes [the revelation of] all the esoteric truths of the Torah in addition to the ingathering of the exiles and the liberation from foreign domination.

As mentioned above, the [concept of the] Seven Sciences is implied in the verse, "Wisdoms have built her house; her hewn pillars are seven" (Proverbs 9:1). [Accordingly, all branches of science can be divided into the following seven categories]:[26]

1. Mathematics, astronomy, and geometry[27]

2. Natural science and chemistry

3. Medicine and pharmacology[28]

4. Logic, grammar, and syntax[29]

5. Musicology and its esoteric theory[30]

6. Engineering and construction[31]

7. Parapsychology and the brain sciences[32]

Our master attained complete mastery in all these sciences.[33] He knew all the fundamentals of healing, but he never actually practiced medicine or pharmacology. This was in deference to the command of his father, who said that if he would completely master this wisdom on a practical level, he would be obligated to save lives, and all those living in his immediate vicinity would rely on him. If, on the other hand, they could not rely on his services, they would certainly arrange for another doctor [in his stead]. The Gaon would thus be freed from having to sacrifice from his time, which was dedicated solely to his God-given mission of revealing the esoteric teachings of the Torah and the mysteries of wisdom that are hidden within it.

[The Gaon also] mastered the science of philosophy. He found nothing of any worth in [philosophical speculation], however, except for isolated points that had actually originated with the Torah sages. "The remainder," he said, "lacks any logical [foundation] or moral justification and is based on foolish skepticism."[34]

8. Both qualitatively and quantitatively, the forces that underlie the most powerful material properties of the world of nature are infinitesimal in comparison with the Light of Supernal Wisdom — the supernal transcendent light of the Divine Wisdom — from which they originate.

With the gradual opening of the gates of wisdom above and below, however, the messianic revelation that will begin from the year 5600 (1840) will resemble the wisdom of King Solomon in his day.[35] Through our arousal from below, this revelation will result in the development of [larger and more powerful] telescopes that will allow mankind to reach the limits of telescopic observation and actually glimpse the Wondrous End (*Ketz HaPlaot*) that lies in the far reaches of the universe.[36]

This [flood of scientific knowledge] will occur through the inscription of the name "Israel", like the radiance (*nogah*) from the luster of the holy celestial creatures (*chayot haKodesh*). This is the meaning of the midrash: "One celestial creature, with its name, Israel, engraved on its forehead, stands in the center of the firmament."[37] The words, "Who is like Your people Israel, one nation in the world?" (2 Samuel 7:23), will then shine forth in brilliant colors. And the verses: "All the nations of the world will see that you are called by the name of God, and they will be in awe of you" (Deuteronomy 28:10) and "[God] will grant you ascendancy above all the nations that He has made, for praise, fame, and glory" (ibid. 26:19), will be fulfilled.

This revelation will first manifest in the holy city of Jerusalem, in accord with the verse: "Your name is upon Your city and upon Your people" (Daniel 9:19), and in accord with the words of the sages: "In the future, Jerusalem will be a beacon to the nations of the world, as it is said: 'Nations shall walk in your light"' (Isaiah 60:3).

The first to merit the supernal [light of] Understanding (*Binah*) and Wisdom (*Chochmah*) was Yoseph the *Tzadik*, as the verse attests: "There is no one with as much understanding and wisdom as you" (Genesis 41:39). It is from [the prototype of] Yoseph that the mission of Mashiach ben Yoseph derives in every generation. This is especially true during the period of the final "Footsteps of the Messiah" (*Ikveta DiM'shecha*).

9. It is well-known that many highly educated men, both Jews and non-Jews, and including ministers and rulers, who were learned in the wisdom of the natural sciences, used to frequent our master, the Gaon. They came seeking solutions and advice from him for difficult questions [that they had encountered] in their investigations of natural phenomena. The Gaon answered all of their perplexing questions in an astounding and expedient manner. When our master saw that this was becoming a burden and taking up too much time, however, he [changed this practice and] avoided such inquiries. Instead, he referred them to his disciples, especially his disciples from the sages of Shklov. Still, every reply that he did give to those versed in the sciences sanctified God's Name and brought tremendous honor to [the people of] Israel.

10. The following episode left a powerful and indelible impression on all of us [who were present at the time]. It happened in the year 5536 (1776) when I was a young man of eighteen. News spread that a number of anti-Semitic Ukrainian priests were preaching inflammatory sermons in their churches against the Jews. Drawing on false libels that had no basis in fact, they denigrated the ethical conduct and material life of the Jews. One of the priests in the city of Kiev was a Jewish apostate, who spoke out of hatred for his own people. Among other outrages he declared, "The Jews think of themselves as a wise and understanding people. With what are they wise? They swindle and conspire against the gentiles in order to exploit them." The words of the priest stirred up great waves [of hatred] among the masses who heard him.

In the wake of this foreboding news, the heads and leaders of our community in Shklov gathered to confer on what course of action to take in order to forestall any evil. Individuals were chosen from the leaders of the community: my father R. Benyamin [Rivlin], R. Yehoshua Zeitlin,[38] my cousin R. Nota Natkin,[39] and R. Dr. Baruch [Schick].[40] As is known, all of these men were respected in the court of the king.

They traveled to the capital, Petersburg, and they were received there with honor. This was partly due to a number of important innovations in the area of cures for infectious diseases, as well as in the science of geometry, etc., that had previously been developed by members of this group and which the government was already using. They recounted the actions of the aforementioned priests to the king's ministers. In return they were given positive assurance that a strong order would be issued to prevent the provocations of the priests and their lies about the Jews from continuing.

Upon their return from Petersburg they all traveled to Vilna to our master, the Gaon, and I also traveled with them. They spoke at length with our master about the matter. The Gaon said to them, "Happy are you that you have merited to perform a great mitzvah! For not one alone has risen up against us to annihilate us. And the Holy One sends worthy messengers and rescues us from their hands."[41]

Our master continued: "We must know, however, that not only with this do we fulfill our obligation, and not only with this will the matter always be rectified. It is well known that the greatest weapon of the enemies of Israel is the oft-uttered expression: 'Where is the "wisdom of the Jews" with which they are glorified in their scriptures as a "wise and understanding nation"?' They ridicule us in every generation with similar insults."

"True, there have been unique individuals from among the Torah sages of Israel who have applied their great wisdom to understanding the underlying principles of nature, and thus succeeded in producing significant inventions. To our great sorrow, however, the majority of Torah sages have abandoned the study of the laws of nature, which are all contained and hidden within the wisdom of our holy Torah. [They have done so] despite the fact that this is God's desire, as revealed in our Torah when it states: 'She [the Torah] is your wisdom and your understanding in the eyes of the nations' (Deuteronomy 4:6)."

"We can learn with sufficient clarity what the Torah's intention is [with regard to defining the exact obligation that is implied] in this verse from its actual wording. Nevertheless, at first sight, there is an apparent difficulty [in whichever way one tries to make sense of it]. If, on the one hand, the gentiles would be able to understand the wisdom of our Torah from its simple, literal meaning alone, behold, they can already do this themselves [by simply studying the written Bible]. If, on the other hand, the verse is referring to the wisdom of the Torah that is hidden in the depths of its kabbalistic mysteries, behold, they will never fully know or comprehend this."[42]

"The question is, therefore, how, and under what circumstances, will the gentiles recognize the wisdom of Israel as stated in the verse: 'She is your wisdom and your understanding in the eyes of the nations?'"

"There is no other way to explain the intention of the verse except as follows: First the gentiles will recognize Israel's superior wisdom in the natural sciences. Then they will realize that this wisdom is derived from the esoteric secrets of the wisdom of the Torah. Only then will the verse be fulfilled: 'She is your wisdom and your understanding in the eyes of the nations.' And they will proclaim [the concluding words of the verse,] 'This great nation is surely a wise and understanding people,' i.e. great in wisdom (chochmah) and understanding (binah). Only thus will the verse be fulfilled, 'God will grant you ascendancy above all the nations He has made, for praise, fame, and glory.'"

"There is no other avenue to attain this ascendancy except through extensive and well-founded training in both extremities, i.e., from the depths of the earth [science] to the heights of the heavens [Kabbalah]. This is the intention of the verse: '[Yours, O God, is the greatness and the power, the harmony, the eternity, the splendor and] all that binds heaven and earth' (I Chronicles 29:11).[43] We must be well versed in the secrets of our Torah that derive from the Supernal Wisdom. And we must be equally well versed in the secret depths of the laws of nature that derive from the wisdom of the Torah. These [two extremities] are interdependent, as indicated in the statement of the holy *Zohar:* 'In the six hundredth year of the sixth millennium, the gates of wisdom above, together with the wellsprings of wisdom below, will be opened up, and the world will prepare to usher in the seventh millennium.'"

"It is impossible to climb a ladder whose top reaches towards the heavens without first stepping on the rungs of the ladder that are stationed near the earth. [In the same way it is impossible to grasp the full implications of spiritual truth without understanding its relationship to scientific fact.] This is the essential idea that was conveyed to our father Jacob in his vision of the ladder."[44]

"There is no greater way to sanctify God's Name and save the honor of Israel in the eyes of the nations than to achieve this great end. This is true to an even greater extent now that we are approaching the most opportune time for this vision of the *Zohar* [to unfold], i.e. from 5600 (1840) onwards. Why should we abandon this great repository of the wisdom of our holy Torah, or any part of it, to others, when it will only result in profaning the Name of Heaven and increase the humiliation of the Torah?"

Our master said these things and spoke at even greater length with such powerful fervor that it is impossible to describe in words or in writing. He expressed his happiness and his recognition for those of his students who had, with God's help, expended every effort to fulfill this great mission for the sanctification of the Name of Heaven and the [elevation of the] name of Israel.

11. Our master said that every single Torah scholar, especially of those initiated into the esoteric wisdom of the

Kabbalah, is obligated to learn at least one of the Seven Sciences enumerated above and teach it to other God-fearing Torah scholars. According to his aptitude and his natural and intellectual inclination, each one should choose one of these wisdoms.

[As a result] many of the sages of our community in Shklov, as well as those from other cities, came to our master the Gaon in order to request his advice in this matter. The Gaon would determine the area of study that was suitable for each and every individual based on his particular aptitude and inclination. In addition, with his divine inspiration (*ruach hakodesh*), he would reveal where each individual's name and mission was alluded to in certain verses of the Bible. At times he would do this by means of a [special system of] divination (*goral*).[45]

12. On the basis of a number of scriptural verses mentioned above, we explained that the revelation of the underlying principles of the [seven] sciences [during the period of Mashiach ben Yoseph] is dependent on the rebuilding of Jerusalem, the ingathering of the exiles, and the re-flourishing of the Holy Land. This explains the fervent yearning of our master's soul [to initiate] the ingathering of the exiles and [to fulfill] the commandment concerning the resettling of the Holy Land. An oft-repeated expression of his was, "To the extent that one lacks knowledge of the properties of the natural forces, he will lack one hundred-fold in the wisdom of the Torah. And to the extent that the Torah sages attain [knowledge of] the underlying principles of the properties of nature, they will increase [their understanding of] the wisdom of the Torah one hundred-fold."[46] [This confluence is, however, dependent on the Jewish nation's return to the Land of Israel.][47]

13. All of these missions, whose initial emergence from potential to actuality will begin, according to the *Zohar*, from the year 5600 (1840), were vouchsafed from heaven as the destiny of our master the Gaon. He merited being an illumination of Mashiach ben Yoseph, through whose agency the exiles will be gathered.

The study of the natural sciences for the purpose of grasping the [inner] wisdom of the Torah will serve to uphold the honor of the Torah and strengthen the love for Torah and the awe of Heaven among the Jewish people. It will also serve to sanctify God's Name and establish the ascendancy of Israel's wisdom in the eyes of the entire world.

14. Already from his youth, our master, the Gaon developed an interest in, and began to investigate, the forces and properties of natural [phenomena] in order to grasp their [inner] purpose. With his great powers of analysis he found the [corresponding] spiritual principles for all of these [properties] in the secret teachings of the Torah and of the [talmudic] sages, in the mystery of the [22] letters and the [10] vowel points [of the Hebrew language].[48] As is known, our master composed a number of works on Hebrew grammar.[49] [By mastering this wisdom] he also hoped to achieve an even greater understanding of the secrets of the Torah. He used to say that all that had been revealed [in previous generations] and all that was being revealed [now] through natural research was no more than a drop in the ocean compared to what was [still] concealed in the wisdom of the Torah, and which will be revealed in the future together with the teachings of the righteous Mashiach.[50] Nevertheless, this wisdom would be revealed to select individuals "little by little"[51] during the period of *Ikveta DiM'shecha*.

Our master knew how to unlock the wondrous forces and properties of natural phenomena [because he had found the keys to nature] hidden in the Torah. No mystery eluded him; the pathways of the heavens were lit up for him like the pathways of the entire Torah.[52] On a number of occasions our master told us that the most opportune place for attaining the "gates of wisdom above and the wellsprings of wisdom below" is the holy city of Jerusalem, may it be rebuilt and established.

Our master merited to have attained his extensive knowledge of the Seven Sciences in three ways:

   1. Through the Supernal Wisdom — "the gates of wisdom above" — all the details of which are

hidden in the secrets of the Torah.

2. Through investigating the forces of nature — "the wellsprings of wisdom below."

3. Through his high level of divine inspiration (*ruach hakodesh*) [he was able to perceive] the Supernal Light to such an extent that the pathways of the heavens were lit up for him like the pathways of the wisdom of the Torah. [As a result of his high level] he also knew how to operate an esoteric formula [of Divine Names], which he used in order to identify the essence of all spiritual and material properties. Finally, with his great and awesome power he also knew how to create a living *golem*.[53]

Our master's knowledge of the Seven Sciences was [thus] not limited to theory; it was [notably] practical. There are many well-known examples of this. Our master authored a number of ingenious inventions in the fields of engineering, natural pharmacology and medicine, music theory, and others. [Concerning medicine,] he once discussed the sublime concepts contained in the verse, "But for you who fear My name, the sun of righteousness shall rise with healing in its wings..." (Malachi 3:20). [Concerning music,] he spoke at length during a meal in celebration of the New Moon on the verse, "Upon an instrument of ten strings and upon a harp; to the melody of the lyre" (Psalms 92:4). He then proceeded to tune my violin in an exceedingly wondrous way.

15. Yoseph the *Tzadik* was the first to attain [the archetypal levels of] Understanding (*Binah*) and Wisdom (*Chochmah*). This is the mystery of the verse, "My sheaf suddenly arose and stood upright" (Genesis 37:7).[54] [Yoseph understood that] the essence of his dream and vision [concerned these two levels]. He therefore saw it as an indication of his great mission: he was to become the conduit (*yesod*) for [revealing the supernal] *Chochmah* and *Binah*. This is why he later said to Pharaoh, "Now Pharaoh must seek out a man who is understanding (*navon*) and wise (*chacham*)" (Genesis 41:33). He was referring to himself.

[Yoseph] mentioned "understanding" before "wisdom"

because this took place prior to the giving of the Torah [which is the level of the Supernal Wisdom]. It is for this reason that, after the giving of the Torah, "wisdom" precedes "understanding," as in the verse: "She is your wisdom and your understanding in the eyes of the nations... this great nation is certainly a wise and understanding people" (Deuteronomy 4:6).

[According to tradition, Yoseph attained these levels] in the following manner: The night before his release from prison he was taught the Seventy Languages by the Archangel Gabriel and the Seven Sciences by the Archangel Metatron.[55]

When Yoseph had recounted his dreams to his brothers, he made sure to include their interpretations, namely, that they indicated his superior understanding and wisdom. This, of course, was the main reason for their jealousy, as the verse states: "They hated him even more for his dreams and for his words" (Genesis 37:8). "His words" refers to the interpretations that he gave to his dreams.

Our master found an allusion to this: [the phrase] "my sheaf arose" (*kama alumati* = 481) is numerically equivalent to [the phrase] "Seven Sciences" (*Sheva Chochamot* = 481). Our master revealed another amazing allusion [that indicates Yoseph's link with "wisdom and understanding"]. During the Exodus from Egypt, "Moses took Yoseph's bones with him, for Yoseph had bound the children of Israel by an oath, saying, 'God will surely redeem you; you shall therefore bring my bones out of here with you'" (Exodus 13:19)]. The *gematria* of the second letter in each word of the phrase *Vayikach Moshe et atzmot Yoseph imo* (10 + 300 + 400 + 90 + 6 + 40 = 846) is numerically equivalent to the phrase *Sheva Chochamot* = 846.

[Since Yoseph is the archetype of the Messiah of the Beginning] all of this indicates that the revelation of the secret wisdom of the Torah will come about primarily through Mashiach ben Yoseph during the period of the Footsteps of the Messiah (*Ikveta DiM'shecha*). Together with the ingathering of the exiles, this will signal the period of the

Beginning of the Redemption (*At'chalta D'Geulah*).

16. Five things aid in grasping the wisdom of the Torah:

- •Correction of character traits (*Tikkun HaMidot*)[56]

- •Fulfillment of the Torah's commandments and acts of kindness

- •Study of the Kabbalah

- •Study of [Hebrew] grammar

- •Study of the properties of nature through the Seven Sciences

Our master wrote extensively on the laws of Hebrew grammar in his holy works on the Kabbalah. In addition, as mentioned, he composed separate works on the theory of grammar and the wisdom [that is contained in biblical Hebrew]. He admonished us concerning the absolute necessity and importance of this study: firstly, for the sake of precision, and secondly, in order to grasp the wisdom of the Torah and the fundamental principles of creation [that are embedded in it]. It is known [from the Gaon's writings] that all the details of creation are included in the Torah. The totality of the wisdom of the Torah is hidden, in turn, in the mystery of its [22] letters and [10] vowel points.[57] This is the meaning of the *Zohar*'s statement that "God gazed into the Torah and created the world."[58] Similarly, the sages taught that [in engineering the construction of the Sanctuary in the wilderness] "Betzalel knew how to combine the letters with which the heavens and the earth were created."[59] This combination (*tzeruf*) of the Hebrew letters is accomplished primarily through knowledge of the rules of grammar and vowel points.

A supernal and majestic wisdom is hidden within the theory of Hebrew grammar. Even the simplest level of construction of the Holy Tongue manifests a wondrous and divine wisdom. This is evident in its brevity of expression, as well as in its root structure and paradigms. The wisdom of Hebrew grammar is the transcendental soul of our holy language, the language of our Torah. It is the language of the Living God and the language of the ministering angels. It is for this reason that the teachings of the Kabbalah repeatedly refer to the mystery of the [22] letters and the [10] vowels points.

As mentioned in *Sod Kedoshim*, speaking in the Holy Tongue actually gives pleasure to the Creator. We express this idea in our prayers when we say, "[The ministering angels] sanctify their Creator; they cause Him pleasure with their pure speech and sweet melody."[60] [This pleasure] is compounded when the Holy Tongue is spoken in the Land of Israel, as per the Midrash, "One who dwells in the Land of Israel, speaks the Holy Tongue, and eats his everyday food (*chulin*) in a state of ritual purity, is guaranteed an inheritance in the World to Come."

Regarding the gravity of grammatical precision, the Talmud says, "One who recites the Shema must be careful to pronounce each letter [properly]." The reason for this is that the world itself was created with this holy language.

Thus, one who is immersed in the Hebrew language and knows the secrets of its grammatical rules becomes a partner in creation with the Holy One. Beyond the requirement to speak the Holy Tongue, it is equally important to know its cantillation notes and its laws of grammar.

---

[1] The Gaon and R. Hillel Rivlin repeatedly refer to Seven Wisdoms, or seven branches of scientific knowledge. Traditionally, the division between these branches of knowledge is somewhat arbitrary. R. Bachya (1263-1340) lists them as logic, mathematics, geometry, physics, astronomy, music, and metaphysics (commentary to Pirkei Avot 3:18). Nachmanides (1194-1270) states that "the philosophers themselves agree that the great benefit of studying the six branches of wisdom is that this brings one to study the seventh branch, which they call metaphysics, i.e., the study of that which pertains to the Divine" (*Torat HaShem Temimah* p. 155; English edition, p. 76). See below par. #7. When the term *chochmat hateva*, literally "knowledge of natural science", is used throughout the text it is referring to any or all of the many and ever growing branches of human knowledge.

[2] A similar interpretation of this verse is attributed to the founder of Hasidism, R. Yisrael Ba'al Shem Tov: The Ba'al Shem Tov homiletically interpreted the verse: "In His hand are *mech'karei aretz*" (Psalm 95:4). Instead of reading *mech'karei aretz*, "deep secrets of the earth," read as if it is written *me'chakrei aretz*, "investigators of the earth." The Hand of God

represents here the aspect of *Malchut*-Kingdom, the last [and most manifest spiritual] level that is now operative. It is in this Hand of God that all the progress and success of the gentile investigators lies". R. Aaron Marcus, *Keset HaSofer*, Bereshit 2, p. 8. See also above note in The Living Legacy of Kol HaTor, Section: The Kabbalah Teachings of the Gaon of Vilna.

[3] See Part I, Chapter 1, *The Living Legacy of Kol HaTor*, Section: *The Kabbalah Teachings of the Gaon of Vilna* and note for an explanation of the traditional correspondence between the six days of creation (micro-time) and the 6000 years of history (macro-time). The Gaon began receiving his "Vision of Zion" in the year 5500 (1740), that corresponds to "dawn" of the sixth millennial day and is, alternatively, called the "Doorstep of the Beginning of the Redemption" or "Initiation of the Beginning of the period of Mashiach ben Yoseph." One example of how the Gaon anticipated the approach of the year 5600 (1840) is found in *Kol HaTor* (Chapter 1, par. #4):

> Our master began revealing the secrets of the Torah at the age of 20, in the year 5500. This year corresponds to "dawn," the first hour of the sixth millennial day. It was then that the spirit of God, the spirit of Mashiach, began to inspire his soul to begin fulfilling his task as the first Mashiach by slowly revealing the secrets of the Torah, revelations of the most mysterious secrets of secrets [of the period] of *Ikveta D'Meshicha*. No secret escaped him. Then, in the year 5542 (winter 1781), the beginning of the second hour of the sixth day, the storm wind of his soul began to rage, the storm wind of Elijah (2 Kings 2:11), to accelerate the process of the ingathering.

[4] In numerous places throughout *Kol HaTor,* the Gaon is described as the Illumination of Mashiach ben Yoseph. *Kol HaTor* is not alone in this radical, and obviously controversial, assertion. See R. Isaac Kahana's gloss on the Gaon's commentary to *Sefer Yetzirah*: "Mashiach ben Yoseph comes in each generation in order to reveal the secrets of the Torah to those who are worthy. And my heart tells me that it is for this purpose that a holy angel descended from the heavens, the great teacher, the Gaon, our master, Eliyahu, of blessed memory. His task was to reveal [the unity of] the revealed and the concealed Torah to us. Only due to our great sins we were not considered worthy of this privilege and, therefore, the majority of his writings concerning concealed matters, which comprised ten-fold more than his writings on revealed matters, have been lost" (*Toldot Yitzchak*, section #2, pp. 140-141).

As explained in Part II, *Messianic Conspiracy*, the concept of Mashiach ben Yoseph functions on three levels: meta-historical, the actual personality of Mashiach ben Yoseph, and any individual who contributes to the messianic process. In this regard, the character of the biblical Yoseph was just one manifestation of this archetype. See below, note 21.

[5] This refers to the Torah. Although the Torah is usually divided into Five Books, there are two verses in all Torah scrolls that are preceded and followed by two inverted letters (a "*nun*" at the beginning and end), thus further dividing the five books into seven; see Numbers 10:35-36. Concerning these two verses the Talmud (*Shabbat* 116a) says: The Holy One made signs to offset this section of the Torah. Why? Rebbe said, "Because it

is considered a Book on its own." The Talmud states further: In this instance Rebbe is following the opinion of R. Shmuel bar Nachmani who said in the name of R. Yonatan, "There are seven books to the Torah, as the verse states, 'She has hewn her seven pillars (Proverbs 9:1)." See also *Bereshit Rabba* 64:8, *Vayikra Rabba* 11:2, *Mesechet Soferim* 6:14. See below, note 17.

[6] See below, note 17.

[7] See Part II for the explanation why the Last Generation is called *Ikveta D'Meshicha* – the Heels (or Footsteps) of the Messiah.

[8] This is *tikkun hamidot*, literally "correction of character traits," as per the Gaon's statement: "The service of God depends entirely on *tikkun hamidot*;" *Even Shleimah* 1:1.

[9] The phrase *razei Torah*, "secrets of the Torah," is often used to designate the entire body of kabbalistic teachings. The importance of this study with regard to the Final Redemption is emphasized throughout *Kol HaTor* and is the basis of one of the Gaon's most emphatic statements: "This [final] Redemption will come only as a result of Torah study, chiefly the study of the Kabbalah;" *Even Shleimah* 11:3.

[10] Chapter 61 of Isaiah speaks of the time when God will call back the captivity of His people and replace their mourning with gladness (1-3). The desolate cities of Judea will be rebuilt, its fields replanted; the children of Israel will no longer be ashamed; they will rejoice in their portion and inherit back their land (4-7). They will be beloved among the nations and recognized as a people "blessed by God" (9). This prophecy is immediately followed by two verses, which compare Israel's redemption to the joy of a bride and groom (10) and a garden that brings forth its produce (11). According to R. Hillel the analogy of the garden alludes both to the people of Israel, whose existence in exile is likened to the scattering of seeds, and to the Land of Israel (especially Jerusalem), which awaits their return; cf. Radak on Isaiah 61:11; Hirsch on Hosea 2:2 and Psalm 126:5; Targum on Isaiah 61:10-11.

[11] Correlating words and verses with each other via their common *gematria*, or numerical value, is considered a sacred science and has been a universally accepted practice by all Orthodox rabbinic schools (exoteric as well as esoteric) since ancient times. The reason for this is that there are no numerals in the Hebrew language; rather each letter also has a numerical value and can thus be read as an equation as well as a word. On the surface, the use of *gematria* can seem trite and superfluous. The Gaon himself points this out in his commentary on the portion of the *Zohar* (3:127b) known as the *Idra Rabba*. [This can also be found at the beginning of the Gaon's commentary to *Tikkuney Zohar*.] The *Zohar* states: "The reapers of the field are few, and even they work only at the edge of the vineyard," on which the Gaon comments: "This refers to those who do not master the wisdom [of Kabbalah] but rather occupy themselves with *gematria,* which is 'at the edge of the vineyard.' Even in this respect, however, they fail to clearly grasp the real intent." The closing statement seems to imply that if *gematria* were really understood, it too would yield true knowledge. This is supported there by the Gaon's comment on the prophetic verse, "Every valley will be elevated..." (Isaiah 40:4): "The [concept of the valley] refers here to the wisdom of *gematria* which now appears to be lowly but will be shown to be of

great importance in the Messianic Future."

R. Shlomo Zalman Rivlin writes that the scholars of Shklov and their descendants made regular use of *gematria* in their sermons and writings. In addition to the Goral of the Gaon (see below, note 45), these calculations served as a form of divine inspiration to aid them in directing their business affairs, social interaction, and marriages, as well as in strengthening their belief in their individual and collective missions; (*Chazon Tziyon*, p. 16).

[12] The Gaon's father also instructed him to "study the occult sciences, which were known to the members of the Sanhedrin and the *Tanaim* [in order to cross-examine witnesses and suspects], as explained in the talmudic episode of R. Shimon ben Shetach, quoted in the introduction to *Pe'at HaShulchan.*

[13] R. Yom Tov Heller (1579-1654) was a student of the Maharal of Prague. He is known for his classic commentary on the *Mishnah, Tosafot Yom Tov.* In order to complete this work he acquired an extensive knowledge of mathematics, astronomy, and natural science.

[14] The Talmud there states, "There is no surer sign that the Revealed End (*Ketz Meguleh*) is approaching than, 'As for you, O mountains of Israel, you shall shoot forth your branches and bear your fruit for My people Israel when their return is close at hand' (Ezekiel 36:8). The intention is that the "Revealed End" is a preparation for the Final Redemption. The Revealed End (*Ketz Meguleh*) is the term used in the Talmud. As explained by R. Hillel in *Kol HaTor,* it refers to the 250-year period (1740-1990) from "dawn" till "noon" of the sixth millennial day (see note 3 above). This crucial end-period is that of Mashiach ben Yoseph. It is called "revealed", despite the fact that its *modus operandi* is completely through natural means and evolves "little by little" through a slow, gradual process. It is only during this time that the power of human action can be directed to actually stimulate and accelerate the Concealed End (*Ketz HaMechuseh*), which is also known as the era of Mashiach ben David. It is "revealed" to us in the sense that the redemption process is in our hands, and we are able to affect and "artificially induce" the last and final end-time, which will begin anywhere from "high noon" to "sunset" of the sixth day, i.e., during the 250-year period from 1990 to 2240.

[15] Apparently based on Esther 3:14: "The copies of the document were to be promulgated in every province and be published [i.e., revealed] to all nations..."

[16] See the Gaon's commentary on the portion of the *Zohar* known as the Book of Concealment (*Sifra DiTzniuta* Chapter 5, p. 34a), quoted above in Chapter 2, *The Messianic Mission of the Gaon of Vilna,* Section: *The Chamber of the Gaon.*

This same idea is expounded by R. Yitzchak Izik Chaver (see above, Part I, Chapter 2, *The Messianic Mission of the Gaon,* and note).

[17] Based on Talmud, *Chagigah* 12b, where all of creation is seen as resting on 12 pillars (alluding to the 12 "simple letters" of the Hebrew alphabet and the 12 diagonals that connect the 10 *sefirot*) or, according to others, on 7 pillars (alluding to the constellation of the seven lower *sefirot*).

[18] These highly esoteric concepts in Part II Chapter 3, *Leviathan.*

Fundamentally, the concepts of *chashmal* and *nogah* are the nucleus of understanding the Gaon's utterly unique perspective of the messianic role of science. Without this understanding, the Gaon system cannot maintain coherency and will certainly lack the cosmological paradigm shift required to integrate this aspect of the Gaon into all his other teachings.

[19] *Zohar.* See note 16 above.

[20] Bereshit Rabbah 17-5. The term *naval*, here translated "distillations," literally means "faded," "worn," or "withered." In the context of this midrash the analogy is to a leaf that has fallen off of the Tree of Supernal Wisdom and floated down into our physical dimension. (From *Kol HaTor's "Tachtit HaHar,"* modeling perspective using the new science of fractal geometry, "*novlot,*" here are simply the essences of the primeval Torah scaling itself "down" as it iterates upon itself and reveals newer and "lower" dimensions of itself.) See Appendix *Tachtit HaHar.* See further volume II, Sacred Serpent, where the three letters that spell [sacred] *nachash*/serpent are the three beginning letters of the rabbinic phrase, *novlot chachma shelema'ala* - "distilled supernal wisdom". (R. Ya'akov Zvi Yolles, *Kehillat Ya'akov,* part II, 11a, Lemberg, 1870).

[21] See above, note 4, where it is explained that Yoseph was the archetype of Mashiach ben Yoseph.

[22] In the same manner the "wellsprings of the great deep" are activated in response to the opening of the "floodgates of the heavens."

[23] This internal/external relationship is also mentioned by two other authoritative Kabbalists from the school of the Gaon. In his *Pitchey Sh'arim,* Part 2, *Netiv Partzuf, Zer Anpin,* par. #30, p. 54 (27b), R. Yitzchak Izik Chaver writes:

> Even when the totality of creation is not in its perfected state, such as when Israel is exiled among the nations and God's light is undetectable, still, we can see that all things are arranged and conducted with wondrous wisdom. All of this, however, is called external wisdom. It involves the natural sciences, the study of astronomy, and all that the wise men of the nations have spoken concerning the nature of all created things. Again, this is nothing but the external wisdom of the Creator, which is the mystery of the membranes of the [right, left, and middle] brains, as well as the brain matter itself relative to the vital forces — *Nefesh, Ruach,* and *Neshamah* — that reside within the physical structure of the brain. As long as the world and all of its creations are not in their perfected state, only the external aspects of God's Wisdom (*Chochmah*), Understanding (*Binah*) and Knowledge (*Da'at*) are recognizable.

In his *Leshem Sh'vo V'Achlamah, Sefer De'ah* 2:4:22:4, p. 181 (91a, bottom), R. Shlomo Eliyashiv comments on the talmudic account of the four men who entered the *Pardes* (Paradise) of kabbalistic mysteries (Talmud, *Chagigah* 14b):

> As these men were preparing themselves to enter into the *Pardes,* their intention was to contemplate the deepest inner depths of the

created universes and to ascend from every external level to the inner level above it... The first level that one must master in order to enter the *Pardes* consists of knowledge of the physical world, "the heavens and earth" of this world. This involves the analytical wisdom that distinguishes all true science. All of this, however, is only the external aspect of lower dimensionality, which is the domain of the sciences. The inner aspect of this is the vital force — *Nefesh* — which sustains nature and activates it continually.

One of the Gaon's foremost disciples, R. Menachem Mendel of Shklov also writes (*Mayim Adirim, Biurim V'Likutim*, p. 60), "... The upper waters represent the mystery of Supernal Wisdom above, while the lower waters represent the mystery of secular wisdom below. These are united in man's mind..." See below in note 24.

[24] The intention here is that reality consists of two "sides," a spiritual "top side" and a physical "bottom side," which exist in an inverse relationship to each other. The "bottom side" or "underside" of the mountain, to which the Torah refers, is the world of nature, i.e. the details of external reality. Accordingly, the "topside" or "face" of the same mountain is the Torah proper, i.e. the details of inner reality. Although the usual translation of *tachtit hahar* is "at the foot of the mountain" (Rashi), the Gaon understands these words according to their literal and more common meaning (as does the Talmud, *Shabbat* 88a, albeit for a different exposition).

Similarly, R. Hillel writes (*Kol HaTor*, end of Chapter 2, par. #5, Kasher, p. 506): "With his divine inspiration, our master established [the necessity] of learning the Seven Sciences from below. It is known that they are like the patterns and models on the "bottom side of the mountain" that can be used to explain the wisdom of the Torah and accelerate the redemption." In both editions of *Kol HaTor* the word that we have translated here as "patterns" is written in the original as *rekachot*, which means mixture or spices. Indeed, R. Menachem Mendle of Shklov wrote regarding the Gaon's mastery and utilization of the sciences that, "They served him as spices (*rekachot*) and herbs (*tabachot*) for the wisdom of our holy Torah" (Introduction to the Gaon's commentary to Avot).

The second term used here in *Kol HaTor*, however, is *dugma'it* which means model or example. This suggests that *rekachot*/spices may be a typographical error for *rekamot* meaning designs or patterns. Additionally, the word for model, spelled here as *dugma'it* and meaning modeling as an adjective may also be a simple typo (i.e., the letter "*yud*" should be a "*vav*") for *dugmaot* meaning models in the plural, although the same meaning is imparted. In any event, even if we maintain the spelling of *rekachot* meaning mixtures, this also can refer to "mixtures" and "compounds, i.e. *formulas and patterns* on the bottom side of the mountain." Regardless of the spelling, for the author of *Kol HaTor*, however, the messianic concept of *Tachtit HaHar* is much more than a simple understanding of "spices and herbs". This is clearly the intention with the juxtaposition here in *Sha'ar Be'er Sheva* of "toy models and similar devices, as well as simple diagrams."

[25] See end of previous note. The belief that scientific models and metaphors can play a crucial role in helping to better understand Judaism's own

esoteric traditions and ushering in the Messianic Era is also discussed by Chabad Hasidut (which is generally considered to be mystically antithetical to the Gaon's school of thought); See further discussion in Part I, Chapter 1, *The Living Legacy of the Gaon of Vilna*, Sections, *The Kabbalah Teachings of the Gaon of Vilna* and *Messianic Synthesis* with corresponding notes.

[26] See above note 1.

[27] The Gaon himself composed works on mathematics (*Ayil Meshullash*, 1833) and on geography (*Tzurat HaAretz*, 1822). He wrote another work containing treatises on trigonometry, geometry, and algebra (published as *Eliah Wilna und Sein Elementargeome Trisches Compendium*, 1903).

[28] Lit. *Chochmat haRefuah veHaTzemicha*. *Tzmichah* apparently refers to pharmacology. Similarly, "healing and plants" (*haRefuot veHaTzmachim*) are coupled together in an abridged version of the logic of Maimonides, attributed to the Gaon (*Kitzur klalim leChakhmat pilosophia haNogea gam ken leChakhmath haDikduk meHaGaon haMefoar deKehilat Vilna*) , and found in the book, *HaTzadik R. Yoseph Zundel meSalant veRabotav*, (ed. Eliezer Rivlin) Jerusalem, 1927, pp.102-107.

[29] The Gaon also composed a number of treatises on Hebrew grammar. One such published work is *Dikduk Eliyahu* (Vilna, 1833; Jerusalem, 2001). Also, *Biur milim haNirdafot*, an anthology of his commentaries on synonyms, in: *Toledot haGra*, (ed. Y.L. Maimon), Jerusalem, 1970, pp. 233-241.

[30] The second term in this category, holiness/*kedushah* (*haNeginah veHaKedushah)*, could also refer to the holiness of the cantellation and songs of the Levitical service. In the introduction to his *Pe'at HaShulchan*, R. Yisrael of Shklov writes: "Without the knowledge of music, it is impossible to understand the cantellation notes of the Torah, the songs of the Levites, or the secrets of the *Tikkunei Zohar*."

[31] Similarly, "*nagarut veHaBinyan ma'ase asiyah*" (*HaTzadik R. Yoseph Zundel meSalant veRabotav, op. cit.*, p. 107)

[32] The term "parapsychology" was chosen as an idiomatic translation of *bain geshem v'ruach*, which literally means "the interface between the physical and the spiritual" or "the interface between physicality and consciousness." For the same reason the term *kochot haNefesh*, literally, "soul powers," has been translated into modern scientific terms as "brain sciences." However, see the *Eight Chapters* of Maimonides, ch. 1, where he refers to the *kochot haNefesh* as the faculties of the soul in the ethical sense.

[33] The Gaon's mastery in all fields of wisdom is illustrated in an account quoted above in Chapter 2, *The Messianic Mission of the Gaon of Vilna*, Section: *"There Is No One Like Him"* with corresponding notes.

[34] In his *Pe'at HaShulchan*, R. Yisrael of Shklov quotes a similar statement: "The Gaon said that he had studied the length and breadth of all the great philosophical writings and had found only two ideas worthy of serious consideration. All the rest, he said, is of little consequence." As is the case with almost all kabbalists, the Gaon's strong opposition to philosophy is well known. See also his glosses on *Shulchan Aruch Yoreh Deah* 179:6:13 and 246:4:18 where he strongly critiques Maimonides and R. Moses Isserles (the

Rema) for being influenced by such ideas.

[35] King Solomon's wisdom is described in 1 Kings 5:9-13: "God gave Solomon wisdom and tremendous understanding; He expanded [Solomon's] heart to comprehend [the details of wisdom that are as endless] as the grains of sand on the shore. Solomon's wisdom then exceeded the wisdom of the East (Babylon and Chaldea), and the wisdom of Egypt. He was wiser than any man... He spoke [of the healing qualities] of trees, from the cedar of Lebanon to the hyssop that grows out of the wall; he spoke of animals, birds, insects and fish...."

See also the Nachmanides' introduction to his commentary on the Torah (pp. 12-13 in Chavel edition).

In his *Leshem Sh'vo V'Achlamah, Sefer De'ah,* 2:4:21:2, p. 85a (169), R. Shlomo Eliyashiv comments further on Solomon's wisdom: "The details and fine minutiae of the nature, potential and character of all creatures were revealed to Shlomo. He knew the [spiritual] root of each and every one... He knew the root-channel of everything that exists in the physical world, all the way up to the beginning of *Beriyah* (World of Creation) and above that to the aspect of *Malchut* of *Atzilut* (World of Emanation) that is clothed within *Beriyah...* ."

[36] The telescope was first used to chart the planets and stars more than four centuries ago. More recently, a new mode of observation was developed which, together with space stations, has completely altered our perception of time and space: Radio Astronomy has revealed awesome inhabitants at the farthest reaches of the universe such as pulsars — rapidly spinning crushed stars left behind after a supernova explosion — and radio galaxies — blasting out so much energy that the known laws of physics are inadequate to explain. See Part II, *Messianic Conspiracy,* for an in depth explanation of this paragraph.

[37] *Pirkei Heichalot* 10, (*Otzar Midrashim*), *Midrash Konen,* end, *Zohar* II, p. 4b: "There is one *Chayah* whose name is Israel." For a literal suggestion as to the meaning of this cryptic statement, see *The Great Era,* Rabbi M. Kasher. Within the "Additional Material", at the end of his book, p.559, he does include this one paragraph from *Sha'ar Beer Sheva,* (although deleting the whole section from the book itself, as explained above). Kasher writes, "These words [*Kol HaTor,* quoting the midrash] are cryptic. Perhaps this is an allusion here to the advancement of the "wisdom from below," and it is [prophesying] the invention of the airplane that flies in the 'heights of the firmament'. The inscription 'Israel' is the insignia of the Israeli Air Force who conquered Jerusalem [in the Six Day War] and were victorious in war..." In Volume II, Chapter 4, *Metatron,* there is a lengthy exposition of the kabbalistic secrets presented in this section of *Sha'ar Be'er Sheva.*

[38] See Part I, Chapter 1, *The Living Legacy of the Gaon of Vilna,* Section: *The History of Kol HaTor and the Rivlin Family.*

[39] He died 1804. He was a champion of the improvement of the status of Russian Jewry. He presented the Russian government with a project for the establishment of large-scale agricultural colonies for the Jews, as well as plans for industrial plants. In spite of the fact that Shklov was a center of

opposition to the Hasidic movement (with R. Benyamin Rivlin at its head), R. Natkin was responsible for freeing the first Lubavitcher Rebbe when he was imprisoned in Petersburg by the Russian government on false charges supplied by other opponents. R. Natkin even owed his success in this *mitzvah* to R. Benyamin Rivlin himself. It was due to the pressure he applied on the officials in charge that the Rebbe was finally freed.

[40] Born circa 1740, died some time after 1812. He was a *dayan* (rabbinical court judge) and physician. He wrote on medicine, hygiene, astronomy, trigonometry, geography, the arts and sciences. He is known for having translated Euclid into Hebrew, at the Gaon's request. For more about R. Dr. Schick, see below, Part II, Chapter 3, *Leviathan*.

[41] This is a paraphrase of the Passover Haggadah: "Not one alone has risen up against us, but in every generation they rise up against us to annihilate us. And the Blessed Holy One rescues us from their hand."

[42] Many aspects of Jewish mysticism are not relevant to gentiles, nor are they obligated to know the entire system of Torah observance upon which many of the particulars of the Kabbalah theosophically depend.

[43] The 69th of the 156 Aspects of Mashiach ben Yoseph is: "for all that is in heaven and earth." R. Hillel provides two numerical equivalences that connect this verse to Mashiach ben Yoseph. First, *Ki Kol* ("for all") equals 80, as does the word *yesod*. Second, *Kol B'Shamayim V'Aretz* ("all that is in heaven and earth") equals 741 as does the phrase Mashiach ben Ephraim. According to the *Bahir* and *Zohar* the phrase "all that is in heaven and earth" corresponds to the *Sefirah* of *Yesod* (Channel), which stands between the eight upper *Sefirot* from *Keter* to *Hod* (Heaven) and the tenth *Sefirah Malchut* (Earth). *Yesod* thus acts as a channel through which Divine illumination (*shefa*) flows from God's Will (*Keter*) into the lower dimensionality of the physical world (*Malchut*). It is in this sense that it "binds" heaven and earth; *Bahir* 22, 78; *Zohar* 1:31a, 2:116a, 3:257a. See *Sha'arey Orah* 2 (p. 29a); *Sha'ar HaKavanot, Inyan Sefirat HaOmer, Drush* #10. For a diagram of the *Sefirotic* template ("Tree of Life"), see the Appendix.

[44] This is based on Genesis 28:12: "[Jacob] had a vision in a dream. A ladder was standing on the earth, and its top reached toward heaven." Jacob is traditionally associated with the *Sefirah* of *Tiferet* which is in the center column of the *sefirotic* Tree of Life (see diagram above). The ladder that Jacob sees "standing on the earth and reaching toward heaven" is this center column that "binds" all of the upper *Sefirot* with the ones below it. This is in accord with what we said in the previous note, namely, that the *Sefirah* of *Yesod*, associated with Yoseph, "binds" all of the *Sefirot* from *Keter* to *Malchut*. This is because every upper triad of *Sefirot* is the "root" of the ones below it. Thus, *Keter* (via *Chochmah* and *Binah*) is the root of *Da'at*; *Da'at* (via *Chesed* and *Gevurah*) is the root of *Tiferet*; *Tiferet* (via *Netzach* and *Hod*) is the root of *yesod*. This also connects to what we said above (note 17) that the root of *yesod* extends all the way back to the *Kav Or Ain Sof* that "extends from one end of the universes to the other." In a sense, all of these *Sefirot* are points or rungs along the ladder that reaches from heaven toward earth and back.

[45] Along with the systematic usage of *gematria* the scholars of Shklov also

employed the *Goral* of the Gaon. This is a well-known methodology revealed by the Gaon for using the Scripture as a source of divination.

The Gaon takes this line of thinking to its logical conclusion. In this case, however, the text of the Written Torah [actually the entire Bible or *TaNaKh*, which is an acrostic for Torah (the Five Books), *Nevi'im* (Prophets) and *Ketuvim* (Writings)] becomes the means of divination. Based on the sacred number seven as alluded to in the verse, "Upon one stone are seven facets" (Zechariah 3:9), the practitioner holds a special edition of the Tanach that is printed with two columns on each page and silently meditates on the question he wishes to ask. He then (1) opens "randomly" to any page; (2) turns seven additional pages; (3) counts seven columns; (4) counts seven open paragraphs; (5) counts seven lines down; (6) seven sentences; (7) seven words. The *Goral* was used during the Israeli War of Independence to identify the graves of ten men who were buried. See *Chazon Tziyon*, p. 16; Simcha Raz, *A Tzadik in our Time*, pp. 162-170 (1977, Feldheim, Jerusalem). See above Part I, Chapter 2, *The Messianic Mission of the Gaon of Vilna*, Section: *Gematria, Transmigration, and Divination*.

[46] As pointed out in the Introduction (See above Part I, Chapter 3, *The Messianic Mission of the Gaon of Vilna*, Section: *Master of the Seven Sciences* and notes), the first half of this statement was recorded by R. Dr. Baruch Schick of Shklov in the introduction to his Hebrew translation of Euclid (which, he writes, was undertaken, along with other scientific works, at the encouragement of the Gaon). The question of whether the Gaon could have made such a statement (with the implication of a necessary confluence between Torah and Science) has been challenged (see e.g., Betzalel Landau, *HaGaon HeChasid MeVilna*, p. 117). We may point out, however, that Schick's Euclid was published eighteen years before the Gaon passed away and thus, was certainly known to him. In addition, this same quote appears in the introduction to *Pe'at HaShulchan* by another of the Gaon's disciples, R. Yisrael of Shklov. The quotation here from R. Hillel Rivlin is thus a third independent source. It should be noted, however, that the second part of the Gaon's statement quoted in *Kol HaTor* is not found in the other sources.

[47] Although this statement does not appear in the original text, the implication, however, is evident. Par. #12 can be divided into three parts: (1) the revelation of the underlying principles of "secular" wisdom, i.e. the opening of the "wellsprings of wisdom below," depends on the return of the Jewish nation to the Land of Israel; (2) these two factors together will make it possible to understand the wisdom of the Torah one hundred-fold, i.e. the opening of the "gates of wisdom above." The unstated conclusion is: (3) the revelation of the confluence between Torah and Science depends again on the return of the Jewish nation to the Land of Israel. This reading is further supported by R. Hillel's statement (in par. #14, below): "On a number of occasions our master told us that the most opportune place for attaining the "gates of wisdom above and the wellsprings of wisdom below" is the holy city of Jerusalem, may it be rebuilt and established."

[48] *Sefer Yetzirah* (1:1) speaks of 32 paths of wisdom. These 32 paths are sub-divided into the 10 *Sefirot* and the 22 letters of the Hebrew alphabet (1:2). The 10 *Sefirot*, in turn, are designated by the 10 vowel points (*Patach, Kamatz, Cholom, Shuruk*, etc.) that enable us to vocalize the letters; see

commentary of Gaon ad. loc. This means that the vowel points (and, by extension, the *Sefirot*) are the "soul" of the letters. When we combine the letters and make words (in the language of the *Sefer Yetzirah,* this is called combining "stones" to make "houses") we are able to draw down the higher energy of the *Sefirot* into our speech. As R. Hillel states below (par. #16), "the combination (*tzeruf*) of the Hebrew letters is accomplished primarily through knowledge of the rules of grammar and vowel points." He cites the tradition that "Betzalel knew how to combine the letters with which the heavens and the earth were created." This explains the inner connection between the Gaon's insistence on knowing the science of Hebrew grammar and his ability to create a *golem.*

[49] See above, note 29.

[50] Compare with the midrash quoted above (note 20) that, "the distillation of the Supernal Wisdom is the present Torah." This idea is preserved even more forcefully in another midrash (*Ecclesiastes Rabba* 2:1): "All the Torah that a person learns in this world is vanity (*hevel*) compared to the Torah of the next world" (see *Leshem Sh'vo V'Achlamah, Hakdamot V'Sh'arim* 1:8, p. 7a (13).

[51] See above, note 14, for explanation of "little by little."

[52] This is a paraphrase of the statement in Talmud, *Berachot* 58b about the sage and physician Shmuel that "he knew the pathways of the stars like he knew the streets of Nahardeah."

[53] See the account of R. Chaim of Volozhin, the Gaon's most famous disciple, from his introduction to the Gaon's commentary on *Sifra DeTzeniuta* (p. iv), quoted above in Chapter 2, *The Messianic Mission of the Gaon of Vilna*, Section: *Master of the Seven Sciences* and in full in the Appendix.

The Gaon's reported supra-natural mastery over material forces is related in another first-hand account by R. Menachem Mendel of Shklov (in his introduction to the Gaon's commentary on *Pirkei Avot* and *Mesechtot Ketanot*), quoted above in Part I, Chapter 2, *The Messianic Mission of the Gaon of Vilna*, Section: *The Censored Mystic.* Also see *Leshem Sh'vo V'Achlamah, Sefer HaK'lallim*, p. 42a.

[54] In the 133rd of the 156 Aspects of Mashiach ben Yoseph, R. Hillel writes: "Whenever the term "arising" is used in the Torah it alludes to Mashiach ben Yoseph, as the verse states, 'My sheaf suddenly arose and stood upright'" (Kasher, p. 497; see also *Chazon Tziyon*, p. 16). As we have seen, the character of Yoseph parallels the *Sefirah* of *Yesod* (Channel). *Yesod*, in turn, parallels the male reproductive organ, which draws down illumination (*shefa*) or intelligence (*mochin*) from the upper *Sefirot* (*Chochmah* and *Binah*) in order to unite with *Malchut*. This union can only be affected, however, when *yesod* is in an "active mode" or, in the words of this verse, when "my (Yoseph's) sheaf suddenly arose and stood upright." It is only then that *yesod* can become, as R. Hillel Rivlin states, "a conduit for revealing *Chochmah* and *Binah*." In terms of the messianic process, this means that a number of conditions have to be met in order for Mashiach ben Yoseph to reveal the Supernal Wisdom through the higher synthesis of Kabbalah and science. This involves the spiritual concept of circumcision. When the sages

of Israel succeed in uniting the "topside" and "bottom side" of Supernal Wisdom, Kabbalah and Science, into one transcendent unity, this is equivalent to "circumcising" the Supernal *Yesod*. In this case the Supernal Wisdom flows down through *yesod* in such a way that God's presence is revealed in the world. When, however, these two inverse surfaces of a single side (see the Mobius strip model in the Appendix) of the Supernal Wisdom are separated from each other, this is equivalent to covering the Supernal *Yesod* with an *o'rlah*/foreskin. In this latter case Wisdom still flows down into the world, but its effect is to diminish the awareness of God and forestall the Redemption. This is discussed at length in Volume II, Chapters 3 and 4.

[55] See *Sha'ar HaGilgulim* p. 33a where the Ari explains that before Yoseph was released from prison he merited to asend to greatness in the aspect of Enoch who is Metatron. Also, "Yoseph learned the seventy languages that night through the root-soul of Metatron who is in charge of the seventy languages", *Sefer HaGilgulim* p. 69a. "Yoseph and Metatron are from the *Zihara Ii'laah* – the Supernal Radiance of the soul of Adam", *Sha'ar HaGilgulim* p. 45a. "That night Gabriel came and taught him the seventy languages", *Sha'ar HaGilgulim* p. 33b. The identity and function of Metatron is explained in more detail in Volume II, Chapter 4, *Metatron.*

[56] See above, note 8.

[57] See above, note 48.

[58] 2:161a; *Bereshit Rabba* 1:1.

[59] Talmud, *Berachot* 55a; 2:152a, 2:234b. Betzalel was chosen by God to oversee the construction of the Mishkan-Tabernacle (Exodus 31:1-11, 35:30 - 39:43). According to tradition (*Pirkei Rabbi Eliezer* 3; *Tanchuma Pekudei* 2; *Zohar* 2:162b) the Mishkan was a microcosm of the entire creation. It is for this reason that Betzalel had to know the secret of "the letters and vowels of the Hebrew language," i.e., the genetic code with which "the heavens and the earth were created." We can now better understand what the Gaon meant when he said, "Once, I actually began to create a *golem*" and "I would show him [Aristotle] the orbits of the planets around the sun together with the stars shining right here on this table just as they light up the firmament of the heavens [i.e., create a microcosm of the universe]." See above Part I, Chapter 2, *The Messianic Mission of the Gaon of Vilna*, Section, *The Censored Mystic.*

[60] *Shacharit*/Morning prayer. This phrase is usually translated: "They sanctify their Creator with a serene spirit (*b'nachat ruach*), with pure speech and sweet melody." In the context of this prayer, however, the expression *b'nachat ruach* can be read two ways. It can refer to the angels themselves, who "with a serene spirit" sanctify God. It can also refer to "serenity of spirit" or "pleasure" that God has when the angels recognize and praise His sanctity and transcendence. While the first reading does not define exactly what it means to "sanctify God," the second reading does. In this sense it is actually closer to the kabbalistic meaning of prayer and follows from R. Hillel's introductory statement: "Speaking in the Holy Tongue actually gives pleasure to the Creator."

A "Missing Page" from *Kol HaTor*

As explained above, following the publication of the two editions of *Kol HaTor* in 1968 a "missing page" from the original 1947 edition was discovered. It has now been added to the more recent and most complete edition of *Kol HaTor* (Yoseph Rivlin, 1994).[1] It is clearly the end of the first section of Chapter 5. This is indicated by R. Shlomo Zalman Rivlin's extract preceding each chapter, where, regarding the fifth chapter, contains almost word for word the first paragraph of this previously "missing page". Furthermore, R. S.Z. Rivlin refers to the content of this section as, "further in chapter 5" in two of his earlier notes.[2]

In addition to the full translation of *Sha'ar Be'er Sheva, The Secret Doctrine of the Gaon of Vilna* contains numerous translated sections from throughout *Kol HaTor* necessary to understand the Gaon's messianic confluence between Torah, Kabbalah and the sciences. Additionally, this "missing page" has also been translated and added here (but without extensive commentary) to close *Sha'ar Be'er Sheva* for four reasons:

1. It contains another reference to the providential role of science in the Messianic Era. It is an additional source besides *Sha'ar Be'er Sheva* of the messianic role of science and technology. (There are still other references to this prophecy in other parts of *Kol HaTor*, as well.)

2. Throughout *Kol HaTor* the crucial eras beginning in 1740 and 1840 are explicit. The turning point ("high noon") of the daylight of the sixth millennium, although clearly implied as being the actual numerical date of the year — 5750/1990, is not explicit except for here in this last page of Chapter 5, Part I. This passage is the only explicit mention in *Kol HaTor* of the pivotal era, beginning in 1990, when the overlapping of the eras of the Twin Messiahs converge, explained below in Part II, Chapter 1.

3. This page, along with the twelve pages of *Sha'ar Be'er Sheva* and six pages of a section entitled "The Sin of the

Spies," is omitted in the Bar Lev English Translation of
Kol HaTor.

4. It must be remembered that *Sha'ar Be'er Sheva* is just
    one section from *Kol HaTor* and the Gaon of Vilna's Secret
    Doctrine of Redemption. As explained throughout this
    work, the messianic relationship between Judaism and
    science is only one cog in the complex machinery of his
    complete blueprint for global redemption. His highly
    interdependent system also includes the historic mission
    and destiny of the Jewish people, return to the Land of
    Israel, strict *halachic* observance of Torah, intensive study
    of Talmud, Jewish law and Kabbalah, that all together
    help effect the universal "arousal from below" in order to
    trigger the "arousal from above." It is, thus, fitting to
    recast the section of the *Gate of the Well of Seven Sciences*
    from *Kol HaTor* back into its larger context by closing
    with this section.

The reader should note, however, that although the
style of language used here is very terse and cryptic, it is
representative of much of the body of *Kol HaTor*. This should
re-emphasize a point from the introduction that, in truth, *Kol
HaTor* was intended for only an elite circle of Torah scholars,
particularly those initiated into the esoteric cosmology of the
Gaon of Vilna (which subsumes knowledge of Talmud, Zohar
and   Lurianic   Kabbalah).

Furthermore, aside from the tension involving science
and Torah, the extremely controversial nature of the last
paragraph of this "missing page" reveals the other great
tension intrinsic to the Gaon's paradoxical Doctrine of
Redemption. This is the question, in the various Orthodox
Jewish communities, of the positive or negative cosmological
role of the secular State of Israel that was created in 1948.
According to this section from *Kol HaTor*, the very date of
Israel's national autonomy — the twentieth day of the
Counting of the Omer, corresponding to the 5th of Iyar — was,
in fact, predicted by the author of *Kol HaTor,* following his
living tradition from the Gaon of Vilna. According to Rabbi
Hillel's account, the Gaon's messianic seeds of redemption,
carried from Vilna to Shklov and then from Zefat to

Jerusalem, were intentionally planted in the ground on that day only to sprout one hundred thirty-six years later.

The difference of opinion regarding the paradoxical nature of this fruit, and how it will continue to evolve, is another reason there is such a wide range of passionate opinions concerning the authenticity of *Kol HaTor* among members of the different non-Zionist, secular Zionist, anti-Zionist, religious Zionist, and "mystical" Zionist groups. But then again, this is exactly what we should expect in the mystery of the hiddenness of Mashiach ben Yoseph — "And Yoseph recognized his brothers, but they did not recognize him."

---

[1] The text used for translation here was first published in 1986 as "A New Chapter from *Kol HaTor*" in *Nitzaney Aretz*, a journal of Yeshivat Mercaz HaRav, which received the document from the Organization for the Dissemination of *Kol HaTor* (who published the 1968 B'nai B'rak edition). The text published in the more recent Yoseph Rivlin edition has some variations in the text.

[2] Chapter 1, notes #50 and #53.

A "Missing Page" of *Kol HaTor*

Kol HaTor
Chapter 5, End of Section I

"To everything there is a season; there is a time for everything [under the heaven]" (Ecclesiastes 3:1). [In this verse] are recondite allusions to the beginning process that will lead to the redemption. [Since this process involves a concealment of the Divine, it will be necessary for the Messiah of the Beginning, Mashiach ben Yoseph, to know] the mystery of "revealing that which is concealed." [He must also know] the mystery of the end times, as per the verses, *"The blossoms have appeared, the time of singing has come, the voice of the turtledove is heard in our land"* (Song of Songs 2:12), and *"Arise, have compassion on Zion, for the time to favor her has arrived; the set time has come"* (Psalms 102:14).

There are seven of these end times [that proceed the period of *Mashiach ben David*]. These correspond to the seven "hours" that begin from the year 5500 (1740), the beginning of the first "hour" of daylight of the sixth millennium, the era of the end of days and the final generation. They continue until the end [of the sixth "hour" of daylight, "noon" of the sixth millennium, 5750 - 1990], the period of the Wondrous End *(Ketz HaP'laot).*

"The time of singing has come." The "time of singing" comes in seven stages [which constitute the seven end times] of the Beginning. Each stage in turn is divisible into seven levels or segments, and each segment has seven aspects. The first stage commenced in the year 5500 (1740), the beginning of the first "hour" of daylight of the 6th millennium. [As the Gaon taught, the events of this first hour are alluded to in the sixth chapter of the book of Deuteronomy (*Ki Tetze*), which corresponds to the 6th-century of the sixth millennium (5500-5600, 1740-1840).]

It is there, at the end of *Ki Tetze* that the great mission of our master, the Gaon is alluded to. First, the Gaon found a hint to his own name in the verse, "You shall retain a perfect and just weight..." (Deuteronomy 25:15). Immediately following this, it is written, "You shall blot out the remembrance of Amalek from under the heavens" (25:19), and then, "When you come into the land that God has given you as an inheritance, you shall occupy and settle it..." (26:1).

The next stage will signal the beginning of the 7th-century of the sixth millennium, and will commence in the year 5600 (1840). From this point on, the messianic revelation will actually begin. This involves the mystery of [a progressive revelation of] the Higher Wisdom, together with [a parallel elevation of] the Lower Wisdom. The [acceleration of this messianic revelation] is dependent on our stimulation from below. This, in turn, is intimately related with the natural evolution of scientific knowledge.

All of this is in accord with the [prophecy of the] holy *Zohar (VaYeira* 117a): "In the six hundredth year of the sixth millennium the gates of wisdom above, together with the wellsprings of wisdom below, will be opened..." From this year, that is 5600 (1840 C.E.) and onwards, [the period of] "the call of the turtledove" will begin. It is then that the light of our master, the Gaon will begin to "shine ever more brightly until the height of noonday" (Proverbs 4:18).

This matter is also alluded to in a secret letter of our master.[1] At his behest, this letter was sealed and not to be opened until one hundred years will have passed, i.e., until "the time to favor her has arrived."

We[2], the disciples of our master, the Gaon, arrived in the land of Israel in the year 5569 (1809), [in accord with the verse], "Ephraim, My firstborn" (Jeremiah 31:8). With this, the first stimulation of the "morning light," referred to by the sages, has been implemented. It is this beginning stimulation that will bring the "time to favor her" closer. This is the mission of the first Messiah, the Messiah of the Beginning, Mashiach ben Yoseph. He will do this in the same way that Ezra and Nehemiah [brought the Jews home] during the reign of Cyrus during the days of the [rebuilding] of the Second Temple. Our master, the Gaon, made numerous references to this [task of Mashiach ben Yoseph/ in his sacred kabbalistic writings, for our master's mission was in the illumination of Mashiach ben Yoseph, in the aspect of "Good" [the active mode of the *Sefirah of Yesod*].

When we established our residence in the holy city of Jerusalem, may she be rebuilt and restored, in the year 5572 (1812) [in the secret of] "His dwelling place [is in Zion]" (Psalms 76:3), it was the commencement of the third "hour"[3] of the *At'chalta* (Beginning) of a "time of singing," in the secret of *Kol HaTor* ("the call of the turtledove" (Song of Songs 2:12).

And it was on one of the days in the year 5572 (1812) that we laid the foundation stone for the establishment of the Beit Midrash Eliyahu (the House of Study of Elijah)[4] in honor of the name of our Master the Gaon. Together with this was a crucial preparation for the rebuilding of Jerusalem. It appeared to us — the disciples of our master, the Gaon — with an unmistakable clarity, that in that very hour the first window was opened up in the "iron partition" in order for the unification of the merit of the Covenant of the Fathers, (the unification of the *Yesod* of *Tiferet* via *Malchut*)[5] which had been interrupted from the time of the destruction of the Holy Temple. That day was the twentieth day of the counting of the Omer, which is the *Yesod* of *Tiferet,* as is known to those initiated into the hidden wisdom.[6]

---

[1] See above, Chapter 2, The Extraordinary Letter

[2] According to the Rivlin edition, in the manuscript a note was inserted here that read, "An exposition by R. Moshe Magid (the Preacher), son of R. Hillel the author of *Kol HaTor*." He notes, however, that a line in the original was made through these words, indicating that it was incorrectly inserted and was to be removed.

[3] The period from 5542-5584 (1782-1824) constituted the second daylight "hour" of the sixth millennium. As explained above, by dividing this period into seven segments, we find that the year 5572 (1812) commences the second to the last stage.

[4] This would be next to the Hurva synagogue in the Jewish Quarter. This area later became the *Eitz Hayim* compound (see reference in the Approbation).

---

[5] This parenthetical explanation appears in the original text.

[6] This event took place in the year 5572 (1812) on the 5th of Iyar after the followers of the Gaon, by his command, had traveled for six months by caravan, by boat, and by foot, in order to initiate the "reawakening from below" in the heart of Jerusalem. It was on that specific day that they laid the foundation stone for the establishment of the Beit Midrash Eliyahu, in honor of their master the Gaon, and planted the seeds of redemption that would finally bear fruit one hundred thirty-six years later on the very same day.

The twentieth day of the Omer is always on the 5th of Iyar. One hundred thirty-six years later, on the 5th of Iyar in the year 1948, the State of Israel received her political independence. It is a tradition from the Gaon that two days in the Omer were of a unique nature — the twentieth and the forty-second. The forty-third day of the Omer is Yom Yerushalayim — the Unification of Jerusalem, following the Six Day War. The actual battle for Jerusalem itself was completed on the fifth day of the war — the forty-second day of the Omer (which is the *Malchut* of *Yesod*). The book, *Midrash Shlomo* (R. S.Z. Rivlin), also points out that the numerical value of "The twentieth day of the Omer" equals 999, in the secret of Formula 999 in *Yesod* (see below Part II, Chapter 1, Fractal 6: Formula 999). See also regarding the Gaon's tradition of the twentieth and forty-second days of the Omer in *Ohr Shmuel*, (R. Shmuel Rivlin, pp. 195 and 343, Israel, 1984, Hebrew).

Part II

Messianic Conspiracy

Chapter 1

Mashiach ben Yoseph
and the Twin Messiahs

- Fractal 1: "But They Did Not Recognize Him"

- Fractal 2: The Split Messiah

- Fractal 3: A Crack in the Foundation

- Fractal 4: The Twin Messiahs

- Fractal 5: Among Us in Every Generation

- Fractal 6: Formula 999

- Fractal 7: Moses and the Twin Messiahs

- Fractal 8: "In Its Due Time I Will Accelerate It"

Chapter 1

Mashiach ben Yoseph
and the Twin Messiahs

Fractal 1:
"But they did not recognize him"

The Gaon of Vilna's esoteric Doctrine of Redemption draws upon virtually all the sources of the biblical and rabbinical traditions — the Prophets, the two Talmuds, the Midrashim, the numerous books of the *Zohar,* and the extensive writings of the Ari (Lurianic Kabbalah). Yet, the one theme that runs throughout the entirety of *Kol HaTor,* as well as in the Gaon's school of Kabbalah, is a concept known as *Mashiach ben Yoseph* (lit. Messiah son of Joseph) — the Josephic Messiah. Although foreign to the vast majority of people — Jewish or not (including scholars) — this concept is axiomatic to a deeper understanding of the history and destiny of mankind and especially to the Jewish Nation. Certainly, Mashiach ben Yoseph is fundamental to the Gaon's unique formula for the confluence of science and Kabbalah. Yet, this foundation principle has remained strangely hidden from the world — even from the orthodox Torah world.

R. Menachem Mendel Kasher (who published one of the two editions of *Kol HaTor* in 1968) was a world recognized Torah authority and, at one point, Rosh Yeshivah of the Gerrer Yeshivah in Jerusalem. In the preface to his edition of *Kol HaTor* he wrote:[1]

> Behold, I have inquired among numerous Torah scholars, including a number of leading rabbinic authorities, whether they are familiar with the subject of Mashiach ben Yoseph. All of them, without exception, replied that they could not explain this concept with any clarity. There was also a portion of them who did not know that it is mentioned in the Babylonian Talmud, thinking that it is found only in Midrashic literature. To the majority of them

this was a new concept which needed to be studied and understood.

In order to briefly illustrate to the reader the intrinsic hidden nature of the Gaon's doctrine of *Kol HaTor,* two examples will be mentioned. Talmud Tractate *Succah* 52a, (and discussed in Volume II of the Secret Doctrine, Chapter 4, *Metatron*) devotes half a page to the subject of Mashiach ben Yoseph and its relation to a number of fundamental Torah concepts. This tractate is studied by most yeshivah students at one point or another. This particular section of *aggada* deals with the future apocalyptic slaying of the Evil Inclination and is well known in Torah circles. In spite of this, and as R. Kasher himself concludes, the personage of Mashiach ben Yoseph that is also explicitly mentioned there has somehow become obscured and forgotten from an ocean of talmudic minds.

No less enigmatic is the fact that Mashiach ben Yoseph is also mentioned in tractate *Baba Metzia* (114b), which is studied by *every* student of Talmud. Here, a description of Mashiach ben Yoseph appears, not in the main text of the *Gemara*, but at the end of a long gloss by the school of *Tosafot.* Now, every *talmid chacham* knows that the commentaries of the *Tosafot,* along with Rashi's commentaries, are fundamental to understanding the main text. In fact, the yeshivah world holds the observations and critiques of the *Tosafot* to be virtually as sacred as the text of the *Gemara* itself, and all their words are analyzed and scrutinized as the most precious gems. Yet amazingly, the assertion of the existence that there is a *Tosafot* commentary which speaks about Mashiach ben Yoseph, and especially located in Talmud tractate *Baba Metzia,* will be met with disbelief by almost everyone — from the talmudic aspirant to the seasoned Torah master. (Even R. Kasher's appended anthology of all the earlier and later rabbinic sources that refer to the Mashiach ben Yoseph in his introduction to *Kol HaTor,* did not mention this source.)

Of course, any Torah scholar can occasionally overlook a conspicuous piece of information, as the sages themselves point out (Talmud, *Eruvin* 90a), "In his sharpness he overlooked the obvious" (*agav churpey lo 'ayain bah*). Rather, what is strangely conspicuous regarding the subject of Mashiach ben Yoseph is that, especially in the present period of the *Ikveta DiM'shecha* (Heels or Footsteps of the Messiah), it has been overlooked by the Jewish Nation as a whole, including most of its scholars and leaders. The question then is: what can be the explanation for such a *collective* phenomenon?

Primarily, since the publication of *Kol HaTor* in 1968, and over the last decades, the name of Mashiach ben Yoseph has become more known. In the overall picture, however, and certainly in its plethora of arcane details, it continues to remain unknown. Yet, this phenomenon is precisely so. Hiddenness and unrecognizability are part of the essence of Mashiach ben Yoseph. He is a master of the art of disguise. This is also the Torah's intention in the verse: *"Yoseph recognized his brothers, but they did not recognize him"* (Genesis 42:8).

R. Hillel Rivlin of Shklov writes:[2]

> "Yoseph recognized his brothers, but they did not recognize him" — This [hiddenness] characterizes Yoseph, not only in his generation, but in every generation in which the Mashiach ben Yoseph recognizes his brothers but they do not recognize him. It is part of a diabolical scheme that the qualities of Mashiach ben Yoseph are concealed in [the final period of] the Footsteps of the Messiah. Due to our many sins, he is scorned, as well. If this were not the case, our suffering would already have ended. If only Israel would recognize Mashiach ben Yoseph's "footprints" [i.e., the signs of his presence], the ingathering of the exiles, etc. [enumerated throughout *Kol HaTor,* including the messianic role of science], we would already have seen the complete Redemption.

As outlined above, this hiddenness characterizes the

entire history of the document *Kol HaTor* itself until today. This alone justifies its being called a "secret" doctrine. Yet, the controversy and the cloak of mystery that surround *Kol HaTor* must be expected *ipso facto,* because it is crucial to the story of Mashiach ben Yoseph himself. Aside from the original source material, only the Ari, the school of the Ramchal, and the Gaon and his school of Kabbalah discuss the subject at length. Even then, aside from a single work by the Ramchal (Part II of *Kinat HaShem Tzevaot,* which also has had a difficult history for the past two hundred fifty years, until its first full publication in 1980), *Kol HaTor* is the only piece of rabbinic literature that is devoted exclusively to the subject of Mashiach ben Yoseph.[3] Even among the voluminous writings of the Hasidic masters, which finely develop a number of esoteric truths of the Kabbalah, the concept of Mashiach ben Yoseph is seldom found, and certainly never developed at length. Although some of the principles of Mashiach ben Yoseph are implicit in its theosophy, it did not require, or permit, the explicit revelation and development of this doctrine. This pattern within Hasidut has continued up until today.

Kol HaTor is a manual and practical guide to the understanding and application of the cosmological principle of Mashiach ben Yoseph. Yet, for virtually all non-Jews, secularized Jews, and even for most of the Torah community, it continues to remain hidden *even after it has been published!* For those who do know of its existence, its authority is often rejected and, by some, even ridiculed. Yet, an intimate familiarity with this principle is essential for an understanding of the historical process of global evolution in general, and the Gaon's unique path to Redemption in particular.

We will now present to the reader a general introduction to the subject of the Messiah, as viewed from the perspective of the Kabbalah teachings of the Gaon of Vilna. It must be emphasized that this presentation is only an overview of some of the major principles involved in this vast esoteric doctrine. Other important keys to unlocking the great mystery of Mashiach ben Yoseph, particularly as it interfaces with science and technology, will be found in the following chapters. Even still, the reader must bear in mind that much of the material being presented is in the category of what the sages refer to as "the Hidden Matters of the All Merciful One" (*kavshey d'rachamana*).[4] Each one's ability to probe these matters depends, not only upon careful analysis and cross-referencing of the material, but also upon the root of one's soul and the permission bestowed from the source of these hidden matters — the All Merciful One.

Fractal 2:
The Split Messiah

What makes Mashiach ben Yoseph such a complex subject is that it is only one half of a larger picture. The other half, which is more familiar to everyone, is known as Mashiach ben David, the King Messiah, or simply *the* Messiah. Together, they are known in the *Zohar* and in the Gaon's commentaries as the *Trein M'shechin* - the *Zohar*'s Aramaic term for the Two Messiahs — Mashiach ben Yoseph and Mashiach ben David. Mashiach ben Yoseph can only be understood together with its complementary force of Mashiach ben David. It is the symbiotic union — or antagonism — between these two cosmological forces that forms the hidden landscape upon which the drama of the entirety of world history unfolds. Kabbalah and science are simply one of the many manifestations and applications of Mashiach ben Yoseph and the *Trein M'shechin*.

It must be emphasized that in the language of the Torah masters and Kabbalah sages, the appellations of ben Yoseph and ben David refer to much more than the historical Yoseph and David. These two "messianic" forces were in existence potentially and manifestly not only before the historical Yoseph, viceroy of Egypt, and King David, but even before creation. Rather, Yoseph and David are specific constellations of the forces of the *Trein M'shechin* incarnating, as it were, in historical time and space. The historical Yoseph and David then reciprocally become prototypes for the *Trein M'shechin* from whence we derive many of the subtle yet crucial details of the phenomenon of the *Trein M'shechin*.

Now, before we begin our journey into the difficult and often serpentine topography of *Kol HaTor* and the esoteric writings of the Gaon, a definition of the concept of *Mashiach* is called for. It will be a simplified definition, which will require qualification and much elaboration afterward. But it is essential in allowing us to approach the *Trein M'shechin* with some sense of perspective.

Why two messiahs?[5] Why any messiah at all? What is the purpose of a *Mashiach*? The *Mashiach* is an individual who is responsible for, and who, either overtly, or covertly, spearheads a collective process of *tikkun*. *Tikkun* is perhaps the single most important concept in all of Judaism, and certainly this is the case from the perspective of the Gaon's Kabbalah. The word *tikkun* means "rectification" or "mending." In the Kabbalah, *tikkun* also refers to a process of "elevation" and "transformation." Whereas the second definition implies taking something that is already complete into a more refined state, the first definition implies that something has broken, or become torn, and the immediate goal is only to return it to its original state of completion. These are the two processes, or modes, of *tikkun*.

When something has been broken, it obviously is not complete, and it cannot function to its full capacity. It is, in a sense, in a state of "fallenness" or "captivity," until it receives its proper *tikkun*. Its *tikkun* is then its redemption from its captive state. The one who performs that act of restoration is said to be its redeemer (*goel*), which is another quality and name for messiah. As we shall see, the Torah teaches that a certain type of breakage, or primordial "fall", took place which affected and continues to affect the entirety of creation. Therefore, the Messiah is simply the one who is responsible for the restoration – the *tikkun* - and the redemption of creation.

Yet, even the second definition of *tikkun,* as elevation and transformation, also implies a subtle form of captivity, which requires a process of redemption. Something can be complete, but still have the capacity to evolve to a higher level. As long as it has not yet attained that higher level, then it too, relatively speaking, can be said to be in a state of captivity that requires redemption. The one who performs that act of transformation is said to be its redeemer, for he has released it from the bondage of its static level of completion. This type of redeemer is also a messiah.

At present, we can understand the need for the first type of Messiah — one who will restore the world to its former state. But where does the second type fit into the picture? When was the world so complete that it needed only to be elevated to higher and higher levels of completion and perfection?

The answer is the Garden of Eden. Originally, when Adam HaRishon (the being, composed of both masculine and feminine) was created, he was placed into a higher dimensional reality that was essentially perfect. His mission was to elevate and transform that which was already in a completed state. In spite of the fact that nothing had broken and nothing had been torn, all life was still undergoing a staggering spiritual evolution. The entire hierarchy of life — human, animal, plant, and mineral — was rising up higher and higher. The one orchestrating this was Adam. Even in the original utopian description of the Garden of Eden, Adam was life's redeemer and the World Messiah.

After the proverbial eating from the higher dimensional fruit of the Tree of Knowledge of Duality, reality and Adam's mission radically changed. The "fall" of man was a cosmic shattering and an existential rip that reverberated throughout the entire fabric of creation. Adam now had a new task to perform, for through his actions everything had collapsed into a lower world order. A new mode of *tikkun* was therefore required — the *tikkun* of rectification, restoration, and purification. This does not mean that his original task of higher transformation had been nullified. It only means that until he mends that which has been torn asunder, his original task gets delayed awhile. In the end, he must, and will, return to complete it as well.

Thus, Adam, presently wearing the form of world humanity, is now two steps removed from God's true intent. First, we have to fix up what has been shattered, and then we have to take up where Adam left off and finish his original work of elevation and transformation. Where there was originally intended to be one singular mode of *tikkun,* now there are two modes. Where there was originally intended to be one redeemer for all of creation, now there are two — one for each mode of *tikkun.* These two modes of *tikkun* are referred to in Torah literature as the *Trein M'shechin* — the Two Messiahs. Adam had, in effect, split his own self into two personae. Adam is the Split Messiah.

(The creation of a dual world order, now dependent upon a two-staged *tikkun,* is the actual origin of all duality — good/bad, male/female, heaven/earth, sun/moon, "This World"/"Next World," etc. — that is the bedrock of our present reality. These sharp distinctions did not exist in the higher world of transformation, which functioned according to a law of singularity, known as the Tree of Life. All duality is a direct consequence of Adam's act of partaking from the Tree of Knowledge of Opposites, which, as its name implies, is the primal source of all duality.)

In general, the redeemer, whose mission is fundamentally one of restoration and purification, is known as *Mashiach ben Yoseph.* The redeemer, whose mission is fundamentally one of elevation and transformation, is known as *Mashiach ben David.* Similarly, the period of time that we are in now, i.e., after Adam's fall and expulsion from Eden, is broadly designated as the Era of Mashiach ben Yoseph. This is the period of time for his mode of *tikkun.*

As explained in the Introduction, the present world order is scheduled to exist for six thousand years. It is during this time that the *tikkun* of rectification must take place in small increments. (Although, in general, this entire period is the providence of Mashiach ben Yoseph, it is the second half of the six millennium, i.e., from the year 5,600-1740, which is the essential period for the *tikkun* of Mashiach ben Yoseph, as will be explained momentarily.) After this *tikkun* will be completed, i.e., near the very end of the six millennia, then we will enter the period of time designated as the Era of Mashiach ben David, since it will then be time to finish the mode of the original *tikkun* of transformation.

Surprisingly, the famous Era of the Messiah (ben

David) so much described by the prophets and formulated by the sages, yet so clouded in obscurity, is none other than a return to the original, but unfinished Garden of Eden, and *Mashiach ben David* is none other than the original *Adam HaRishon* himself before the Fall![6] This is certainly a return full circle if there ever was one. (This principle is included in the rabbinic formula, *sof ma'aseh b'machshavah techilah* — "the final act [returns to] the original intended thought.)

The statement that there are two distinct modes and periods for each of the *Trein M'shechin* must now be qualified. In truth, there is much overlapping between the two. The *ben David* mode is always present in the immediate background of the *ben Yoseph* mode and vice versa. In other words, a fractal spark (*nitzotz*) of the lower *tikkun* of Mashiach ben Yoseph is always present within the higher *tikkun* of *Mashiach ben David*. Conversely, a fractal spark of the higher *tikkun* of *ben David* is always present within the lower *tikkun* of *ben Yoseph*.

This interpenetration of the Two Messiahs is true on two levels, and thus, the term *Trein M'shechin* has two meanings. The processes of Mashiach ben Yoseph and Mashiach ben David occur together, at all times, in every generation, and in all places. The Messianic *Era* of Mashiach ben Yoseph and the Messianic *Era* of Mashiach ben David, however, refer to large scale time-frames where there is a sharper line of demarcation between the two modes of *tikkun*. The first aspect of the *Trein M'shechin* that functions on the generational or micro-time scale, i.e., on an annual and daily basis, we will call the generational *Trein M'shechin*. The second aspect of the *Trein M'shechin,* that functions on the millennial or macro-time scale, we will call the millennial *Trein M'shechin*.

In short, this is what Mashiach ben Yoseph and the Two Messiahs are all about. There is, however, a very basic question that must be asked. What was it in the structure of creation itself that allowed for this dimensional break to have occurred in the first place? When something breaks, although it may appear to split or crack at random, in truth it is following a structural pattern that is not visible to the naked eye. The same is true with the Split Messiah. It is also following an underlying structural pattern. But for this we must look into the hidden foundations of the creation itself and see what lies beneath us.

Fractal 3:
A Crack in the Foundation

We are now going to penetrate deeper into the cosmological roots of the Split Messiah in order to see the depths to which this phenomenon goes and how all history, and especially the confluence between Kabbalah and science, literally molds itself to its surface. Although it was explained above that the split, or double, *tikkun* was a consequence of Adam's Fall, this (as usual) is only part of the story. The truth is that the hidden foundations for this cosmic crack were already prepared long before the story of Genesis and Adam's drama unfolded. But let us begin slowly with the surface evidence.

The Talmud states (Talmud, *Berachot* 34b):

R. Chiya bar Abba said in the name of R. Yochanan: "All the prophets only prophesied with regard to the Messianic Era. As for the World to Come, 'No eye has seen it, aside from You God' (Isaiah 64:3)." These rabbis differ from Shmuel; for Shmuel said: "There is no difference between the present world order and the Messianic Era except [that in the latter Israel will no longer suffer] the subjugation of foreign powers, as it says (Deuteronomy 15:11): 'For the poor will never cease out of the land [i.e., not even in the Messianic Era].'"

Shmuel's statement has since become well known, codified, and authoritative. In his *Mishnah Torah (Hilchot Melachim* 12:2), the Rambam (Maimonides) writes: "The sages have said, 'There is no difference between the present world order and that of the Messianic Era, except for the subjugation of foreign powers.'"[7]

Commenting, however, on the divergence of opinion

between Rabbi Yochanan and Shmuel, the Gaon writes,[8] "These and these are both the words of the Living God, because *there are two messianic periods"* [i.e., the supra-natural order that was envisioned by the prophets is the period of *Mashiach ben David,* and the natural order described by Shmuel is the period of Mashiach ben Yoseph].[9]

The existence of two messianic time periods is axiomatic throughout the Gaon's system of Kabbalah. This is because these two periods are not only historical time frames, but also spatial-like structures based upon specific universal laws of the Kabbalah. As explained in the Introduction, the Gaon was a master of all the fields of Kabbalah, but his specialty was the dimension of time. For the Gaon, time is not simply a river that flows from the past through the present and into the future. Rather, it is just the protruding edge of a larger and more encompassing divine structure. This structure has its own higher dimensional form with specific co-ordinates mapped onto its "body."

In this sense, the Gaon's formulation of time is more analogous to the modern scientific notion of a space-time continuum, i.e., the three dimensions of space are inextricably interwoven into the dimension of time, and both are, in fact, aspects of a larger and more encompassing structure. This "body of space-time" is what is known in the Kabbalah as the *Shiur Komah,* the "Stature of the God-Image," or *Adam Kadmon,* "Archetypal Man." The infinitesimal unit of the surface of this divine space-time structure, to which we currently have direct access, consists of six sub-units, to be followed by a seventh unit, which is of a different nature all together. These six units are what mankind currently experiences as the six millennia of history to be followed by a unique seventh millennium — the Great Shabbat, the "World to Come" (*Olam HaBah*).

Using the terminology of the Kabbalah, the Gaon identifies the six millennia of space-time with the six lower *sefirot* — *Chesed, Gevurah, Tiferet, Netzach, Hod*, and *Yesod*. All six of these are then channeled (via the thrusting power of *yesod*) into the seventh *sefirah, Malchut*. The quality of *yesod* is associated with the personality of Yoseph, while the quality of *Malchut* is associated with David. Nevertheless, while it is true that Mashiach ben Yoseph is associated with the sixth millennium, it does not necessarily follow that *Mashiach ben David* is associated with the seventh millennium. We will now explain why and what difference this makes.

There is an astounding and bizarre phenomenon that, due to its other-worldly nature and its need to be concealed from the populous, is only discussed in the books of the Kabbalah. In his commentary to the *Zohar's Sifra DiTzniuta* (Book of Concealment), the Gaon analyzes at length the cosmic "event" known as the Death of the Primordial Kings, or the Shattering of the Vessels, that occurred prior to the events of Genesis in the preceding primeval Universe of the *Tohu* ("void" or "chaos"). He writes there that, due to this orchestrated cosmic "catastrophe" in the primordial creation process, the theoretically indivisible space-time unit of *yesod* fragmented, or cracked, into two parts.[10] In speaking of a "crack" in the foundation — *yesod* also translates as "foundation" — the Gaon is revealing a very profound esoteric principle that, although alluded to in the *Zohar*, is not even mentioned throughout the writings of the Ari – the corpus of Lurianic Kabbalah.[11] The full implications of this seemingly minor tear in the fabric of creation leads into the deepest, and most hidden, recesses of the Gaon's Kabbalah. We shall limit ourselves to the historical and messianic implications of this cosmic division.

On the messianic level, the collective personality that embodies the quality of *yesod* — the Messiah from the House of Yoseph — has itself divided into two parts. Likewise, the *yesod* of space-time — the sixth millennium of history (5,500-6000 = 1740-2240 C.E.) — has also divided itself into two distinct periods. This sixth unit of historical time has had a relative seventh unit of time added on to it, aside from the true final seventh millennium that follows. The original period of Mashiach ben Yoseph itself, which in theory should have remained singular, has now divided into two periods and becomes the millennial *Trein M'shechin*.

This is what the Gaon wrote:[12]

The *atarah* (crown) of the *yesod* split off... This is the secret of the Messianic Era [of *ben David*] that will occur at the end of the sixth millennium, at which time "Death will be reabsorbed [back into its source] forever" (Isaiah 25:8)... It is the secret of the removal of the *orlah* (foreskin) from the *atarah* of the *yesod*... and the secret of the duration of the Messianic Era [of *ben David*], which is equal to the measurement of the *atarah* [relative to the length of the measurement of the *yesod* itself]. If there is sufficient merit, then Mashiach ben Yoseph will come first and reign, as did King Saul [who was the Mashiach ben Yoseph of his era], before King David. ...Then [the Talmud's statement in the name of Shmuel will be fulfilled], "There is no difference between the present world order and that of the Messianic Era [of Mashiach ben Yoseph], except for the subjugation of foreign powers." However, when the period of Mashiach ben David will be reached, then, "Death will be reabsorbed [into its source] for eternity."

In his commentary on the *Tikkuney Zohar Chadash* the Gaon is very explicit concerning the existence of these two modes of redemption:[13]

"The left hand repels and the right hand brings close" — This is the meaning of the verse, "For a small moment I have forsaken you, but with great mercies I shall gather you" (Isaiah 54:7). The final Redemption will come from the "right" side [of *rachamim*-mercy]. In the meantime, however, it will begin from the "left." This same principle is the basis of the verse, "His left hand is under my head, but His right hand will embrace me" (Song of Songs 2:6). The beginning that will come from the left is called *pekidah* (remembrance). It will be similar to the beginning of the Second Temple Era when Cyrus allowed all the Jews to return, yet most of them did not leave [the Diaspora]. Following this, however, the Redemption will come from the right side.

Aside from the Gaon's own statements throughout his extensive writings,[14] the existence of two processes of messianic redemption is an accepted part of the Gaon's tradition. Both R. Yitzchak Izik Chaver and R. Shlomo Eliyashiv, the two foremost expounders of the Gaon's Kabbalah, state the same principle. Commenting on the Gaon's own reference to the two messianic eras, R. Yitzchak Izik Chaver writes:[15]

> Israel's redemption from the physical subjugation of other nations will come about specifically through Mashiach ben Yoseph. It is for this reason that his mission involves the [initial] ingathering of the exiles. Ultimate spiritual liberation from the Angel of Death, however, will only be brought about through Mashiach ben David.

R. Shlomo Eliyashiv writes:[16]

> This matter [of the primordial split in the *Tohu*] is also the secret of the two eras of Mashiach ben Yoseph and Mashiach ben David.

Thus, even before we quote from *Kol HaTor* it is evident that there are two messianic periods in the Gaon's cosmology and that they are in conformity with immutable spiritual laws of creation. Furthermore, both periods are manifestations of esoteric principles etched into the primordial plan of creation; they have equally vital roles to play. It would also seem apparent that recent global events, as well as events revolving directly around Israel and the Jewish people, are not happening in a vacuum. According to the Gaon's system, the present period places us dead center in the overlapping period between the Messianic Era of Mashiach ben Yoseph and the Messianic Era of Mashiach ben David.

Some two hundred years ago, R. Hillel Rivlin wrote:[17]

According to our master, the Gaon, if we do not
have the full merit, the beginning of the
Redemption will be initiated via [a natural
process of] "awakening from below," as was the
case in the days of Cyrus during the rebuilding
of the Second Temple. This [redemption] came
from the "left" side, that is, the quality of
constriction (gevurot) as formulated in the
verse, "His left hand is beneath my head,"
which is a reference to the process of Mashiach
ben Yoseph. [Likewise, the beginning of the
final Redemption] will be through the
permission of the nations of the world. Only
afterwards will the complete Redemption
commence from the "right" side, that is, the
quality of expansion (chesed) [as formulated in
the continuation of the verse, "...and His right
hand embraces me"] and through the re-
balancing of the middle quality of mercy
(rachamim) in accord with the verse, "With
great mercies I will gather you."

R. Hillel continues:

According to our master, the Gaon, the
ingathering of the exiles, via the awakening
from below, comes through a process of
reclamation and redemption. This follows from
the verse, "God's redeemed will return and they
will come singing to Zion... they shall obtain joy
and happiness" (Isaiah 35:10 and 51:11). This
redemption will take place under the leadership
of Mashiach ben Yoseph. It will involve a
redemption from bodily subjugation and
redemption from the subjugation of the soul.
"God's redeemed (plural) will return" implies
this two-fold process: "They will return to Zion"
in body [i.e., the material body of Israel], and
"they will come singing to Zion" [i.e., the
religious spirit of Israel]. They will then [both]

return in *teshuvah*-repentance. This is implied in the continuation of the verse, "They shall attain joy and happiness."

R. Hillel further writes:[18]

According to our master, the Gaon, all activities and all efforts — in all their particulars, down to the most minute details — that are directed to the ingathering of the exiles, the building of Jerusalem, the expansion and resettlement of the Land of Israel, and the return of the *Shechinah* (Divine Presence), are dependent upon the mission and destiny of the Messiah of the Beginning, the first Messiah — Mashiach ben Yoseph. He is the supra-natural force that aids every activity, which is "aroused from below," through the natural occurring process. In this sense, Mashiach ben Yoseph is that aspect of redemption that manifests "from the earth" [i.e., from below], and Mashiach ben David is that aspect that manifests "from the heavens" [i.e., from above]... In another sense, Mashiach ben Yoseph himself contains both of these manifestations. As the son of Rachel, he manifests "from the earth." As the son of Jacob, he manifests "from the heavens."[19]

In other words, any human labor and pursuit involving the ingathering of the exiled of Israel, the rebuilding of Jerusalem, the expansion and resettlement of the Land of Israel, the dissemination of the Jewish esoteric tradition and the spiritual reclamation and integration of scientific knowledge — although appearing on the surface as part of a natural "man made" process – is, in truth, being directed by a supra-natural providential force — Mashiach ben Yoseph.

From the ultimate perspective, there is only one source of providence, yet, as the Gaon explained above, the substructure of the present sixth millennium split into two parts, with each part containing aspects of the other. When the supra-natural law of *ben David* (the *atarah* of the *yesod*) is revealed on this side of current reality's cusp, we find it clothed in the guise of human struggle and naturally occurring events. It is then known as Mashiach ben Yoseph and is bound under a specific set of laws and principles — the laws of "nature." When the same source of God's providence will be revealed, in the near future, of the messianic era of *ben David,* then — although stretching the limits of our imagination — the *ben Yoseph* aspect (the *yesod* of the *atarah*) will find itself clothed in the guise of divine revelation and miraculously occurring events!

The *Trein M'shechin* are two sides of one *cosmic* coin. Using another model from modern science — the equivalence of matter and energy ($E=mc^2$) — we can better grasp that the material events of Mashiach ben Yoseph are just another mode of the selfsame spiritual reality of Mashiach ben David. Only because the natural process of Mashiach ben Yoseph — the "arousal from below" – chronologically precedes that of the supra-natural process of Mashiach ben David — the reciprocal "arousal from above" — is Mashiach ben Yoseph known as the first Messiah and Mashiach ben David as the last Messiah. In the end, however, both of the messiahs are united together by a power that is even greater than both.

Thus far we have presented the Gaon's definition of the messianic split, as it functions on the larger millennial level rooted in an archetypal crack in the very foundations of creation. Now let us look at the Gaon's definition of the *Trein M'shechin* on the smaller, and more immediate, generational level.

Fractal 4:
The Twin Messiahs

We just learned from the Gaon that a primordial split occurred in the substructure of the *yesod* of space-time, generating for itself its own relative *Malchut* (the *atarah* of the *yesod*). There is, however, another type of split in the *yesod,* which is better known in the Kabbalah and does not require as much esoteric detective work. Whereas the first type of polarity is known as the *Yesod/Malchut* paradigm and is more applicable to the millennial messianic process (as just discussed), the second type of polarity is known as the

Netzach/Hod paradigm and is more applicable to the generational messianic process, which will be discussed momentarily.

What emerges, however, is that there are two types of "splits" in the archetypal *yesod*. The one discussed above is "vertical" in nature, i.e., the division and/or unification is along the *Yesod-Malchut* axis. The one to be discussed now is "horizontal" in nature and divided between the right and left sides. These two modes of splits are actually two different forces that operate in two different dimensions, according to two different sets of laws. The two dimensions are the large millennial scale and the immediate generational scale. Although each set of cosmic laws can only be properly applied to its own domain, both types of forces of the Split Messiah share a common higher source. It is there where their two fields of influence unite and are revealed to be simply two aspects of a greater third, and more encompassing, force.

By way of analogy, this relationship parallels that of electricity and magnetism. Throughout history these two forces had always been considered as two distinct phenomena — one would attract iron filings and cause a compass to.point north, while the other would light up the sky with its bolts of lightning and could be generated by rubbing one's feet on a carpet and then touching a piece of metal (static electricity). In the middle of the 19th-century, however, science produced the first "unified field theory." It was demonstrated that electricity and magnetism were not distinct forces at all, but actually two sides of the same coin! A vibrating electrical field can create a magnetic field, and vice versa, and hence its new name — electromagnetism.

Magnetism has its own mode of positive and negative polarity, and can be used here to represent the first type of *Trein M'shechin* polarity, namely the *Yesod-Malchut* split. Electricity also has its own polarity of positive and negative currents, and can be used to represent the second type of *Trein M'shechin* polarity, namely the *Netzach-Hod* split. The unified field, where these two cosmological forces interface and affect each other, lies in the supernal root of the *Trein*

M'shechin. This super-force is known as Metatron, and will be discussed briefly below and at greater length in Volume II, Chapter 4, *Metatron – the Mystery of Israel.*

Netzach and *Hod* are the seventh and eighth of the *Ten Sefirot* and correspond to the two legs of the human form. Just as the two legs "split" the singular trunk of the body into two branches, so also, *Netzach* and *Hod* "split" the higher unity of divine providence into two parallel modes of influence. They are, therefore, known in the *Zohar* as the *"trei palgei gufa"* — Two Halves of the [One] Body. Although emphasizing different aspects within each other, they are quite literally mirror images of one another. They are the greatest manifestation of the paradox of the "dual," or "twin unity," that is found throughout the Kabbalah, and it is the model of the *trei palgei gufa* that is constantly referred to by the Gaon and his school when deciphering cryptic passages in the *Zohar.* This is especially true here in our case, where the *trei palgei gufa* are in the *yesod* itself, i.e., the parallel currents of *Netzach* and *Hod* themselves are both in the cosmic *yesod* of Mashiach ben Yoseph.

R. Hillel writes:[20]

Od Yoseph Chai (Yoseph lives on) — All three of these aspects are in the *sefirah* of Yesod. *"Od"* is the left current, the *Hod* of Yesod. *"Chai"* is the right current, the *Netzach* of Yesod. Yoseph is the middle current, the *Yesod* [of *Yesod*].

Thus, the relationship of the *trei palgei gufa* is the underlying structure of the generational *Trein M'shechin.* The Two Generational Messiahs are not only dependent upon each other. Each one defines the other, because each one contains the other. It is now possible to understand the *Zoharic* and talmudic expression *Ikveta* (Plural) *Di'M'shecha* as the Two Feet (or Heels) of the Messiah — one for Mashiach ben Yoseph and one for Mashiach ben David.

R. Hillel explains at length:[21]

On the macrocosmic level of redemption the

first messiah is Mashiach ben Yoseph, and the completer is Mashiach ben David. The same is true on the microcosmic level regarding every individual act. Every action undertaken throughout all of the stages of the beginning process that is initially "awakened from below," via natural effort and in incremental stages, is, according to the great principle of our master, divinely directed, first through the agency of Mashiach ben Yoseph, and then [it is completed] through the agency of Mashiach ben David.

The two generational messiahs are the supra-natural forces that maintain the existence of the Nation of Israel, strengthen them throughout their entire exile, and miraculously assist them [especially] during the period of the *Ikveta DiM'shecha*. Mashiach ben Yoseph is the miraculous force that supports and strengthens Israel's material existence, and Mashiach ben David is the miraculous force that supports Israel's spiritual existence in general and in particular. As explained in the writings of our master, the functions of the Two Generational Messiahs have many different aspects.

The Two Messiahs act in partnership with each other and assist each other. They live and exist in each and every generation. Mashiach ben Yoseph is the secret of "Yoseph lives on," and Mashiach ben David is the secret of "David King of Israel lives forever." Although they operate in their own individual roles, each one is dependent upon the other, and they influence each other, according to each one's unique characteristics.

Without the power, vitality, and protection of their influence, Israel could not continue to exist for even a single moment, God forbid. It is only because Israel and the Shechinah are in exile that their forces and manifestations are hidden in our lower dimension. It is therefore extremely important to know that these two great forces can only function and activate their powers to their fullest degree when there is no dissension and division between them.

Although working in different spheres of influence, the polarity within the generational *Trein M'shechin* parallels the polarity within the millennial *Trein M'shechin*. In both cases, the aspect of Mashiach ben Yoseph is just the other side of the aspect of Mashiach ben David. On the large scale, or on the small scale, although one may precede the other chronologically, in the end, both of the messianic energies are united together by a power that is even greater than both:

> *And the word of the Lord came to me, saying: "Son of man, take one branch, and write upon it, for Yehudah* [the source of the Davidic line]; *...then take another branch and write upon it, for Yoseph, the branch of Ephraim... Join them together into one stick; and they shall become one in your hand... and they shall become one in My hand"* (Ezekiel 37:15-19)

R. Hillel explains these words of the prophet (Aspect #101):[22]

> *Etz Yoseph* (the Branch of Yoseph) — refers to Mashiach ben Yoseph. The entire Redemption is dependent upon the unification of the two branches — the Branch of Yoseph and the Branch of Yehudah — as explained in this chapter. They are the *Trein M'shechin,* which will initially "become one in your hand" through the natural path of arousal from below. Afterwards they shall "become one in My hand" — the Hand of God — through the supranatural path "upon the clouds of heaven."

The two modes of the *Trein M'shechin* — on the larger time scale or the smaller time scale – are two branches of one root. Nevertheless, they often appear to function in distinct and even opposing paths. According to a deeper truth, however, there is a manner in which the two can synergistically interact with each other in a unique union. Each will maintain its distinct mode of function, yet combine with the other to produce something more than both. The primordial tear in the fabric of God's creation is being mended into a seamless unity. Each stitch is another aspect in the slow process of the cosmic *tikkun,* and each aspect reflects another face — and phase — in the cosmic personality of Mashiach ben Yoseph.

Fractal 5:
Among Us in Every Generation

To anyone not initiated into the Gaon's Secret Doctrine of Redemption, the text of *Kol HaTor,* will appear to be filled with strange and conflicting descriptions of Mashiach ben Yoseph. In one instance Mashiach ben Yoseph is identified with the Patriarch Abraham, in another he is Moses our Teacher, in another Queen Esther, and in another even the Gaon himself! And then it states that *anyone* involved in the Torah's messianic conspiracy for global evolution is Mashiach ben Yoseph!

In Chapter 2 of *Kol HaTor*, R. Hillel lists 156 different attributes, characteristics, and aspects derived from scriptural verses, which are all necessary in order to comprehend the gestalt that makes up the complex nature of Mashiach ben Yoseph. (*Yoseph* and *Zion* both have the same numerical value of 156.) It is not possible to present all of these aspects in the present work, however, a number of them have already been discussed above, and others will be brought below and in the following chapters. Along with these aspects it is essential to understand that Mashiach ben Yoseph always functions on three levels.

1. Mashiach ben Yoseph is a super-archetype, i.e., an all encompassing collective consciousness, which networks a vast matrix of smaller and distinct, yet interdependent, archetypal processes. These can remain on their collective root level and/or they can also manifest in the form of (2)

and (3) below. An archetype in Torah literature can also be known as an archangel, such as Michael, Gabriel and Raphael. In this case, however, Mashiach ben Yoseph is the *meta*-archangel known throughout the Talmud (including the standard commentaries of Rashi and *Tosafot*), Midrash, and *Zohar,* as Metatron. In spite of the initial strangeness of this concept, Metatron plays a critical role in the Gaon's Kabbalah, and especially throughout *Kol HaTor*.[23]

2). Mashiach ben Yoseph is any individual — man or woman — who is involved in the specific activities of Mashiach ben Yoseph, i.e., returning to the Land of Israel (including its expansion and rebuilding,) learning and dissemination of Torah, and — for the Torah scholar — mastery of the Kabbalah and scientific knowledge. Such an individual's mission is then considered a "cell" in the larger body of Mashiach ben Yoseph.

3. Mashiach ben Yoseph is an actual individual who exists in each and every generation. This is the deeper meaning of the verse, "The *tzadik* is the foundation channel (*yesod*) of the world" (Proverbs 10:25). How, where, and in what role he or she, will manifest is dependent upon a multitude of factors. His ability, however, to evolve from a *potential* to a fully actualized Mashiach ben Yoseph, in union with the aspects of Mashiach ben David, depends upon the collective merit of humanity, especially that of the Nation of Israel.

We will discuss the first two categories of Mashiach ben Yoseph in Volume II, Chapter 4, *Metatron.* Here, we will present an overview of the third level — the actual Mashiach ben Yoseph who lives in each generation.

The idea of the Messiah being a living individual walking among us in every generation is a bit strange, until *Kol HaTor* supplies us with a few examples from throughout history (which are quoted from various rabbinic sources).[24]

R. Hillel writes:[25]

"Yoseph Lives On" — Included in the category of the generational Mashiach ben Yoseph are the Patriarchs, many of the Prophets and Kings of Israel, many of the *Tanaim* and *Amoraim* [sages of the Mishna and Talmud], and many of the great men of Israel and persons of note throughout history. The first among them was Avraham Avinu (Abraham our Father), in the secret of [his statement], "How will I know that I will inherit it [the Land of Israel]?" (Genesis 15:8). It is known that any usage of the term 'inheritance' in conjunction with the Land of Israel is in the category of Mashiach ben Yoseph. Likewise, this is alluded to in the word "I will inherit it" (*irashenah*) which has the same numerical value as Mashiach ben Yoseph [566]. Abraham began the *Atchatah D'Geulah*, the initial process of redemption of holiness (*kedushah*) from below, which is the actual earth of the Land of Israel.

Yitzchak Avinu (Isaac our Father) began his mission as Mashiach ben Yoseph from the day of the *Akeida* (Binding)... Ya'akov Avinu (Jacob our Father) began from the day that he struggled and overcame the Oversoul of Esav... Yehudah began from the day he saved Yoseph; Yoseph from the day of his first dream, and Moses our Teacher from the day that he carried Yoseph's bones out with him from Egypt. Yehoshua ben Nun (Joshua) began when he engaged in the battle for God against Amalek. Saul and David also engaged in battles for God and, as it is known, all battles fought for the Sanctification of God's Name are in the mission of Mashiach ben Yoseph. [And this list goes on.]

In the latter generations, the holy Ari and his unique disciple, the holy and pure one, R. Chaim Vital, as well as, the holy master, the author of the *Or HaChaim* [R. Chaim ben Attar

1696-1743], were in the category of Mashiach ben Yoseph.

The generational Messiah's mission extends beyond the Jewish Nation to the Gentiles. The prophet Jonah was commanded by God to bring the entire non-Jewish city of Nineveh to repentance.

In the 75th Aspect of Mashiach ben Yoseph R. Hillel writes:[26]

> Admonisher to Repentance — Not only is Mashiach ben Yoseph to admonish the Jewish people, but the nations of the world, as well. This is shown in the mission of the prophet Jonah, who was the Mashiach ben Yoseph of his generation (as explained in the *midrashim* and in the holy *Zohar*).[27]

The Gaon's revolutionary understanding of the messianic process directly includes women as well as men.

R. Hillel writes:[28]

> According to the explanations of our master, the *Trein M'shechin* have various aspects, in accord with their many different functions. ...The first historical manifestation of the *Trein M'shechin,* during the period of the Egyptian exile, was the two Hebrew midwives (Yocheved and Miriam). This is what our teacher wrote in his commentary on the *Tikkuney Zohar Chadash* [36c] on the verses:

> "The midwives feared God... they saved the infant boys' lives... God gave them great houses of their own" (Exodus 1:17-20). They merited this because they were involved in saving the nation of Israel. Likewise, in each and every generation there is an actual pair of messiahs, which then also act as the source for the other messiahs of the generation, and their helpers,

according to their respective categories.

Concerning the 8th Aspect of Mashiach ben Yoseph, R. Hillel writes:

> The Morning Star — "To the chief Musician upon [the appearance of] the Morning Star, a Psalm of David. My God, my God, why have You forsaken me?" (Psalms 22:1-2). This was the prayer of Queen Esther, who was the Mashiach ben Yoseph of her generation. The sages explained that the Redemption of Israel will occur in stages, like the appearance of the Morning Star [at the darkest moment before the dawn]. This is the entire matter of the *At'chalta D'Geulah* that is Mashiach ben Yoseph's mission.

Even a non-Jew, who does not yet fully appreciate the revelation of God in the world or the vital mission of the Jewish People in bringing about that revelation, can be chosen for a mission of Mashiach ben Yoseph. The case given in *Kol HaTor* is that of Cyrus, the Persian King, who, upon conquering Babylonia, permitted the exiled Jews to return to Israel and to rebuild the Temple. The Prophet Isaiah had already predicted the meteoric rise of a certain Cyrus: "Thus says God to his anointed (*"Mashiach"*), to Cyrus ... I call you by your name, I surname you, though you do not know Me" (Isaiah 45:1-4).

In the 130th Aspect of Mashiach ben Yoseph, R. Hillel writes:

> *Tzedek* (Righteousness) — It is written concerning Cyrus, "I have raised him up in righteousness, and I will make straight all his ways; he will build My city, and he will send forth My captives, not for price nor for bribe, says the Lord of Hosts" (Ibid. 13). As it is known, Cyrus was under the directive of Mashiach ben Yoseph.

He also writes (Aspect #70):

"He will perform all My pleasure" — This is referring to the rebuilding of Jerusalem by Ezra and Nehemiah, via the agency of Cyrus. This is the intent of the verse, "[God] says of Cyrus, 'He is the shepherd of My flock; he will perform all My pleasure, saying to Jerusalem, "You shall be rebuilt"; and to the Temple, "'Your foundations shall be laid'" (Isaiah 44:28). All of this is from the quality of *din* (constriction), from the "left side" in the mission of Mashiach ben Yoseph.[29]

And finally, the role of Mashiach ben Yoseph is not limited to well known biblical personalities.[30]

R. Hillel writes:[31]

Our master, who was the illumination of Mashiach *ben Yoseph*,[32] would recite the prayer "Yoseph Lives On" daily.[33] ...In this prayer he also mentioned the merit of his great grandfather, R. Eliyahu Hasid [the progenitor of the genealogy of both the Gaon and the Rivlin family], who was Mashiach ben Yoseph in his generation.

And again:[34]

In this last generation our master, the Gaon, is also an illumination of the light of Mashiach ben Yoseph, and his guiding light will continue to increase and to ascend before us until the height of the [sixth millennial] day. Specific individuals from among his disciples, who fulfilled his commandments regarding the Vision of Zion, also merited to receive and to become extensions of his spirit and great light in this capacity [of Mashiach ben Yoseph].

Od Yoseph Chai! It is axiomatic to the Gaon's

Doctrine of Redemption that Mashiach ben Yoseph lives among us in every generation. It is he who acts as the central conduit for the messianic process to become manifest, and it is he — or she — who carries out the various missions of earthly and cosmic *tikkun*. The cosmology of *Kol HaTor* reveals, moreover, that there is an actual mechanism, a force that is animating the phenomenon of Mashiach ben Yoseph. This is the key that unlocks the power of the messianic process. This is Formula 999.

Fractal 6:
Formula 999

In one of the Gaon's works on Kabbalah — *Secret of the Letters* — he writes in his signature cryptic shorthand:[35]

999 is in *Yesod* [the ninth *sefirah*]. As is known, the letter/number Tet/9 signifies [the ultimate] Good, as the sages stated,[36] "Seeing the letter *Tet* [=9] in a dream is a good sign."

The inner connection between the ultimate Good of the number 9 and Mashiach ben Yoseph is repeatedly emphasized in *Kol HaTor*.

In Aspect #51 R. Hillel writes:

Tov-Good is in *Yesod* — According to our master's explanation (ibid.) this refers to the letter/number *Tet*/9 [of the word *tov*]. As the sages stated, "...the letter *Tet* [=9] in a dream is a good sign." This pertains to the character of Yoseph, concerning whom it is written, "One whose eye [looks for] good is blessed; he gives of his bread to the poor" (Proverbs 22:9). This is [the formula] of 999 in *Yesod*.

The numbers 999 and 1000 are the keys to the inner mechanism of Mashiach ben Yoseph, and they appear throughout *Kol HaTor*, virtually on every other page. Not only does the value of 999 lie at the inner essence of Mashiach ben Yoseph, but his continued existence hinges upon it.

In *Kol HaTor*,[37] R. Hillel lists seven fundamental principles that must govern our actions during the period of *Ikveta DiM'shecha*. The first principle is:

> *Od Yoseph Chai* (Yoseph Lives On) — Our master based his entire doctrine on the underlying principle of "Yoseph lives on," i.e., Mashiach ben Yoseph is not only alive; he will continue to live, and the decree that he is to be slain by Armilus the Evil One [the spiritual leader of Gog and Magog] has been nullified [discussed in Volume II, Chapter 4, *Metatron*]. The entire *At'chalta D'Geulah* (Beginning of the Redemption) depends on him. The decree has therefore been atoned for by virtue of the length of [Israel's] exile and the suffering he endures by carrying our afflictions (Isaiah 53:4)... It has been nullified in the sense that it has been broken up into numerous smaller parts. This is the meaning of the analogy brought in the midrash: "It is comparable to a king who became angry at his son and swore that he would hurl a massive stone at him. Later, he regretted this and had compassion on the boy. In order to fulfill his own oath, however, he had the stone broken up into small pebbles. These were thrown at the boy, one by one." In the same way, Mashiach ben Yoseph will not suffer the death penalty. He must, however, still suffer the pain of the smaller rocks. These represent the *Chevley Mashiach* (Birth pangs of the Messianic Era) that come, little by little, together with the 999 phases [lit. *Ikvot*] of the *Mashiach*. This occurs in such a manner that the decree is also divided up into 999 smaller segments.

The number 999 is also the highest stage that the inner power of Mashiach ben Yoseph can achieve before it evolves into the number 1000 and thus trigger the climactic response of the power of *Mashiach ben David*. Formula 999 is the point of critical mass in the slow and incremental process of the "arousal from below."

R Hillel writes:[38]

> In conjunction with the verse [discussed
> below], "The least one shall become a thousand
> and the smallest one a strong nation; I the Lord
> will accelerate it [the Redemption] in its time"...
> our master told us that even its predetermined
> time will be accelerated. And when will this
> occur? When... "The least one will become a
> thousand and the smallest one a strong
> nation." The "least one" and the "smallest one"
> both refer to [the archetype of] Ephraim [ben
> Yoseph], which is [another aspect of the
> principle of] Mashiach ben Yoseph. Now, it is
> known that the extreme threshold level of
> *Mashiach ben Yoseph* that is achieved through
> [the process of] the "arousal from below" is [the
> power of] 1000 minus 1, that is [the formula
> of], "999 in *Yesod*."[39] "The least one shall
> become a thousand" [thus] means that when
> [the messianic process of *Mashiach ben Yoseph*]
> will reach a degree just up until [the climatic
> conclusion of] 1000 — then, "I the Lord, even in
> its due time, will accelerate it [the
> Redemption]."

Based upon principles of the Kabbalah found in the
Gaon's other writings [notably the concept of the *yesod*
splitting into two — the *trei palgei gufa*], R. Hillel continues to
explain just how the stimulation of Formula 999 operates.
This universal *yesod*, represented by Yoseph, produces a
"tuning fork" effect in which the two messiahs resonate back
and forth with each other. Likewise, the full power of the
higher root of *yesod* — represented by Formula 999 — is also
divided into two halves — 499½ on one side and 499½ on the
other. Now, when these two negative and positive polarities
attract and stimulate each other, their combined energies
produce the necessary threshold point of 999, which then
"miraculously" jumps into the higher energy state, known as
the Great Thousand — the collective *Keter*-Crown of

Mashiach ben David.

In one of many examples R. Hillel explains:[40]

"There is hope (*tikvah*) for your end..."
(Jeremiah 31:16) — This entire prophecy was
said regarding the Redemption that will come
about through Mashiach ben Yoseph, i.e.,
through our "arousal from below" that
[eventually] reaches up to its final phase of 999
in *Yesod*. This *yesod* is split into two — 499½
from the left side, representing the quality of
Din [the negative pole of constriction] and 499½
from the right side, representing the quality of
Chesed [the positive pole of expansion]. This is
the intention of the verse, "The least one shall
become a 1000." For the number 1000 will be
completed from both sides simultaneously,
there now being 500 in the letter *Vav* [of the
Divine Name] and 500 in the letter *Heh*. This is
the [inner] meaning of "There is hope (*tikvah*)
for your end." [The first two letter/numbers of
tikvah — the *tav* (400) and the *kuf* (100) —
have the combined value of 500. The last two
letter/numbers *vav* and *heh* correspond to the
Vav and *Heh* of the Divine Name. The *Vav* is
the masculine/heavenly/positive current of
Mashiach ben David, relative to the final *Heh,*
which is the feminine/earthly/negative current
of Mashiach ben Yoseph. Thus, the word
tikvah-hope in this verse contains a coded
equation, mapping out one of the hidden
mechanisms of the *Trein M'shechin*.]

The Twin Messiahs are the two pulsating currents of
divine energy — *Din* (or *Gevurah*)-Constriction and *Chesed*-
Expansion — manifesting within the historical space-time of
each and every generation. Although each messianic current
is a distinct force field of energy that appears to repulse the
other, it is the very tension they generate that, when
channeled and directed, becomes the most powerful force for
personal, national, and planetary change that has ever

existed. Their paradoxical natures are continually present in every thought and action, and they are waiting to be channeled.

R. Hillel explains:[41]

> A fundamental rule is that during the performance of every *mitzvah* and every *tefilah,* one should contemplate the unification [of the *Trein M'shechin*] and bind oneself to the "Two Armies of God" — [these being the two divine names] *E-lohim Tzevaot* (God of Armies) and *Y-HVH Tzevaot* (Lord of Armies), *Din* (constriction) and *Chesed* (expansion). One must [then] calculate the line of balance between their two numerical values — 499½ from the left side and 499½ from the right side.

Each of the two messianic polarities has within itself a number of sub-currents that interact together in a cacophony of pulsating social, political, and religious events to generate the ever rising threshold of Formula 999. In a divinely orchestrated fashion they all act according to specific laws contained within the 156 Aspects of Mashiach ben Yoseph. It is they who make up the members of the Two Armies of God. In *Kol HaTor*'s Messianic Conspiracy, they are the Appointed Agents of God.

R. Hillel writes:[42]

> The thrice-woven cord of "Signs," "Designated Times," and "Appointed Agents" appears simultaneously in a three-pronged campaign. The "agents" react to the "signs" and thus accelerate the arrival of the "designated times." This is alluded to in the verse, "The blossoms have appeared in the land; the time of singing has arrived, and *kol hator* — the call of the turtledove — is heard in the land" (Song of Songs 2:12). "The blossoms have appeared" — these are the signs; "the time of singing has arrived" — these are the designated times; "the

call of the turtledove is heard" — these are the appointed agents.

These agents are vehicles for the different aspects, or mini-personalities which, like pieces in a puzzle, only when they are fit together constitute the totality of Mashiach ben Yoseph.[43] They include, for example, titles like Ephraim ben Yoseph, Shirya ben Dan,[44] Eliyahu HaNavi (Elijah the Prophet), the archangels Gabriel, Sandalfon, and Metatron, Neriya, Menachem, Ezra and Nehemiah, Yehoshua ben Nun, Sasson and Simcha. (Sasson and Simcha are explained in Volume II, Chapter 4, *Metatron*.)

There is, however, one all encompassing Mashiach ben Yoseph archetype that we must mention briefly. Initially it appears to confuse an already overly complex pantheon of messianic archetypes, yet it is precisely here where all the various aspects of Mashiach ben Yoseph come together. This is the climatic evolution of Formula 999 into the Great Thousand. This is the cosmic image of Moses our Teacher together with the Two Messiahs.

Fractal 7:
Moses and the Twin Messiahs

The separate personalities of the *Trein M'shechin,* are, in fact, a singular reality. Their dynamic unification constitutes a paradoxical "dualistic singularity." Their potential seamless interdependency is the key to accessing and activating the messianic role of modern technology, as well as virtually all other dualities in the world. But what is the unified field behind the *Trein M'shechin* that is able to bind them together? What force is powerful enough to unite these two great cosmic terminals? On the Gaon's map of cosmic *tikkun* and global evolution this supra-natural force is none other than the soul of Moses our Teacher.[45] Commenting on the Talmud's assertion that the order of the *Shemoneh Esrey* (Standing) Prayer of "Eighteen Blessings" hints to the ultimate Redemption, the Gaon writes:[46]

The future Redemption will occur through the *Trein M'shechin,* Mashiach ben Yoseph and *Mashiach ben David,* and "Shiloh," who is

Moses... Indeed, it will occur mainly through Moses, who will appear [together with *Mashiach ben David*] and redeem [the nation] as he did in Egypt. Moses' return as the final redeemer is hinted in the initial letters of the phrase, **ma'sh'haya hu sh'yihyeh** — "that which was shall be [again]" (Ecclesiastes 1:9) which is an acrostic for Moses.[47]

This point is also brought out in the 38th Aspect of Mashiach ben Yoseph:

"The Call of the Turtledove (*Kol HaTor*) is heard in our land" — The call of the turtledove is the sound that precedes the actual appearance of the turtledove. The turtledove is Moses our Teacher himself, who comes with *Mashiach ben David*, the Last Redeemer.

Until now we have spoken of Mashiach ben Yoseph alone, or Mashiach ben Yoseph together with *Mashiach ben David*. It is only logical, however, that Moses should finally enter into the picture. He is known as the First Redeemer — from the first exile in Egypt — and the Last Redeemer — from the last and final exile, that is, from the bondage of the six thousand years of creation. In fact, in a number of rabbinic statements Moses is depicted as *the Mashiach*. And to further complicate matters, sometimes Moses appears alone, sometimes together with *ben David,* and sometimes together with the Twin Messiahs.

On the other hand, as we have seen, sometimes ben David and ben Yoseph each appear alone, and sometimes they appear together as the Twin Messiahs without Moses. So, who is the real Mashiach — ben David, ben Yoseph, or Moses? The answer is that although the three can appear separately, together they are components of an even larger gestalt. The Gaon bases this on a number of sections in the *Zohar.*[48]

Moses, similar to the dove that Noah sent and which found no dry place to alight upon, so you were also sent into Egypt. What is written there, "Moses looked all around and found no man" (Exodus 2:12)? It means that not one Israelite was found in whose merit they could be found worthy of Redemption. For this reason you [Moses] refused to redeem them, and you pleaded, "Please, God, send someone else to redeem them" (ibid. 4:13). Behold, Moses, it is the same now as it was then. Then, Israel was like the body of a dove and you (Moses) and Aaron were the two wings with which they flew into freedom. Now, in this last exile, you are a body without wings. I will therefore send you the *Trein M'shechin* as your wings.

Again, using other traditional imagery of the Kabbalah, the *Zohar* states:[49]

[Moses] will then arise with the *Trein M'shechin*. They are his two legs and he is the sign (of the covenant) between them...

The Gaon explains this passage in his commentary:

The sign of the covenant is "Mt. Zion," which is the *"Tzadik"* in the secret of Yoseph the *Tzadik*. Yoseph and Zion thus share the same numerical value (156), as is known. Moses stands between them, as is written in the section of the Faithful Shepherd.[50] Mashiach ben David is on his right side and Mashiach ben Yoseph is on his left side. Judah [the progenitor of the Davidic line] is personified [in the prophet Ezekiel's vision of the Divine Chariot] as a young lion and is to the right, and Yoseph, who is personified as a first-born ox, is to the left.

The Gaon discusses this triune relationship within the context of the previous discussion of Formula 999 and the *trei palgei gufa:*[51]

...and see what I wrote in *Sod HaOtiot* (Secret of
the Letters) that they are [each] 499½, male
and female, with the 1000 completing them.

He then explains that the letter *Vav* of the Divine
Name is the collective channel that connects the lower and
upper realms. When this *Vav* is expanded, or written out in
full, however, it is spelled *vav aleph vav*. The two *vavs* then
signify the *Trein M'shechin* and the *Aleph* between them is
Moses.

Moses is really *HaEleph HaGadol* (the Great
Thousand) who "fell" and became the small *Aleph* (the
number one) [who will again arise, via Formula 999 in
Yesod].

He writes further:[52]

This is the meaning of the verse, (Genesis
49:10), "The scepter will not depart from
Judah, nor the staff from between his feet,
until *Shiloh* will come." [*Shiloh* is an appellation
for the King Messiah — Rashi]. This is what the
Zohar is referring to here, namely, that at that
time there will necessarily be two messiahs,
i.e., the two *vavs* (the scepter and the staff) and
Moses (*Shiloh*), who is the *Aleph* between the
vavs.

Finally, R. Hillel pulls the Gaon's teachings together
into the context of a practical doctrine of *tikkun,* in order to
actively, and consciously, accelerate the universal process of
redemption. He writes:[53]

With all of the power of our hands, through
action and calculations, we will draw down the
supernal effulgence of the power of redemption
from the attribute of *Chesed* of the Great
Thousand (*HaEleph HaGadol*). We will continue
until the [required] degree of "arousal from
below" will have been reached... and their
qualities become equalized, i.e., 499½ from the

left side and 499½ from the right side, which is the level and power of the "Two Armies of God"... of *Chesed* and *Din* in *Netzach* and *Hod*.

Both of these two levels must be attained... in an exact balance... with their numerical values equalizing, right and left, up and down. For they parallel the letters *Vav* and *Heh* of the Name and the *Trein M'shechin,* which are united together in a single encompassing value — 1000 minus 1 [Formula 999].

Then immediately, in the blink of an eye, the supernal effulgence of the Great Thousand will descend via Moses our Teacher, peace be upon him. He is the Final Redeemer, and it is he who completes the number 1000 in the mystery of (Song of Songs 8:12), "The thousand is yours, Solomon."[54] Thus, the numerical value of Mashiach ben Yoseph (566) plus Mashiach ben David (434, [when the name David is spelled with the letter *yud,* as it appears in special instances in Scripture]) equals 1000.

In the final analysis, the question asked above, as to who is the real and last Mashiach, does not really ever start. In the Gaon's cosmology the different names of Mashiach are just different stages, within different processes, within different levels, that eventually all fuse together into the great constellation of synergistic forces, collectively known as Mashiach ben Yoseph. Even the historical Yoseph himself was an extension of the larger and more encompassing archetype of Moses and the Twin Messiahs, even though the historical Moses had not even been born yet![55]

Returning to our original definition above of the concept of Mashiach, the rule is this: All processes of *tikkun,* redemption, and purification throughout the period of the six millennia of the present reality — even those of spiritual redemption and subtle forms of purification (i.e., those processes which are "aroused from above" via Mashiach ben

David) — are all within the concept and mission of Mashiach ben Yoseph. From whichever way one looks at it, the name of the game is Mashiach ben Yoseph. The rules are also all his, and it is he alone who makes the last and final move (even when he is called Moses our Teacher!) The only question that remains is whether or not we can put the finishing touches of the excruciating drama of the divine game of life into fast forward.

Fractal 8:
In Its Due Time I Will Accelerate It

The novel, and utterly fantastic, thrust of the Gaon of Vilna's synthesis of science and religion is found in his unique explanation of a well known statement of the sages, regarding the conditions under which the Messianic Era will be initiated. It is a theme which runs throughout the whole of *Kol HaTor*.[56]

As quoted above, Isaiah (60:22) prophesies, "The least one shall become a thousand and the smallest one a strong nation: I, the Lord, will accelerate it in its time." The Talmud states (Tractate *Sanhedrin* 98a):

> R. Alexandri said: R. Yehoshua ben Levi pointed out an [apparent] contradiction. It is written [as to when the messiah will come], 'in its time' yet, it is also written I (the Lord) will accelerate it' [which implies before the due time and thus the phrase appears self-contradictory]. [There is no contradiction.] If they are worthy, I will accelerate it. If not, [the Redemption will come] in its due time.

R. Hillel writes:[57]

> Our master told us that in the final analysis a scriptural verse can never be divorced from its plain meaning *(ein mikra yotzei midei p'shuto)*. The literal intention [of this verse] is that even "in its due time I will accelerate it" [i.e., both aspects will occur simultaneously, and not one way or the other, which is the homiletic

interpretation offered by the Talmud]. And when will this occur? When, "The least one shall become a thousand and the smallest one a strong nation." The "least one" and the "smallest one" both refer to [the archetype of] Ephraim [ben Yoseph] which is [another aspect of the principle of] Mashiach ben Yoseph. Now, it is known that the extreme threshold level of Mashiach ben Yoseph that is achieved through [the process of] the "arousal from below" is [the power of] 1000 minus 1, that is [the formula of], "999 in *Yesod*." "The least one shall become a thousand" [thus] means that when [the messianic process of Mashiach ben Yoseph] will reach, through its activity, a degree just up until [the climactic conclusion of] 1000 — then, "I the Lord, even in its due time, will accelerate it." The intention is similar to the verse (Deuteronomy 32:35), "The things that come upon them make haste" according to the explanation of our master [in his commentary *Aderet Eliyahu*].

R. Hillel continues:

Many times I saw our master pacing back and forth in his study and speaking in an awesome stormy spirit saying, "Master of the Universe, do You not have a middle path between 'in its due time' and 'I will accelerate it'?! We are relying with all of our strength upon the plain and literal meaning in the words of Your promise, 'I, the Lord, will accelerate it in its due time.'"

It is difficult to understand what the Gaon could be referring to when he pleads before the Master of the Universe that He fulfill the literal meaning of the scriptural prophecy by revealing a "middle path." What can he possibly have in mind? There are only two avenues through which the final stage of global evolution — the Messianic Era — can occur:

- If *Teshuvah* — collective world Jewish repentance — will not occur, and the present condition of Israel and humanity will continue to deteriorate, then the Messianic Era of ben David will, perforce still come, but only after a complete causal process of "natural" deterioration. This is the path of *B'Itah* — the End in its natural due time.

- If, however, complete *Teshuvah* of the Jewish people does occur, this will trigger an immediate redemption, and the natural process will have been miraculously "jumped" forward to the Messianic Era of ben David. This is the path of *Acheeshenah* – a supra-natural acceleration of the End *before* its due time.

Thus, the Messianic Era — signaling the End of Time (as we know it) — can only come naturally, in its due time, or be supra-naturally triggered to appear before its due time. It is either this or that. There does not appear to be any room for a third alternative. Furthermore, the same section of *Gemara* presents another similar contradiction, and answers that the apparent contradiction is referring to two distinct modes of action:

> R. Alexandri said: R. Yehoshua ben Levi opposed [another] two verses against each other. It is written (Daniel 7:13), "And behold, one like the son of man came with the clouds of heaven," whilst [elsewhere] it is written (Zechariah 9:9), "[Behold, your king comes unto you...] lowly and riding upon a donkey." [There is no contradiction.] If they are worthy, [he will come] with the clouds of heaven (i.e. miraculously swift). If not, [he will come] lowly and riding upon a donkey.

Once again, the only apparent alternatives for the messianic arrival are either that of the natural path (riding on a donkey) or that of the supra-natural path (riding on the clouds). What then, is the third path to which the Gaon of Vilna refers? Is there a process that is both natural and supra-natural? Can an event be accelerated and yet still arrive *in its due time*?

The answer to this riddle lies in the deeper understanding of the synergistic relationship between the *Trein M'shechin* that was explained above. On the surface, the two modes of revelation, inherent in the two Messianic eras, appear to function in distinct, and even opposing, paths. These potentially opposing forces of the *Trein M'shechin* are reflected in the homiletic explanation of the Talmud itself. Yet we now know that these two branches emanate from the same identical root. If we could tap into that higher root, then we would, indeed, have access to a third alternative path of redemption. It is this higher union of the *Trein M'shechin* that is reflected in the plain meaning of the verses (which, according to the Gaon, always contains the deepest level of *sod*). It is this union to which the Gaon was referring, and attempting to awaken, through his supplication, "We are relying with all of our strength upon the plain and literal meaning in the words of Your promise, 'I, the Lord, will accelerate it in its due time.'"

Thus, according to the deeper truth hidden in the verse, there is a manner in which the two messianic forces can synergistically interact with each other in a unique union. Each will maintain its distinct mode of function, yet combine with the other to produce something more than both — an amazing third path. This is achieved by stimulating the "heavenly" supra-natural force from "below," which in turn will reciprocally "artificially" stimulate the natural process to quicken and speed up its otherwise natural and gradual rate of accretion. The third path in the Gaon's Doctrine of Redemption is the phenomenon of artificially accelerated global evolution.

In the sphere of knowledge, as well as in the domain of everyday earthly life, such "artificial stimulation" is being achieved through advanced technology. In this process, so much momentum is reached that all reality, and human consciousness along with it, is literally stimulated to "jump" into a higher dimension, while simultaneously triggering that higher dimensionality to receive it into its midst. According to the formula of the *Zohar,* quoted above, ever since the beginning of the 19th-century, the divine process (Mashiach ben David) is "artificially" stimulating the natural growth rate of planetary transformation through scientific "discovery" and applied technology (Mashiach ben Yoseph), in order to accelerate the "arousal from below" which, upon picking up breathtaking speeds, will then furiously trigger the climactic "jump," both from "below" and from "above" simultaneously — the coming messianic world consciousness.

The reader will notice that the Gaon's third path to universal redemption has revealed an entirely new middle state of possible reality, that is not simply natural "in its due time," nor simply supra-natural and miraculously "accelerated" before its time.

Rather, as R. Hillel himself puts it:[58]

It is an extreme qualitative increase in the supra-natural force that aids every act performed, via the 'arousal from below,' through the natural occurring process.

The supra-natural is already completely clothed in the guise of nature (in this case, science and technology) and animating it. Only now, the higher and "other worldly" supra-natural force of Mashiach ben David unites with Mashiach ben Yoseph and accelerates its development at ever increasing speeds. This, in turn, prematurely stimulates its own miraculous development. The end result is that the climactic arrival of its "due time" has been "accelerated." The fact that an escalated arrival of the "due time" (B'Itah) can, in theory, be triggered before its natural "due date," is not an infringement upon the natural laws to which it is bound, since it is still following a precise step by step sequence of events and stages that produce, through strict causality, its ultimate conclusion. Only the progress of its sequence of stages has been "artificially" accelerated, via the staggering power of science and technology. The natural growth process continues, but, as with the addition of fertilizer together with the enhancing of the natural growing conditions, fruition can be achieved at a much quicker rate.[59]

The Gaon's new middle contains both distinct paths and yet, is more than both at the same time. Amazingly, however, the third path is as distinct in its nature from either one of the two other paths as each of the two paths is distinct from the other![60] This is the power of the synergistic union between the Two Messiahs. This is the power of the spirituality of ancient religious truth synthesized with the "hard reality" of evolving scientific discovery. Drawn from the prophetic words of the *Zohar,* this is the Gaon's description of our present and imminent future reality.

The foundation principle in the Gaon's Doctrine of Redemption is that global evolution can be stimulated and accelerated via the "artificial" stimulation that comes from the exploding wave of technological advancement, along with the maps, models, and metaphors being supplied by ever increasing scientific discovery. Moreover, this is only half of the cosmic picture. The other foundation principle in the Gaon's doctrine of Redemption is the "supra-natural" return, over the past one hundred fifty years, of the Jewish people to their homeland after almost two thousand years of torturous exile, coupled with the phenomenal rebirth of the Land of Israel. *Kol HaTor* explicitly outlines this principle in commenting upon two verses dealing with the process of redemption: "Arise and have mercy (*rachamim*) upon Zion; for it is time to favor her, for the fixed time is come. For your servants hold her stones dear, and cherish her very dust" (Psalms 102:14-15).

R. Hillel writes:[61]

How is it possible that the "fixed times" [for the redemption process] can be brought closer... "end times" which are fixed from the beginning? ...[This is possible] because every activity performed, via the "arousal from below" of the earthly principle of feminine polarity from the left side is aided [i.e., reciprocally stimulated], via the heavenly principle of masculine polarity from the right side, as explained further. It thus develops that every "fixed time" is decreased by half its time. This is the meaning of "for the fixed time is come," that is, it is not necessary to go to the fixed time[s] rather the fixed time[s] will come to us since, "For Your servants hold her stones dear, and cherish her very dust [i.e., the source of stimulation is aroused from below by Israel returning to its land]. It will then be completed by the central pole, the [harmonizing] principle of *rachamim* (mercy), the path of the synthesizing middle, as is indicated by the beginning of the verse, "Arise and have mercy (*rachamim*) upon Zion..."

One has simply to look at the course of history to see that the intervals between the appearance of new eras are rapidly decreasing. For thousands of years, all societies were agricultural in nature. Then, at the dawn of the sixth millennial day (1740-1840), the Industrial Revolution burst forth in a series of earth-shaking changes throughout these societies and, correspondingly, began remodeling our view of the world around us. Shortly after, as the millennial clock was reaching high noon of the sixth day (1940-1990), another new era was launched, igniting a rapid series of extraordinary and spectacular changes. This era has been called the Space Age, the Electronic Era, the Global Village, and more. But the common denominator of all of them is technology.

Yet, none of these terms are wholly accurate in terms of conveying the extent and dynamism of the transformation which is thrusting us forward. What is the appropriate metaphor for the age in which we live? The utter phantasmagoria of events, ideas, and images, exploding world wide, appear as an incoherent mosaic of fragments with nothing to hold them together. What is the figure of speech, or the concept, that is sufficiently powerful, and yet pliable enough, that it can encompass such a drama and guarantee that the world will not look like the product of a shattered mind? In an age of blindingly accelerating change, human language can no longer fashion its concepts fast enough to stabilize the shock waves. To plunge on without the benefit of a meta-system, or even without the necessary metaphors, is a dangerous loss. The dawn of a new reality, that is truly global in its nature, is emerging in our lives, snowballing with the enormity of its ideas and the velocity of its changes. The present era is even more accelerative, and it has been projected that it will complete itself in a just a few more thundering decades.

According to the Gaon of Vilna, the only system which is sufficient to describe the scope, as well as the conflicts, of what has been emerging in the world, and in our daily lives, is that of Mashiach ben Yoseph. This is a super meta-system which serves as a vast data-bank of universal knowledge containing and integrating, clarifying and synthesizing, the serpentine path of planetary transformation. The meta-system of Mashiach ben Yoseph is, in fact, known in its more traditional context as Metatron — the supreme archetype and integrating process of the present era. Without such a systematic framework — a virtual *Shulchan Aruch* (Code of Jewish Law) — for understanding the tensions between religion and science, technology and nature, the ancient and the futuristic, we cannot hope to draw a coherent picture out of the past, current, and coming events. For those who are able to recognize the signs and characteristics of Mashiach ben Yoseph, there stands before us a unique opportunity for active and conscious participation in the acceleration of our own destined evolution.

---

[1] *HaTekufah HaGedolah* (The Great Era), R. Menachem M. Kasher, Torah Shelemah Institute, 1968, p. 421.

[2] *Kol HaTor*, Chapter 2, par. #39 (p. 485 in Kasher).

[3] There are other extensive references to Mashiach ben Yoseph and the *Trein M'shechin* in the Ramchal's more recently published commentary on Tanach and in some of his other works and personal letters. Additionally, the writings of R. Moshe Chaim Valle, a close colleague of the Ramchal have been published from manuscript, e.g., *In The Matter of the M'shechin* (*Ketvei RMD Valle, Likutim,* Part I). Although there is much overlapping, the Ramchal and his school develop different aspects of Mashiach ben Yoseph than the Gaon and R. Hillel. Still the two systems interface with each other, as explained in the Introduction, and certainly are seamlessly dependent upon each other.

[4] Cf. Talmud, *Berachot* 10a, end of page.

[5] For another approach to this question see Rav Kook's "Eulogy In

Jerusalem" and the Maharal's explanation in *Netzach Yisrael,* chapter 37.

[6] According to tradition (*BaMidbar Rabbah* 14:12 and elsewhere) Adam was destined to live for one thousand years and he saw into the future that King David was not destined to live at all. Therefore, Adam gave 70 of his years to David so that he could live. Thus, David's 70 years of life complete Adam's original 1000 years. Adam = David = Messiah = Adam.

[7] But see Rambam, *Hilchot Teshuvah* 8:7, where he also brings the other understanding.

[8] *Biurei HaGra, Berachot* 34b, *Even Shelaimah* chapter 11, p. 53a

[9] *Shnei Luchot HaBrit* (R. Yeshayahu Horowitz) also maintains this view (Beit David, pg. 36, Jerusalem 1972, 17b Jerusalem 1975.) See Kasher, pp. 350, 419 for clarification on the Rambam's position.

[10] Commentary to *Sifra D'Tzeniuta* 1, p. 19 (10a), s.v. *Melech HaSh'mini Hadar.* The mathematical-like details of this process constitute one of the most arcane fields of theoretical Kabbalah and occupies a large place in the systems of both the Ari and the Gaon. Even though this bizarre process is often depicted as a cosmic mishap and divine catastrophe, the obstensibly accidental nature of this archetypal event is only from one perspective. From another, more encompassing perspective, it is following a clear cut "fractal" pattern, and every detailed move was willed and orchestrated specifically by the Divine Mind.

[11] According to the *Leshem Sh'vo V'Achlamah* (*Hakdamot V'Sh'arim,* Introduction to *Sha'ar HaPoneh Kadeem,* p. 118) the Gaon's statement that the essence of the *yesod* was split into two parts at a primal stage in the creation process is drawn from the other tradition of Lurianic Kabbalah, that of R. Yisrael Sarug, as opposed to the "authoritative" teachings of R. Chaim Vital. These "underground" teachings of the Ari were considered sacred by the school of the Gaon (as well as to Hasidic masters) and are assumed to have all been taught to R. Chaim Vital by the Ari, only that he was not granted permission to reveal them.

[12] Commentary to *Sifra D'Tzeniuta* 1, pp. 19-20.

[13] Printed at the end of the Vilna edition of *Tikkuney Zohar,* p. 27a, middle of left column.

[14] See, e.g., the Gaon's commentaries on The Prayer of Hannah and the prophets Habakkuk and Isaiah.

[15] *Likutey HaGra,* pp. 40 and 63.

[16] *Leshem Sh'vo V'Achlamah, Hakdamot V'Sh'arim,* pp. 172-177.

[17] *Kol HaTor,* Chapter 1, par. #3 (Kasher, pp. 463-464).

[18] Chapter 1, par. #2, (Kasher, p. 463 and see p. 469).

[19] This resolves what could have appeared as a possible contradiction between R. Yitzchak Izik Chaver and R. Hillel. In the section quoted above from R. Isaac, he gave Mashiach ben Yoseph the job of redeeming Israel from physical subjugation and Mashiach ben David the job of redeeming us from

the Angel of Death. Here, R. Hillel shows that there is no contradiction. Since the entire period of the *Atarah* of *Yesod* was originally part of the period of ben Yoseph, it can still be called by his name.

[20] *Kol HaTor*, Chapter 1, par. #21 (Kasher, p. 477).

[21] Ibid., Chapter 2, Section b, par. #1 (Kasher, p. 502).

[22] Ibid., Section a, Aspect #101 (Kasher, p. 492).

[23] This aspect or "Oversoul" of Mashiach ben Yoseph is also known in the Zohar and in the writings of the Ari as the "*Zihara Ii'laah*" – the Supernal Radiance of the soul of Adam. We will return to the phenomenon of Metatron in Volume II, Chapter 4, *Metatron.* There it is explained that according to the Gaon the unique collective consciousness of Metatron is the missing link that melds science back into Torah. In fact, it has been my experience in studying and teaching this material for decades now that without an intimate understanding of Metatron, the *modus operandi* of *Kol HaTor* will remain hidden, and the corpus of the Gaon's kabbalistic writing will remain incoherent.

[24] The concept of a messiah living in each generation is far from being unique to *Kol HaTor*. In *Toldot Yitzchak* (p.140b) it is written, "...one of the reasons for which Mashiach ben Yoseph must come in every generation is to reveal the secrets of the Torah to those who are worthy." The Ramchal also writes (*Kinat HaShem Tzevaot,* p. 105), "Two aspects exist regarding Mashiach [ben Yoseph]. One, the supernal soul itself (*Yechida*), which is the [essence of the] actual Messiah, and the other is the individual who is fitting to be the [vehicle for the] Mashiach. This latter aspect exists continually in every generation. Further, he writes (p. 103), "Any murderous death at the hands of the gentiles is a rectification for [the sparks of holiness] that have been given over to the *Other Side.* [This martyrdom] is in order to elevate the [captive] holiness from there. All Jews that are killed are considered to be branches from him, because all of them are extensions of the *tikkun* of Mashiach ben Yoseph." R. Zussman heard from his mentor, R. Ya'akov Moshe Charlap, that "Any Jew killed by a non-Jew has within him the aspect of Mashiach ben Yoseph" (*Torat HaGeulah*).

[25] Chapter 1, par. #23 ,(Kasher, p. 477)

[26] Chapter 2, Aspect #75 (Kasher, p. 489).

[27] See *Sha'ar HaGilgulim*, Hakdamah 32 p. 34.

[28] Chapter 2, Section b, par. #4 (Kasher, p. 504).

[29] See also Aspect #109: "This is also a reference to Cyrus who was in the category of Mashiach ben Yoseph, as the verse says, 'I have raised him up in righteousness.'"

[30] "On a number of occasions my teacher and master, R. David Cohen (the "Nazir") z"l said to me that our master, the Rav z"l [Rabbi Avraham Yitzchak HaKohen Kook], said about himself that he was Mashiach ben Yoseph." *Aleyet HaShachar,* R. Ya'akov Filber, Institute for the Research of the Teachings of R. A. Y. Hakohen. (Hebrew edition).

[31] Chapter 2, Aspect #108

[32] See also Introduction, note 4, from *Toldot Yitzchak*

[33] This prayer is printed as an appendix to *Kol HaTor*, Chapter 5 (Kasher, pp. 530-531).

[34] Chapter 1, par. #23, (Kasher, p. 478).

[35] *Lekutay HaGra, Sod HaOtiyot*, p. 81 (41a), and see the gloss there by R. Yitzchak Izik Chaver, who explains the Gaon in the same context as does R. Hillel.

[36] Talmud, Tractate *Bava Kamma* 55a

[37] Chapter 1, par. 6, (Kasher).

[38] Chapter 1, par. #8, principle #3, (Kasher, p. 470).

[39] *Yesod* is the technical term in the Kabbalah for channel and also the general term for the reproductive organs.

[40] Chapter 2, Aspect #60, (Kasher, p. 487).

[41] Chapter 5, par. #2, (Kasher, p. 524).

[42] Summary at beginning of Chapter 4, (Kasher, p. 519).

[43] "The Mashiach has many names, each one according to its function". *Otzrot Ramchal,* R. Moses Chaim Luzzatto, B'nei B'rak, 1986 p. 24.

[44] *Kol HaTor,* Chapter 2, Aspect # 150. See *Zohar Balak* 194b.

[45] See the Introduction to Part I regarding the Gaon's unique relationship with the soul of Moses.

[46] The Gaon's commentary to Talmud, *Megillah* 17a, quoted in *Even Shleimah* 11:2, note 1, p. 100 (50b).

[47] "Moses is the first Mashiach [from Egypt] and the last Mashiach", Gra, *Yahel Or,* p. 18. "The first Mashiach is Mashiach ben Yoseph — 'His Firstborn Ox' — which emanates from the left side, as is known", Gra, *Tikkuney Zohar Chadash* p. 53

[48] *Zohar, Ra'aya Mehemna, Ki Teitze,* p. 278b

[49] *Tikkuney Zohar Chadash,* p. 30. See also, R. Margoliot, *Nitzotzay Zohar,* Vol. II, p. 120a.

[50] *Zohar, Ra'aya Mehemna Mishpatim* 120a

[51] Gra, *Yahel Or VaEira,* p. 2.

[52] Gra, *Yahel Or, Mishpatim,* pp.18, 19. See also the Gaon on *Tikkuney Zohar Chadash* p. 36b, *"Shevet uMechokek".*

[53] Chapter 5, par. #6 (Kasher, p. 528).

[54] See the Ari in *Sha'ar HaP'sukim* 31c and *Sha'ar HaKavanot, Kabbalat Shabbat.* "King Solomon" is a Kabbalah code word for the *yesod* of Moses,

i.e., the central channel within the spinal column, connecting the lower forces with the higher.

[55] *Zohar* I 21b, *Sefer HaLekutim* p. 9.

[56] Chapter 1, Kasher, pp. 470, 479; Chapter 2, Kasher, p. 484; Chapter 5, Kasher p. 526, and more.

[57] Chapter 1, par. #8, principle #3. See note 28 above.

[58] *Kol HaTor,* Chapter 2, Part II (Kasher, p. 502).

[59] See *Emunah VeBetachon*, p. 29, the example of the gardener and further, in Volume II, Chapter 2, Sacred Serpent.

[60] This is an application of the methodological tool referred to in the Appendix as a coherent superposition.

[61] Chapter 4, (Kasher, p. 521).

Appendix

- Introduction to the Gaon's Commentary on *Sifra DiTzniuta*

- *Tachtit HaHar* – Maps, Models, and Metaphors for New Understanding of Kabbalah for the "Last Generation"

- Template of the *Ten Sefirot*

- The GRA Mandala

Appendix 1

Introduction by R. Chaim Volozhin to the Gaon of Vilna's Commentary on *Sifra DiTzniuta*

Blessed is the one who keeps His promise to the nation of Israel, blessed be His name, who assured us that the true Torah will not be forgotten from the Jewish people. That promise has protected us, from the day Israel was expelled from the Holy Land. Even though when "Israel, its kings and ministers are amongst the nations, there is no Torah," in His eternal mercy, He granted His blessings upon us through saintly messengers that He places in each generation. From their mouths we live, and from their waters we drink. And even in this generation, when sorrow is frequent and livelihood is scarce, and the Nation of God is on a lowly level, the Merciful One continues to have pity on us.

Sorrows trouble our minds, and cause us to act like drunks. For this reason, Rabbi Eliezer decided to require of the Diaspora generation merely the minimal, superficial understanding of the words of prayer, as sufficient to fulfill the requirements of prayer. Yet we know that "understanding in study requires prayer," and this concept applies even to *halachic* studies [which are widely understood by the majority of scholars]. How much more so does this apply to the inner soul of Torah, which the *Tanaim, Amoraim,* and kabbalists expound upon in brief and cryptic terms!

Only a wise man, who is able to deduce the unstated, can comprehend the esoteric Torah. How can the likes of us, drunk from the sorrows that befall us, understand their words that are bound by "one thousand chains"? In His eternal mercy, to ensure that we should not forget the Torah, He sent us a celestial being, a man within whom dwells the spirit of God, our great teacher, the light of the world, whose sanctity in Torah and righteousness is known in all the worlds, the Gaon, Rabbi Eliyahu of Vilna, from whom no secret was withheld, and who enlightened our eyes in revealed and esoteric understandings of the Torah.

The *Sifra DiTzniuta* (Book of Concealment) predated the *Zohar* and was studied by its authors. It contains very few words, revealing few of its secrets. Even though it is quoted in its entirety in the *Zohar*, we have not yet merited to bask in its light. Since the times of the sages who composed the *Zohar*, its light has been concealed from us almost completely, so that it has become like a closed book to us. Printing errors have also added to the enigmatic quality of this book. And even though the Ari has commented upon sections of the *Sifra DiTzniuta*, we lack a methodical explanation from beginning to end.

Great is this day that we have merited this wondrous commentary by our great Rabbi, the Gaon, who explained it thoroughly, and corrected its text from mistakes that befell it. Rejoice, righteous ones, and be filled with joy, all who yearn to bask in God's pure light. Those who understand will be able to see how this book is constructed in the same form as the *Merkava*, the Divine Stature [of Archetypal Man] and the Emanation process, as explained in the *Zohar* and Ari. Its form also parallels the creation of the world, as described in Genesis until the beginning of the life of Noah. It is no less than the dwelling place of God, who revealed Himself to our master. It is a heavenly gateway to understand the two *Idrot*, [two related sections of the *Zohar*] for those who study this book truthfully.

Our master condensed within this work the majority of the teachings of the Ari. The diligent student will see how numerous teachings of the *Zohar* and Ari were included in a few words. The Gaon himself used to say that the Ari left him a place to fill, which is the commentary to this book. In the revealed Torah, Rebbe [Rabbi Judah the Prince] condensed the nine hundred volumes of the *Mishnah* into the six volumes that we know today, in order to prevent us from forgetting the Oral Torah. In order to do this, great efforts were made by Rebbe and those sages of Rebbe's generations to phrase the *Mishnah* in such a way as to include the content of the nine hundred *Mishnah*s in the six volumes. When people were drawn to learn the *gemara* as their main area of study, the level of academic mastery of the Mishnah suffered. To this Rebbe exclaimed, "Always run to the

Mishnah!"

The *Amoraim* learned by resolving apparently contradictory *Mishnah*s, and through this system, were able to reconstruct at will the talmudic dialectic arguments. Later, when our vision became dim by the exile, and people were unable to derive practical *halacha* from the study of the *Gemara*, the sages understood the necessity of compiling the practical laws into the accessible form of the *Shulchan Aruch* (Code of Jewish Law). These laws are the fine sifted flour that resulted from the relentless study of the Talmud, which in turn is derived from the *Mishnah*. To one who is capable, his main study should be in the Talmud. The *halachic* works and the *Shulchan Aruch* (Code of Jewish Law) should only be used as a reminder of all the laws that are scattered in the sea of Talmud. The elite ones in the nation should devote their main study to the *Toseftot* and *Braitot* [exterior mishnaic traditions not included by Rebbe in the six volumes of *Mishnah*], that are ultimately rooted in the sacred *Mishnah*.

The aforementioned principle is true of the study of the esoteric teachings, which are the soul of the Torah. They are also in the category of the Oral Tradition, since we have an oral transmission from generation to generation, dating back to Mount Sinai. Our great sages, the ancient ones, the masters of secrets, in whom dwelled the spirit of God, to whom no gate remained locked, saw fit to write a sacred work, wondrous in its brevity, in order to teach their disciples, in a brief and condensed way, and to prevent the eyes of the unworthy to receive this light from comprehending the holy words. In this work they concealed the highest of divine secrets, which they received in a direct Oral tradition from Mount Sinai. They are concealed for all the righteous in each generation, who are worthy of this light. And thus, they called it *Sifra DiTzniuta* (Book of Concealment), referring to the many wonders that are hidden in it, which are only accessible to the humble scholars.

This cryptic work is to esoteric Torah what the *Mishnah* is to exoteric Torah. Due to the sorrows that befell us during our exile, God's sacred, brilliant light has been concealed from us. Consequently, our ability to understand the Creation/Emanation process and the structure of the *Merkava* diminished. At this point God, in his great kindness, sent us a holy man, our sacred master, the godly Ari, who explained the Creation/Emanation process in detail. The early kabbalists merely hinted about the secrets of the *partzufim* (*sefirotic* personas), while the Ari made these secrets readily available to those scholars wishing to taste these delicacies. All of the Ari's teachings ultimately emanate from the *Zohar* and the *Idrot*, which in turn are based on the *Sifra DiTzniuta*. In time, our ability to comprehend the Creation/Emanation process described in Genesis diminished, until God sent a light from the heavens, the Ari, who explained the Creation process in a wondrous way.

The Ari's writings are based on sources in the *Zohar* and the two *Idrot*, but ultimately the source of everything is the *Mishnah*, which is this *Sifra DiTzniuta*. In truth, this is the task that every scholar in the esoteric studies has to accomplish: to ponder the words of the sages, and to see their words as extensions of sources in the *Zohar* and the two *Idrot*, and consequently to enter the holy domains and understand how their words are contained in, and emanate from, the *Sifra DiTzniuta*.

Unfortunately, few are the scholars that accomplish this task even in the revealed Torah. And even in the esoteric Torah, our eyes have been veiled from seeing how the sages' holy words emanate from the *Zohar* and *Idrot*, and even the disciples of the Ari himself were lacking total comprehension of their master's teachings, (except for R. Chaim Vital, as the Ari himself states). For, who will dare to enter the Holy of Holies and accomplish this exalted task of uniting the sages' teachings to their ultimate source, the *Sifra DiTzniuta*. The day is short, the workers in the field are scarce, and we cannot fathom what tomorrow will bring.

Yet for the sake of the Torah and the wonders hidden within it, God had mercy on us, and sent us a divine being who came with the clouds of Heaven, the likes of which has not existed for many generations. To him were given a heart that understands and eyes that see clearly the pathways of the revealed and esoteric Torah. His holy way was to ponder and meditate and labor in an awesome way that is hard to imagine, as everyone who was witness will testify. With tremendous adherence to his Creator, and in a state of holiness and purity, he managed to cross the threshold of understanding and clearly see the source of all wisdom. In all of his holy words, he shows us the true path to holiness and wisdom, a path that has not been tread upon for numerous generations, a sure path through the esoteric and revealed Torah. Just like in the *Shulchan Aruch* (Code of Jewish Law), he showed us the talmudic sources for all the *halachot*, and in his commentary on the *Mishnayot* he condensed the opinions of all the *Amoraim* and *Tanaim* in both Talmuds. Also in his commentary on the *Sifra DiTzniuta* he revealed to us his holy fire by clarifying and enumerating in meticulous detail the structure and origin of the Creation of Genesis and the secrets of the *Merkava*.

And God in his mercy, showed us that even when we dwell in our enemy's lands, when we find ourselves in the lowest of spiritual levels, He is our light. He showers upon us the dew of supernal knowledge to nourish our souls with pure and divine light, for He will not abandon His nation, and He does this for the sake of His blessed Name. And as I expand upon the great holiness of our master's Torah, I am reminded of something that makes my heart burn like fire and my soul tremble within me: and that is a preposterous claim made by ignorant and vain men from distant towns, who did not merit to see the light of our master's Torah, irresponsible people who speak against the saintly, who are like flies that hover over carcasses, that wish to cause our great master's fragrant ointment to give off a sickly odor — that our master, within whom dwelled the spirit of God, did not value the teachings of the Ari, God forbid. There are those who add that even the *Zohar* was in low esteem in our master's eyes, that he did not study it regularly, and did not see it fit to do so.

For it is clear for anyone to see that all of his works emanate from the *Zohar, Idrot,* and *Ra'aya Mehemna,* including his works in exoteric Torah, to the point that in his commentary on the *Shulchan Aruch* (in the sections of *Orach*

Chaim and *Yoreh Deah*) he used statements from the *Zohar* as supports for *halachic* opinions. And even though "lies do not last" and their words are totally baseless, my heart and ears are pained to have heard such slander. Therefore, I see it as my responsibility to announce to the Tribes of Israel the truth: that our master's knowledge in the *Zohar* was immense, for they were all readily recalled by him from memory, in their proper order and in full comprehension.

His study in the *Zohar* was with a flaming passion and the awe of God, in a state of pure holiness and wondrous adherence, which is difficult to describe. I heard from his own lips that he would intensively review the *Ra'aya Mehemna* ["The Faithful Shepherd", a section of the *Zohar*] numerous times, to the point that he considered himself sufficiently well versed in it to count the number of letters contained in this work by memory. At this point, he turned to other fields of study in exoteric and esoteric Torah. Consequently, our master dreamt that Moses our Teacher visited his house during the time when he was studying the *Ra'aya Mehemna* and then abandoned our master's house when he concluded his studies of the *Ra'aya Mehemna*.

Our master also accepted it upon himself to fulfill in detail all of the stringencies and saintly practices that the *Zohar* and *Ra'aya Mehemna* enumerate. I saw the tremendous respect and honor that our master felt for the Ari, the awesome man of God. For when I spoke of the Ari, his entire body trembled, and he said, "What can we say about a holy, awesome, and sanctified man of God like him? Great hidden secrets were revealed to him, and from the moment that he merited the revelation of Elijah the Prophet, he became able to conceptualize the most awesome thoughts that one can imagine."

Our master also clarified and corrected many of the Ari's texts, especially those not written by Chaim Vital. He worked very hard to show how the Ari's teachings are compatible with, and extend from, the *Zohar*. And even though the diligent scholar will find that our master explained a few texts differently from the Ari, they really were referring to the same point, yet differed in the method used to explain the idea. Happy is the one who is able to resolve an argument between these two sages! Even though there are few who are able to accomplish this task, one should realize that the differences between the Ari and the Gaon are akin to the arguments between two ministering angels in the heavens, and we have only to bend our heads under their feet and drink their words thirstily, for both their words are the words of the Living God.

The extent to which our master toiled over every subject is awesome, for even though he was gifted with an intellect, the likes of which has not existed for a number of generations, he was not satisfied with his perception of a subject until he had intensively weighed it out in his mind a few hundred times. He would not eat, drink, or sleep for a number of days and nights, until his complexion would darken, and he would come close to physical death. At this point, God would reveal to him wisdom that expanded his understanding to new realms. Then the supernal light of the Torah would radiate from his face. I heard from his holy mouth that it is impossible to understand a section of the Zohar unless one toils over it at least a number of weeks.

Once when I spoke to him about prayer, he said to me, "The importance of prayer was once revealed to me through a divine intervention; what occurred was that some while ago I toiled for twelve weeks over a certain statement in the Zohar on the subject of the New Moon, but to no avail. During the morning prayer, on a certain Rosh Chodesh, I had a revelation which enabled me to understand the statement in seven different manners. What was I to do?" I answered him that he could interrupt his prayer for a moment to contemplate and entrust to memory this extraordinary revelation, and then resume his prayer. He said to me, "Truthfully, that is what I did. For fifteen seconds I committed the revelation to memory. After the morning prayers, I found, to my great distress, that I could not remember the vision. It took me a half hour of contemplation to remove the distress from my heart so that I could recite the Hallel praises properly. As I started to pray musaf, low and behold, all the seven perspectives of the Zoharic statement that were revealed to me returned to my mind.

This time, however, I did not pay any attention to them. When I finished praying *musaf*, I found, to my great joy, all seven ways clearly arranged in my mind."

His great toil over the holy words is illustrated by the way he compiled his corrections of *Zoharic* texts. He would come to the point of counting the words and letters on the page in the *Zohar,* until it became clear to him what the correct version was. Even so, he was not satisfied until he would learn the entire *Zohar* with his particular interpretation of this passage in mind and see whether it would solve numerous other problematic passages in the *Zohar*. I heard from his lips that he would not correct a text in the esoteric Torah unless his correction clarified at least one hundred and fifty other problematic verses in the *Zohar*. When I presented him with ten different textual emendations of the *Sefer Yetzirah* [Book of Formation], he told me that the Ari's text was the true one, except for one printing error that befell it and that our master corrected.

His mastery of *Sefer Yetzirah* was evident even in his youth. I once commented that with his level of mastery of *Sefer Yetzirah,* it should not be too difficult to create a *golem,* to which he responded, "Truthfully, I once began to create a *golem,* but in the midst of my attempt to do so, I had a divine vision appear over my head, at which point I assumed that the divine realms opposed my creating a *golem* at such a tender age." When I asked him what age he was at the time, he said, "less than thirteen years old."

Only when he saw clearly how the esoteric Torah emanated from the written Torah, and located the particular sources in the crowns of certain letters in the Pentateuch, did he feel satisfied in his study of *Sefer Yetzirah*. After he would toil and labor over texts, to the point of physical collapse, mercy from the divine realms would become awakened and great secrets would be revealed to him. Many times *maggidim* (divine entities) and angels of Torah would come to him and offer to teach him secrets in Torah without any toil. He would pay no heed to them. Once, a certain *maggid* was very insistent that our master accept his secrets of Torah without toiling over them. He replied to him, "I do not want to receive my understanding of Torah through any envoys; rather I crave that God Himself grant me understanding according to the amount of toil that I exert. He will grant me wisdom from His lips, knowledge to my heart, and He will transform my two kidneys into wellsprings of prophecy. Only then will I be certain that I have found favor in His eyes. Therefore, I do not want free gifts of knowledge from *maggidim*."

I was asked by our master to inform my younger brother (yet greater in wisdom than I) that he should not accept any *maggidim* that would shortly appear to him. Our master explained that even though Rabbi Joseph Karo [author of the Shlchan Aruch (Code of Jewish Law)] did have a *maggid*, that was over two hundred years ago when generations were still worthy, and Rabbi Karo lived in the spiritual purity of the Holy Land. In our bereaved times, in foreign lands, even the secrets of *maggidim* are tainted by impurities.

He especially disdained revelations offered to him whose content was devoid of Torah. Our master also said that "the revelations that the soul is exposed to while the physical body is in the state of sleep are not as valuable as the wisdom acquired in this world through toil in the study of Torah. The greatest way to find favor in God's eyes is by devoting one's time to the study of Torah, which is man's ultimate purpose. The revelations to the soul during sleep are simply gifts that hint to the greatness of the Next World." This implies that our master merited to these ascensions of the soul nightly.

This was confirmed by a close disciple of our master. Once, on the first night of Passover, two of his senior disciples were rejoicing in the gladness of the Lord in the most marvelous manner during the festival days, as we are commanded by the Law. But when they saw that our master's rejoicing was not as full as usual, they asked him about it. At first he refused to answer, but when they insisted he could no longer refrain himself and said, "Though it is not my habit to do so I must tell you about this. I hope to relieve myself of my anxiety by fulfilling the verse: 'If there be anxiety in the heart of man, let him tell it to others.' For last night Elijah the Prophet visited me (if I remember correctly it was Elijah, although it could have been another envoy of the heavenly Academy) and revealed awesome things, some two thousand four hundred and sixty aspects of understanding different passages in the *Zohar*. One of these teachings explains the true nature of the creation and the anatomy of the human body." These occurrences were natural to him, and he did not require doing any meditations to attain these exalted states. This is understandable, since his every word and thought were devoted to the study of exoteric and esoteric Torah. As is well known, he did not walk even four cubits without Torah and *tefilin*. He used to say that the purpose of sleep is to instill into men the insights that he cannot attain in his waking state, since the waking state is akin to a dividing curtain between God and men. During sleep the soul separates from the body and clothes itself with supernal garments.

I witnessed that in his holy writings he states: "True are these divine secrets, which were revealed to me by Jacob the Patriarch and Elijah the Prophet." It is unclear to me if the rest of his novella, where this comment is not mentioned, were attained through revelations in the waking state or through revelations during the sleeping state, when his soul ascended to the Heavenly Academy.

One thing is clear, and that is that he experienced these ascensions nightly. Once, on a rare occasion when the Gaon described to me his waking state revelations, he told me the following: "In Vilna there was a truth-sayer and dreamer, who would know of people's actions and thoughts even behind closed doors. People feared him greatly, for he knew the most personal information about the townspeople. Once, he was brought in front of me. The truth-sayer said, 'Rabbi, allow me to say something. Two weeks ago on Thursday you sat in this room and expounded novella about the portion of the Pentateuch *Ha'azinu* on such and such verses, and Rabbi Shimon Bar Yochai (the author of the *Zohar*) sat at your right and the Ari sat at your left.'" The Gaon was amazed that a human being knew of such things. Our master said, "I remember sending away even my personal attendant from the house that day. I did, indeed, expound on awesome subjects that day." Our master's face then radiated a strong brilliance, which revealed to me the awesomeness of the subjects spoken of that Thursday, which were worthy of being said in front of Rabbi Shimon Bar Yochai.

All of the forty-eight traits, through which the Torah is acquired, were apparent in our master. He labored in Torah for its sake with all of his strength, in the greatest of holy and pure states. He did not leave a great or small subject unexplained, ranging from the Talmuds, *Mechiltah*, *Sifre*, *Sifra*, *Tosefta*, all the Midrashim, *Zohar*, *Tikunim*, *Merkava*, Ari, and other early *Mekubalim*. In all these, he corrected texts and labored to attain full understanding... he would not even look out of his four cubits. His great abstinence from worldly matters was unbelievable, to the point that he did not allow himself to converse with the children. He dwelled in the Eternal Tree of Life, he hardly slept, and as a result he was granted the Torah as a gift. His two kidneys became overflowing springs of knowledge, which became increasingly powerful. Combined with this was his awesome humility. He who did not see his Torah service, spiritual purity, abstinence, and devotion, has not seen a luminary in his days.

My heart trembles when I recall the manner in which he served God, as a ministering angel from on high. Who has seen such a man in this or in numerous past generations? The revelations to which he merited are not wondrous to me, for they were the result of his toil in Torah. For, indeed, we have a tradition from R. Meir that (one who learns Torah) merits many things." He did not enumerate what these "things" are, rather he alluded that one merits to have revelations and experience wondrous events which cannot be described by words. He merited to *Ruach HaKodesh* (Divine

Inspiration), as it says in *Zohar Shemot*: "I (God) do not hide anything from the wise ones, even for a moment, because they know what occurs in the lower and higher realms, and they do not reveal these secrets to the unworthy."

Certain secrets were only granted to the Gaon in order to explore the supernal realms of existence, as it says: "Even the secrets that are hidden from other men are revealed to the sages" (Talmud, Tractate *Avoda Zara* 35). All the gates were unlocked to him, and there was nothing to impede him from entering. As it says: "To one who labors in Torah in times of distress, even the divine separating curtain is opened to him" (Talmud, Tractate *Sotah* 49). He is the one who adheres to God, for "He and the Torah are one...." Happy is the generation that merited to witness our master's greatness. Joyous is our generation that merited to drink from the wellsprings of our master's Torah, which he wrote in his numerous sacred works. Outstanding amongst his works is this *Sifra DiTzniuta,* which enlightened our eyes. Even so, all of his works are like a drop in the ocean when compared to his wisdom, which he did not fully reveal in his works. Still, even these drops are more than enough to quench our thirst, and were it not for God's assurance to us that the Torah will never be forgotten from the Jewish people, we would not even have this. These are the words of a young scholar, who merited to serve his holiness, our master, in a small way. When I recall our master's sacred study of Torah, his abstentious, purity, and humbleness, my whole body trembles...

Appendix 2
Tachtit HaHar

Practical Application of *Sha'ar Be'er Sheva*
For New Understanding of Kabbalah in the Last Generation.

In order to understand and grasp the wisdom
of the Torah contained in the light of the upper
wisdom, it is necessary to learn the Seven
Sciences hidden in the lower world of nature.
This is the mystery of [the verse that refers to
Israel's receiving the Torah at Mt. Sinai]
"...they stood on the *bottom side* of the
mountain" (Exodus 19:17). Our master said
that [the usage of patterns and examples
found in the "bottom side" of reality] is
analogous to a teacher of children who is able
to explain numerous matters in the Torah
[that his young pupils might not otherwise
understand] by using toy models and similar
devices, as well as simple diagrams.[1]

Kol HaTor is not intended to be studied only as a
kabbalistic text or only as an agenda for "religious Zionism."
It is also a spiritual activist's manual of how to actually
implement and stimulate the graduated, but ever-
accelerating phases, of messianic global redemption. The
doctrine of *Kol HaTor* has, clandestinely, inspired and
influenced small groups of Jews over its two hundred year
history and, since its presentation to the public in 1968,
influenced many more today than ever before. However, the
one area of *Kol HaTor* that has received virtually no attention,
and certainly no systematic application, is the secret
"messianic weapon" of *Tachtit HaHar* - the "Bottom Side" of
reality – as detailed in *Sha'ar Be'er Sheva*.

Rabbi Hillel of Shklov is emphatic when he writes:
"The level of the Inner Circles comes about... not only in
thought and meditation upon mystical unifications, but also
together with the integration of the rectified actions

connected with them."[2] The secret of *Tachtit HaHar* requires no less activism, rigorous discipline, and continuous work than the other actions demanded from the Gaon in order to stimulate the messianic process and to accelerate global redemption.

In the world of physics there are six types of tools, dating back to the ancient Greeks, which scientists call "simple machines." All machines, no matter how large or complicated, are made up of combinations of these six simple "tools." (They are the pulley, the wheel and axle, the lever, the inclined plane, the wedge, and the screw.) Over the last few decades, following the Gaon of Vilna's prophetic imperative in the secret of *Tachtit HaHar,* I have discovered, in the "wellsprings from below" of the new sciences, "Six Simple Scientific Tools" that have completely transformed my ability and that of hundreds of students to grasp fundamentals of the Kabbalah – the inner teachings of the Torah. It appears that virtually all the "spiritual machines" of the Kabbalah, no matter how large or complicated, are made up of combinations of these six simple tools.

In this case these "tools" are the mapping, modeling, and metaphoric power supplied by these profoundly simple, yet simply profound, concepts. I have been very successful in using these six simple tools (along with other modern maps and state of the art models) for effective teaching aids. This is what the Gaon intended when he referred to, "...using toy models and similar devices, as well as simple diagrams." This is in order to interface the Kabbalah with the Talmud, the *sod*/secret level with the *pshat*/plain meaning of Scripture and the messianic future with the Torah's ancient and eternal truth.

It is important to emphasize that when the school of the Gaon's Kabbalah is referred to, this is not only the classical Kabbalah of the *Zohar* and the Ari (Lurianic Kabbalah), etc. For the Gaon, the tools of *Tachtit HaHar* also must be applied to include the last unexplored frontier of the secrets of Torah and creation that are hidden and camouflaged within the sixty tractates of the Talmud. This field of kabbalistic *aggadic* study, as outlined above in *Kol*

HaTor, is one of the main missions of Mashiach ben Yoseph in the Last Generation. According to the Gaon, the maps, models, and metaphors being supplied by modern science and technology are absolutely indispensable to begin to comprehend these messianic "time capsules" the talmudic sage-mystics wove and embedded together within the ocean of civil, criminal, and ritual law.

Each of these maps, models, and metaphors requires serious study, first in the secular context in which they are found and then as the vessel or lens to hold and perceive the particular light of the kabbalistic concept. (Separate essays, explaining these models and their Torah applications, can be found at the website: cityofluz.com.) Occasionally, I have seen specific metaphors culled from "the wellsprings of wisdom from below" used in teaching about themes within the Kabbalah. However, it appears that many students and readers do not really have a full appreciation of the details of the "toy models", and thus the depth of the Torah reality is far from being understood and grasped. In other cases, the teacher himself or herself may not yet fully grasp the "light" of the matter, only because the vessel has not been sufficiently explored and grasped.

The following is only a prospectus of six possible examples from a myriad of messianic tools from the "Underside of Mt. Sinai". These simple tools enable the Torah scholar, as well as the novice, an amazingly deep grasp of some of the most profound and subtle secrets of the Torah, preparing us for the Gaon of Vilna's description of the "New Torah" beginning to be revealed in our generation, the Final Generation (discussed in Volume II Chapter 3, Leviathan).

~~~

After thousands of years of travel, humanity has reached the final shore — the Edge of Time. Across this great ocean lies a new territory of consciousness, the Messianic Era of Mashiach ben David, and beyond. Yet, even now, as we stand upon this seashore of earthly time, there are strange and mind-boggling objects being washed ashore from the other side of our present reality.

Although, to the casual bystander, these devices may appear only as intellectual novelties or devices to make our lives easier, the Gaon of Vilna is telling us that they are also secret weapons of an inner technology. These "spiritual toys" of inner technology are merely simple vessels, but the light of the secret wisdom of the Torah they can reveal and enable us to see, is inestimable. Let us now bend down, reach into the sand, and redeem a few small items that have, embedded within them, the fallen fractal sparks (*nitzotzot*) of divinity, in order to better prepare ourselves to actively usher in and complete the Messianic Era of Mashiach ben Yoseph.

1. Flatland and Dimensionality. The greatest difficulty in wrapping one's mind around the texture of the Kabbalah in general and biblical events, such as the Garden of Eden in particular, is a total unfamiliarity with the concept of dimensionality. Truly, the entire Torah world-view subsumes that there is a fourth direction ("dimension"), aside from length, width, and depth of everyday common senses by which all reality is apparently governed. This is the significance of the Tetragrammaton — the four digit alphanumeric Name, or sacred Formula, of God. All the sage-mystics throughout Jewish history knew through direct experience — prophecy, *ruach hakodesh*, revelation, meditation, prayer, etc. — that our immediate 3-D space-time reality is embedded in a four-directional fabric of a "higher" and more encompassing dimension. It is not for naught that the rabbis of the Talmud and Midrash have referred to our limited linear world as *Olam HaShafel*, which literally translates as "Flat Land."

Over a hundred years ago a small book was written by the mathematician and Shakespearean scholar, Edwin A. Abbot, called *Flatland - a Romance of Many Dimensions*. This model is a profoundly simple, yet simply profound introduction into learning how to perceive and experience the higher (and lower) dimensionality of mathematicians and thus, the four dimensional view of the sages of the Kabbalah and Talmud. (A synopsis of *Flatland* and its application is found it Volume II, Chapter 2.)

2. Split-Brain and Polarized Reality. Only in the last several decades has the science of neurosurgery revealed that we have not one, but two brains within us, each with its own mode of perception or "information processing." The concept, for example, of "right brain" holistic "seeing" versus "left-brain" linear thinking, has become ubiquitous in our generation, allowing for new insights into the phenomenon of knowledge itself. Yet, "right brain" (*chochmah*/wisdom) and "left brain" (*binah*/analysis) are inseparable from the nomenclature of the Kabbalah and the cosmology of the Gaon. The *Sefirot* of *Chochmah* and *Binah* are a guiding principle of hidden symmetries found throughout the Torah. The Torah declares, "God made man in His Own image" (Genesis 1:27). We have two distinct brains *precisely* because the Divine Mind operates through two modes of divinity. The split-brain model enables us to grasp the phenomena of self-replicating polarities that the Torah is built upon, e.g., the two Torahs - Written and Oral, the "Jewish mind" and the "Greek mind" (a *"Yiddisheh kop" and a "goyisheh kop"*), "This World" and the "Next World", the two Leviathans, the Twin Messiahs, and an endless host of other dual structures and relationships.

3. Quantum Logic and the Rabbinic Mind. This is a conceptual tool from the "New Physics" that is used to "see" into the quantum layer of physical reality. In this sub-atomic realm, "matter" behaves bizarre and counter-intuitive. Nothing is a simple "this" or "that." In order to quantify anything one must employ a coherent superposition. A "superposition" is one thing or more superimposed upon another. For example, in photography a double exposure is the superposition of one image positioned onto another. What one now has is a mixture of two things, but those can still be broken down into its separate components. A coherent superposition, however, is not simply a composite of one thing superimposed upon another. It is a separate thing-in-itself. In fact, a coherent superposition is as distinct from its components as its components are from each other.

Pure experience is never restricted to merely two possibilities. Our analytical conceptualization of an event is either "this" or "that." This perception is brought about by assuming that experience is bound by the same rules as symbols. In order to understand the rabbinic *chidush* — a novel Torah or kabbalistic understanding — one must utilize a conceptual tool from modern physics and quantum mechanics that will enable the aspirant to begin to grasp, among endless examples, the secret of *machloket* – the classic rabbinical "dispute." With the conscious application of Quantum Logic it becomes joyfully shocking that, in truth, the rabbis are never actually arguing with each other. Instead, they are dancing with each other to consciously produce more than "a this" or "a that," and more than both![3] (An application of a coherent superposition is found above in Part II, Chapter 1, Fractal 8, note 60.)

4. The Möbius Strip and "Singular Duality". The Möbius strip was introduced by the German mathematician and astronomer Augustus Ferdinand Möbius (1790-1868). He described his remarkable paper surface as a strip, which has no "other side." Astrophysicists and cosmologists (who both deal with the origin and structure of the universe as a whole) make use of this unusual topological surface when trying to understand the possible "shape" of our physical cosmos. According to one model, the universe, like the Möbius strip, curves back on itself, and thus has no outside, and having no outside, neither does it have an inside, or, one can say that its inside *is* its outside — the physical universe as non-dual.

Kabbalah, like the sciences, has many diverging branches of study. One of its fields of exploration is analogous to that of cosmology. However, unlike science, which is concerned with the structure and shape of physical reality, Torah cosmology and the Kabbalah school of the Gaon are involved with mapping out the structure and "shape" of the metaphysical relationship between human experience and divine consciousness. Here, the kabbalist asks, "Which geometrical or topological surface best describes the man/God relationship?" The Möbius strip offers a simple, yet precise, model of one of the fundamental "shapes" that molds this hidden landscape. It is also a simple key to understanding the well-known rabbinic and kabbalistic statements: "The end is united with the beginning," and "[Although it appears] last in action, it is first in thought." There is an endless array of other examples and applications. (More about the Möbius model is also in Volume II, Chapter 4.)

5. Holography and the Interconnectivity of Reality. One of the amazing technological developments to appear in the world in the last decades is the hologram. A hologram is a special type of three dimensional optical storage system (commonly known as a "picture"). From a Torah perspective, there is, however, another quality of holography that is even more intriguing than its 3-D life-like appearance. If you take a true holographic photograph of a man and cut one section out of it, say, the foot, and then enlarge that section to the original size, you will get, not a large foot, but a picture of the whole man. In other words, each individual part of the holographic picture contains the whole picture in condensed form. The part (in Hebrew, the *prat*) is in the whole (the *klal*), and the whole is in each part — a type of unity-in-diversity and diversity-in-unity. In other words, every part has access to the whole. With this awareness, the holographic model can help us understand an axiom in the Kabbalah known as *Hitkallelut veHitkashrut haOlamot* — the interconnection and interpenetration of all existence. This teaching is also the basis for the well-known formula: "All of Israel is interconnected one with the other." If the holographic model is studied, and seriously and consistently applied, the hidden principles of the Kabbalah, as well as the entire Torah, will open up.

6. Fractals, Chaos and the Eternally Iterating Torah. The term fractal, coined just in the 1970's, began as a new field of mathematics and geometry, but have now evolved to interface with almost every category of modern knowledge, including the arts. The term, a cross between "fracture" and "fraction," is used to describe the discovery of underlying order to chaotic systems. This amazing new field is known as chaos theory. Chaos is a shorthand term for a movement that has quickly been reshaping the landscape of many diverging fields within the scientific community. Although it is still filtering down into the public mainstream like the terms (if not some of the concepts) of relativity and quantum mechanics, chaos theory, has already been claimed as the third great revolution of the 20th-century in physical science. A leader in quantum physics and modern cosmology has stated: "No one will be considered scientifically literate tomorrow who is not familiar with fractals."[4]

Where chaos begins, classical science ends. It is a new science that spells out, mathematically, philosophically, and graphically, the universal design of how nature functions and flows, rises and falls. It has brought together not only mathematicians, physicists, biologists, and chemists, but also physiologists, ecologists, economists, and meteorologists. It affects our local weather. Chaos conferences and chaos journals are far and near. Government programs and university campuses are afire with chaos.

Fractals have come to represent a way of describing, calculating, and thinking about forms that are fragmented and irregular (like life itself!). The fractal approach embraces the whole structure — in terms of the branching that produces it — and behaves consistently from large scale to small scale. A fractal curve refers to an underlying organizing principle embedded within the monstrous complexities and apparently disconnected fragments. Reality, on all levels, displays a regular irregularity! Here, "fractal" means self-similar. Self-similarity is symmetry across scale. Every *fracture* of the shape replicates a *fraction* of itself on a smaller or larger scale, continuing infinitely. A fractaled view of reality is an infinite recursion of pattern within pattern. Fractal geometry provides a set of tools to navigate the new scientific world of "order within chaos."

Chaos, belying its name, is about order. It is about the sublime order underlying the complexity of apparent disorder. Its major tool is the special techniques of computer graphics that are able to translate otherwise abstract, mathematical descriptions into pictures of utterly fantastic and delicate structures. These forms, which previous to computerization were barely conceivable to even a few mathematical visionaries, comprise a new family of shapes.

Technology is now painting, in infinite detail and color, what the mind can no longer imagine. Even hard core mathematicians and scientists cannot but experience an epiphany, inducing a logical leap of faith into another dimension. Seeing is believing, as a vision of testimonial faith appears on the computer screen. A new geometry, long hidden in the nature of things, has reared it strange head.[5]

Yet, it is this "strange" new science that holds the maps, models, and metaphors to some of the most bewildering and abstruse traditions of the talmudic and Kabbalah sage-mystics. Fractals offer a huge arsenal of power tools to get a serious handle on core teachings of the *Zohar* and Lurianic Kabbalah, such as the Primordial Worlds of the *Tohu* (referring to the secret of the second verse of Genesis: "And the earth was *tohu*/chaos"), the Divine Personas (*partzufim*), and the ubiquitous "*nitzotzot*" – fractal chips or "sparks" of collapsed divinity that are embedded in our present reality.

The entire structure of the Torah, the universe, and the mission of the Jewish Nation, is dependent upon these kabbalistic teachings that are conceptually based upon a "fractaled" picture of existence. There is no question that from the perspective of the Gaon of Vilna, the conscious language of fractals is being revealed in our generation as one of the 999 phases of the messianic process. This is to enable many diverse individuals, as well as seasoned Torah scholars, to grasp relatively quickly, yet firmly and deeply, these most ancient truths to prepare for a complete future paradigm shift in global transformation – *and the future is now.*

Additionally, learning to see, think, and envision *fractally* is the key to integrate other ostensibly strange beliefs in the Gaon's Secret Doctrine that are reiterated through out *Kol HaTor*. These include his absolute adherence to *Gilgul* (doctrine of transmigration of soul fractals) and its everyday application, together with his extensive usage of *gematria,* to calculate and plot the inner geography of the soul's journey and purpose. Fractal theory reveals that the Gaon's usage of *gematria* is not a "numbers game," and his usage of *gilgul* is not about individual "people" reincarnating. Rather it is about recurring cosmic geometric fractal patterns embedded within Torah and the universe. In fact, for the Gaon, *gematria, gilgul,* and Mashiach ben Yoseph are the fundamental bedrock of a fractaled universe.

(As a small application of fractal thinking, the subheadings throughout Part II have been titled, Fractal 1, Fractal 2, etc. Part of the idea here is that, although each section stands on its own, each one is interdependent on all the other subheadings, and in fact, each subject matter is an iterating replication ("fractured fraction") of all the others, each one with its unique nuances. All these patterns originate from one eternal formula — The Tetragrammaton Y-H-V-H.)

~ *Hasadim* and *Gevurot* ~

There is one more mechanism that, although not coming from the science and technology vessels of *Tachtit HaHar*, it is absolutely indispensable to understand and integrate the doctrine of *Kol HaTor* and the Kabbalah of the Gaon. This teaching, from the "Front Side" or "Face" of Mt. Sinai, is the pivotal axiom of an entire Torah-based cosmology. In this case, this ancient Torah tool is coming directly from the Gaon's writings, as amplified by R. Shlomo Eliyashiv, (the great expositor of the Gaon's Kabbalah known as the "*Leshem*".)

The kabbalistic principle of *Hasadim* and *Gevurot* is the key to understanding all branches of Jewish mystical thought, especially the Kabbalah school of the Gaon of Vilna, from whence I have received this initiation. *Hasadim* and *Gevurot*, or *HuG* for short, is the inner mechanism that lies at the very center of the Kabbalah, yet its systematic analysis and conscious application is virtually unknown, even in scholarly kabbalistic circles.

This concept is, without exaggeration, the *modus operandi* to understanding the full spectrum of Judaism, rabbinic or kabbalistic, secular or religious. For want of any comparable Western terminology, the Oriental medical and philosophical concept of *yin-yang* that has entered English usage, is apropos. The masculine/expansive *hasadim (yang)* and the feminine/contracting *gevurot (yin)* are the two underlying forces that animate and define the entirety of creation and human intercourse. But here the comparison with *yin-yang* stops. From the perspective of the Gaon's Kabbalah, the relationship between these two aspects of divinity takes a decidedly Jewish twist. This knowledge generates a wonderful interdisciplinary approach to the different streams of Kabbalah, and it is a prerequisite to being initiated into *Kol HaTor's* secret of the Twin Messiahs. Additionally, the mechanics of *HuG* offer a meta-historical vantage point to observe the divergent denominations and rivalries — religious and political — that are endemic in Judaism today and in the world at large.[6]

---

[1] *Kol HaTor*, Chapter 5, Section II, par. #6.

[2] *Kol HaTor*, Chapter 5, Section I, par. #2.

[3] Source: Gary Zukav, *The Dancing Wu-Li Masters*, 1979.

[4] John Archibald Wheeler, protégé of Niels Bohr and friend of Albert Einstein, quoted in *Introducing Fractal Geometry*, Lesmoir-Gordon, Rood, 2001.

[5] Source: James Gleick, Chaos – Making a New Science, 1987.

[6] For an overview of *HuG* see my *Introduction to Torah Cosmology and Jewish Mysticism,* Lessons 1 and 2.

Appendix 3
Template of the *Ten Sefirot*

Keter
(Crown)
Cranium

Binah
(Discernment)
left brain

Chochmah
(Wisdom)
right brain

Da'at
(Knowledge)
middle brain, spine

Gevurah
(Strength)
left arm/hand
Isaac

Chesed
(Love)
right arm/hand
Abraham

Tiferet
(Beauty)
Torso
Jacob

Hod
(Empathy)
left
kidney/gonad/leg
Aaron

Netzach
(Dominance)
right
kidney/gonad/leg
Moses

Yesod
(Channel)
reproductive organs
Yoseph

Malchut
(Kingship)
reproductive organs/
separated female
David

Appendix 4

The GRA Mandala
Explanation of the Cover Image

The graphic on the cover of this book is intended to be instructional and thought provoking. "A picture tells a thousand stories" — in this case this unusual picture, which is a type of "Torah mandala,"[1] reveals a thousand lights in the mystery of the Gaon of Vilna. The true image of the Gaon — public and private — is historically unique in many ways, if only because there is no single image of the Gaon of Vilna! From among all his sons, relatives, and numerous disciples, as well as from among numerous historians and biographers (both Orthodox and secular), there is no consensus at all as to who the Gaon of Vilna really was and what exactly he was doing throughout his seventy-seven years of earthly existence.

After the reader has read *The Secret Doctrine of the Gaon of Vilna*, the question is specifically: who did *he* think he was, and what did *he* believe to be his life's mission? How did *he* understand his superhuman computer-like brain, capable of processing at lightening speed, literally every single letter of the entire Written and Oral Torah, together with almost every known field of scientific and philosophical knowledge? How did *he* understand his unexpected, inexplicable, and bizarre behavior, from his still-to-this-day unexplained battle with the Hasidic movement; his mysterious aborted trip to the Land of Israel and the enigma of his taking off even minutes of Torah study to research and author a book on trigonometry and other secular disciplines in Hebrew? The list goes on and on.

The cover photo-montage consists of six different portraits of the Gaon which were produced in the past by various artists — Jewish and non-Jewish. Emblematically, each "face" of the Gaon can reflect at least six different "facets," as perceived and envisioned by various individuals and communities over the last two hundred fifty years. There is the image of the Gaon of Vilna who is the strict legalist, ethicist and master Talmudist; the Gaon as the superlative mathematician and scientist; the Gaon as the vigilant anti-Hasidic leader; the Gaon as the master Hebrew grammarian; the Gaon as the kabbalist's kabbalist, revealing new secrets of the Torah for the Final Generation; the Gaon as the incarnation of Moses; the Gaon as the guardian warrior of ancient rabbinic tradition; and the Gaon as the harbinger of a futuristic Jerusalem, functioning as the spiritual and scientific *meta*-tropolis of global consciousness. Will the real Gaon of Vilna please stand up? Truthfully, all these are only some of the aspects and missions of Mashiach ben Yoseph.

From the perspective of *Kol HaTor,* all these images are true, and yet they are not complete for the Gaon contains all these aspects and more. The hidden whole of the Gaon is far more than the sum of his individual parts. The "more" is here represented by the computer animated fractal in the middle. This fractal has an eerie human-like or "Adamic" form to it. This is the root-soul of the Gaon, also known as the Illumination of Mashiach ben Yoseph. Additionally, the *meta*-soul of Mashiach ben Yoseph, as well known in Kabbalah and throughout *Kol HaTor,* is the multi-spectral phenomenon known as Metatron (explained in the chapters above). This fractal image, representing higher dimensional consciousness, reveals the Gaon of Vilna as a living manifestation in the mystery of Metatron. According to R. Hillel of Shklov, the Gaon's guiding metatronic spirit is yet alive and well within the pages of the secret doctrine of *Kol HaTor* and throughout his enormous matrix of writings.

These six "faces" of the Gaon can also signify the six spiritual "phases" of the template of the six lower *Sefirot*, as they emanate and filter down the Light of the *Ain Sof*. The seventh "face/phase" of the Gaon is the *Sefira* of *Malchut* which, as is well known in the Kabbalah, "has nothing of her own", yet reveals all the aspects that are being directed into her vortex. One light of understanding, among many that this mandala reveals, is that the Torah of the Gaon can only be understood through the providential discoveries of science and technology, symbolically embodied here within the computer generated fractal. Without the maps, models, and metaphors of the new sciences we cannot hope to grasp whom the Gaon of Vilna is, what he was really doing, and where he is still trying to take us.

The secret to understanding the *oversoul* of the Gaon is the Hebrew diagram that forms the backdrop of the GRA Mandala. The diagram below on the right was drawn by R. Shlomo Eliyashiv (known as the *Leshem*), the early 20th-century master kabbalist and chief expositor of the Kabbalah of the Gaon.[2] It is a graphic description of his clarification of the Gaon's commentary of a section of the *Sifra DiTzinuta* from the *Zohar*. The diagram is mapping out the cosmic "circuits" of the higher dimensional "brain" of *Arich Anpin* or, in simple theological language, the "Godhead". This is an "aerial view" with the bottom of the diagram being the back of the head ("west"). The fundamental design is that of a central column dividing at its top into two branches that curve around to reunite at its original starting point. This is the form of the cosmic serpent that reveals itself as two serpents only to reunite as one. The diagram below on the left is the same one as on the right only with the serpentine movement clearly indicated.

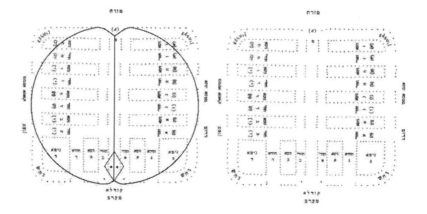

This sacred Uroboros — the motif of a serpent with its tail in its mouth — is very much the backbone of the Gaon's Kabbalah teachings (amplified at length in Volume II of *The Secret Doctrine of the Gaon of Vilna*, especially in Chapter 2, *Sacred Serpent and the Roots of Technology*). This section references the *Zohar's* graphic depiction of what is, with little question, the most unusual and intriguing shape in the entirety of Torah literature. In fact, this strange Uroboros shape is the most unique shape in the annals of comparative religion, mysticism, mythology, and Jungian psychology. This holy "Jewish" serpent, however, is virtually unique in that it is a serpent with *two* tails in its mouth! The Two-Tailed Uroboros is also "fractaling" (a self-replicating fractured fraction of itself, see Appendix 2) the mystery of the two Leviathans that are really one as explained there by the Gaon (and in Volume II, Chapter 3, Leviathan).

The GRA Mandala incorporates the four fundamental teachings (elaborated in the four chapters of Volume II) of the Gaon's Kabbalah — Mashiach ben Yoseph, the Sacred Serpent, Leviathan, and Metatron. These four aspects of reality — corresponding to the four alphanumeric symbols of the Tetragrammaton — are the roots and branches of *Kol HaTor*. Additionally, the Gaon wrote (quoted above) that, "all that now exists and all that will exist until eternity, is all contained in the Written Torah." The small image of the *sefer Torah* (Scroll of the Torah) situated as the crown of the GRA

Mandala alludes to this truth of the Gaon – that all reality/consciousness is ultimately emanating out of the Five Books of Moses. Now, by integrating the six historical images of the Gaon into his metatronic oversoul, superimposed upon the Two-Tailed Leviathan swimming in the higher dimensional ocean of the Godhead, and all of this radiating out of the higher-dimensional Torah, we can just begin to get a small glimpse of the light of the GRA, Rabbi Eliyahu, the Gaon   of   Vilna.

---

[1] A mandala, literally meaning "disc" or "circle", is an ancient form of Oriental art that graphically portrays a schematized representation of the cosmos. Mandalas are often characterized by concentric configurations of geometric shapes, each of which contain images or aspects of divinity. In Jungian psychology the concept of the mandala was borrowed as a symbol representing the effort to reunify the self. Along with other originally Oriental terms, such as "mantra", "tantra" and "yin-yang", the term and imagery of the mandala has become part of the Western language and mind-set. Even a six-pointed "Jewish Star" — an intersection of two triangles — if contemplated for its schematic representation of the cosmos reveals itself as an ancient kabbalistic "mandala". The "GRA Mandala", as with any true mandala, has embedded within it virtually endless symbols and fractaled layers of the enigmatic soul of the Gaon of Vilna.

[2] *Hakdamot v'Sh'arim, Likutim*, p. 197

Index

M

Rivlin, R. Hillel · continued
  goral, gilgul, gematria ·
    81
  Kol HaTor · 25
  leader of Vision of Zion ·
    25
  Secret Goral · 84
  settlement of Jerusalem
    · 26
  seven branches of
    science · 32
  system of Gaon · 32
Rivlin, R. Shlomo Zalman ·
  14, 28, 35, 43, 45, 48,
  69, 108, 164
  Chazon Tziyon · 28
  gematria · 155
  Kol HaTor intro · 31
  Kol HaTor publication ·
    29
  Midrash Shlomo · 28
  Rivlin, Asher · 30
  Rivlin, Shmuel · 30
Rivlin, R. Shmuel · 170
Rivlin, R. Yitzchak Tzvi ·
  29, 84
  "Living Talmud" · 29
  "Master of the Holy
    Tongue" · 29
  "Master of the
    Settlement" · 29
  Kol HaTor publication ·
    29
Rivlin, R. Yoseph (Yosha) ·
  27
  Ashkenazi community
    in Jerusalem · 27
  built neighborhoods · 28
  *Brit Avot B'Se'arat
    Eliyahu* · 28
  Jewish homes beyond
    the Old City walls · 27
  Meah Sh'arim · 27
  Petach Tikvah · 28
  poems of · 28
  Rivlin, Shlomo Zalman ·
    28

Rivlin, Rabbi Hillel
  Kol HaTor · 114
  of Shklov · 2
  resettlement of Holy
    Land · 113
Rivlin, Rav Zalman Chaim ·
  114
Rivlin, Shmuel · 30, 48
  Organization for the
    Dissemination of *Kol
    HaTor* · 30
  role of the Jewish nation ·
    10
ruach hakodesh
  divine inspiration · 1,
    82, 86, 99, 113, 129,
    147, 149, 240

S

Sacred Serpent · 156
  direct experience of · 34
  Gaon's cosmology of
    creation · 15
  role in technology · 15
Salanter, R. Yisrael · 39
Sanctification · 127, 129
  tikkun of · 128
Sanctification of God's
  Name · 127, 196
Sandalfon
  agents · 205
Sanhedrin · 108, 138, 155
Sasson and Simcha · 16,
  75
  agents · 205
  secret of · 16, 75
Schick, R. Dr. Baruch · 21,
  32, 47, 108, 161
  Euclid · 90
  Euclid's Geometry · 51
  Shklov leader · 144
science and technology
  messianic role of · 34,
    164

W

wellsprings of wisdom · 39,
41, 51, 93, 94, 134,
137, 140, 146, 148,
161, 168
forces of nature · 149
from below · 239
Wheeler, John Archibald ·
247
wisdom of Israel · 126,
127, 136, 137, 138
gentiles recognize · 93,
145
in eyes of nations · 138
wisdom, secular
messianic role of · 12

Y

Yaacov Tzvi of Berlin · 45
year 1776 · 143
year 1840 · 12, 24, 39, 97,
134, 142, 146, 147,
153, 164, 168
year 1990 · 11, 24, 49, 86,
97, 155, 164, 167
noon of sixth day · 117
Yehoshua ben Levi · 210,
212
yesod
divine attribute of · 128
yesod
999 is in · 200
Messiah from House of
Yoseph · 184
space-time unit of · 184
yesod of space-time
sixth millennium · 184
yesod of the *atarah*
ben Yoseph · 189

Yesod/Malchut paradigm ·
189
Yisrael of Shklov · 66, 108,
158
music · 158
Pe'at HaShulchan · 161
yonah
dove · 17
Yoseph (Yosha) Rivlin
poems of · 36
Yoseph and his brothers ·
35, 166, 175
Yoseph and Zion · 194
Yoseph Lives On · 87, 123,
196, 199, 201
Yoseph the *Tzadik* · 149,
207
Binah and *Chochmah* ·
143

Z

Zeitlin, R. Yehoshua
Shklov leader · 144
Zietlin, R. Yehoshua · 23,
47
Zimmerman, R. Dr. Chaim
· 50
Zion
healing · 121
Mashiach ben Yoseph ·
124
place of refuge · 124
return to · 24
Torah from · 124
Zionism, religious · 11
Zionism, secular · 6
Zionist groups
mystical · 166

The Author

Joel David Bakst is a teaching rabbi and scholar of Talmud, Kabbalah and Biblical Hebrew who, for 20 years while living in Jerusalem, studied and taught in Orthodox yeshivot. He has lectured and given workshops in Israel, the United States and India. He has written extensively about the confluence of Kabbalah and science with a special interest in the biblical and kabbalistic references to the pineal gland and the DMT model as it relates to higher consciousness and global evolution. He lives and teaches in Southern Colorado.

His other published books are *The Secret Doctrine of the Gaon of Vilna, Volume II: The Josephic Messiah, Leviathan, Metatron and the Sacred Serpent,* and *The Jerusalem Stone of Consciousness: DMT, Kabbalah & the Pineal Gland. Beyond Kabbalah: The Teachings That Cannot Be Taught* will soon be available. His books are available on amazon.com; recordings of his classes and seminars are available at cityofluz.com.

Made in the USA
San Bernardino, CA
09 June 2015